Migration, Minorities and Citizenship

General Editors: Zig Layton-Henry, Professor of Politics, University of Warwick; and Danièle Joly, Professor, Director, Centre for Research in Ethnic Relations, University of Warwick

Titles include:

Christian Joppke and Ewa Morawska
TOWARD ASSIMILATION AND CITIZENSHIP
Immigrants in Liberal Nation-States

Atsushi Kondo (editor)
CITIZENSHIP IN A GLOBAL WORLD
Comparing Citizenship Rights for Aliens

Zig Layton-Henry and Czarina Wilpert (editors)
CHALLENGING RACISM IN BRITAIN AND GERMANY

Jørgen S. Nielsen
TOWARDS A EUROPEAN ISLAM

Pontus Odmalm
MIGRATION POLICIES AND POLITICAL PARTICIPATION
Inclusion or Intrusion in Western Europe?

Jan Rath (editor)
IMMIGRANT BUSINESSES
The Economic, Political and Social Environment

Peter Ratcliffe (editor)
THE POLITICS OF SOCIAL SCIENCE RESEARCH
'Race', Ethnicity and Social Change

Carl-Ulrik Schierup (editor)
SCRAMBLE FOR THE BALKANS
Nationalism, Globalism and the Political Economy of Reconstruction

Steven Vertovec and Ceri Peach (editors)
ISLAM IN EUROPE
The Politics of Religion and Community

Maarten Vink
LIMITS OF EUROPEAN CITIZENSHIP
European Integration and Domestic Immigration Policies

Östen Wahlbeck
KURDISH DIASPORAS
A Comparative Study of Kurdish Refugee Communities

John Wrench, Andrea Rea and Nouria Ouali (editors)
MIGRANTS, ETHNIC MINORITIES AND THE LABOUR MARKET
Integration and Exclusion in Europe

Migration, Minorities and Citizenship
Series Standing Order ISBN 0–333–71047–9 (hardback) 0–333–80338–8 (paperback)
(*outside North America only*)

You can receive future titles in this series as they are published by placing a standing order.
Please contact your bookseller or, in case of difficulty, write to us at the address below with
your name and address, the title of the series and the ISBN quoted above.

Customer Services Department, Macmillan Distribution Ltd, Houndmills, Basingstoke,
Hampshire RG21 6XS, England

The Europeanization of National Policies and Politics of Immigration

Between Autonomy and the European Union

Edited by

Thomas Faist
Professor of Sociology
Bielefeld University, Germany

and

Andreas Ette
Research Associate
Federal Institute for Population Research, Germany

First published 2007 by
PALGRAVE MACMILLAN
Houndmills, Basingstoke, Hampshire RG21 6XS and
175 Fifth Avenue, New York, N. Y. 10010
Companies and representatives throughout the world

PALGRAVE MACMILLAN is the global academic imprint of the Palgrave
Macmillan division of St. Martin's Press, LLC and of Palgrave Macmillan Ltd.
Macmillan® is a registered trademark in the United States, United Kingdom
and other countries. Palgrave is a registered trademark in the European
Union and other countries.

ISBN-13: 978–1–4039–8713–6   hardback
ISBN-10: 1–4039–8713–0   hardback

This book is printed on paper suitable for recycling and made from fully
managed and sustained forest sources.

A catalogue record for this book is available from the British Library.

Library of Congress Cataloging-in-Publication Data
The Europeanization of national policies and politics of immigration :
     between autonomy and the European Union / edited by Thomas Faist,
     Andreas Ette.
       p. cm. – (Migration, minorities and citizenship)
     Includes bibliographical references and index.
     ISBN-13: 978–1–4039–8713–6 (cloth)
     ISBN-10: 1–4039–8713–0 (cloth)
       1. European Union countries–Emigration and immigration–Government
policy. 2. Emigration and immigration–Government policy. 3. Emigration and
immigration–Political aspects. 4. European Union countries–Emigration and
immigration. I. Faist, Thomas, 1959- II. Ette, Andreas, 1975-

     JV7590.E9534 2007
     325.4–dc22   2006051536

10   9   8   7   6   5   4   3   2   1
16   15 14 13 12 11 10 09 08 07

Printed and bound in Great Britain by
Antony Rowe Ltd, Chippenham and Eastbourne

Contents

v

List of Figures and Tables

Figure

Tables

Acknowledgements

Many people and organizations contributed to making this book possible. The original idea for this book emerged out of a collaboration between two groups of researchers. The first consisted of participants in a project on the democratic legitimation of immigration policies at the University of Applied Sciences Bremen, which was part of the Collaborative Research Center 597 'Transformations of the State' and funded by the German Research Foundation (DFG). Headed by Thomas Faist, this group included Stefan Alscher, Andreas Ette, Margit Fauser, Jürgen Gerdes, Kathrin Prümm and Mikael Spång. The second group consisted of doctoral students – Georgia Mavrodi and Imke Kruse – who gathered because of the initiative of Mechthild Baumann. Both groups of researchers met because of their shared interest in the changing multi-level governance of immigration in Europe and its impact on the policies and politics of member and non-member states. The concept of the volume developed in discussions between Mechthild Baumann, Andreas Ette and Thomas Faist. The gratitude of the editors goes to Mechthild who was not able to continue with the project to its completion. Yet without her support the book project would not have been launched in the first place.

Financial support for the project was generously provided by the Europäische Akademie Berlin and the Friedrich-Ebert-Foundation, without which we would not have been able to bring together most of the authors of this volume at a common workshop held in Berlin in September 2005. Following this meeting where we shared our insights into the politics of Europeanization and the highly differential national experiences with the EU, the contributors to this volume drafted and revised their chapters during winter and spring of 2005–6.

As editors of this volume, we offer our deepest gratitude to all of the contributors for their interest in participating in this project. The cooperation has been an interesting academic as well as personal learning experience which has been deeply rewarding. For her support in preparing the manuscript we particularly thank Dr Edith Klein for her proofreading. Despite the time pressure and the fact that most of this volume has been written by authors whose first language is not English, she helped enormously to produce a more coherent style of language and grammar. Finally, we would like to thank the staff at Palgrave Macmillan and Philippa Grand in particular for the steady reminders about a timely delivery of our manuscript and for their efficient publication of the book.

Wiesbaden and Bielefeld
Andreas Ette and Thomas Faist

Notes on the Contributors

Stefan Alscher is a research assistant at the Centre on Migration, Citizenship and Development at the University of Bielefeld. He received his MA at Humboldt University Berlin and is currently completing his PhD thesis. He was a Visiting Research Fellow at the Centre for Comparative Immigration Studies at the University of California, San Diego, in 2004–5. Alscher is also a member of the editorial board of the German-language newsletter *Migration und Bevölkerung* (Migration and Population). His research interests include undocumented migration and border control, with a focus on Europe and North America, and the impact of free trade on migration processes.

Petra Bendel is the Managing Director of the Central Institute for Regional and Area Studies and Lecturer in Political Science at Erlangen-Nuremberg University, Germany. She conducts research in the areas of comparative politics and policies as well as international relations, EU studies and area studies. She is the co-editor of books and articles on Latin American politics, on worldwide democratization, on terrorism as well as on migration and integration policies in Europe.

Andreas Ette is a Research Associate at the Federal Institute for Population Research, Germany, and a PhD candidate at Bielefeld University. Previously he was a Research Fellow of the Collaborative Research Centre 'Transformations of the State' at the University of Bremen. His research interests include population and immigration policies, democracy, comparative politics and the European Union.

Thomas Faist is Professor of Transnational Relations and Development Studies at the Faculty of Sociology, Bielefeld University, Germany. Formerly, he directed International Studies in Political Management (ISPM) at the University of Applied Sciences Bremen. Thomas Faist received his PhD degree from the New School for Social Research in New York. His research focuses on international migration, ethnic relations, social policy and transnationalization. His book publications include *The Volume and Dynamics of International Migration and Transnational Social Spaces* (2000), *Transnational Social Spaces* (2004), and *Citizenship: Discourse, Theory and Transnational Prospects*, co-authored with Peter Kivisto (2007).

Margit Fauser is a Lecturer and Research Fellow at the Faculty of Sociology, Bielefeld University. Her research interests embrace transnational migration, integration, democratization and development. She is currently working on immigration flows and policies in Spain. She has been associated with the Instituto Universitario Ortega y Gasset, Madrid, and the Migration Programme of the Centre for Documentation and Information, Barcelona (CIDOB). Her recent publications include a book chapter on 'Transnational Migration – a National Security Risk? Securitization of Migration Policies in Germany, Spain and the United Kingdom' (*The Transatlantic Security Challenges and Dilemmas for the European Migration Policy Project*, ed. by Krystyna Iglicka).

Andrew Geddes is Professor of Politics at the University of Sheffield where he is also the Director of the Centre for International Policy Research. He has published extensively on European and EU migration policy and politics. Among his recent publications are *Immigration and European Integration: Towards Fortress Europe?* (2000, second edition forthcoming in 2007) and *The Politics of Migration and Immigration in Europe* (2003).

Jürgen Gerdes is a Research Fellow at the University of Bielefeld in Germany. He currently works with the Research Project 'The Democratic Legitimacy of Immigration Control Policy' within the DFG Collaborative Research Centre 'The Political as Communicative Space in History'. He previously worked on an international research project on dual citizenship supported by the Volkswagen Foundation, which compared the politics of dual citizenship in a number of immigration and emigration countries. His research focuses on the relationship between democracy, human rights and immigration. His reviews and papers on questions of multiculturalism, cultural rights and dual citizenship have appeared in numerous journals and anthologies.

Agata Górny is Assistant Professor at the Faculty of Economic Sciences and Research Fellow at the Centre for Migration Research, Warsaw University. Her research interests include patterns of migration and adaptation of ex-USSR migrants coming to Poland, multiple citizenship and the application of qualitative methods in migration research. She is co-editor of *Migration in the New Europe: East–West Revisited* (2004).

Ahmet İçduygu is a Professor in the Department of International Relations, and Director of the Migration Research Programme (MiReKoc), at Koç University, Istanbul. His most recent research deals with the mechanisms and dynamics of irregular migration and its labour consequences, the anatomy of transit migration, the question of how individual citizens experience and perceive their own citizenship in various social settings, and the structure, environment, value and impact dimensions of civil society in a comparative perspective. He is co-editor of *Citizenship in a Global World: European Questions and Turkish Experiences* (2005), has published numerous articles in journals such as *Ethnic and Racial Studies, International Migration, International Social Science Journal, Global Governance, Middle Eastern Studies* and *Mediterranean Quarterly*.

Anna Kicinger works as a researcher in the Central European Forum for Migration Research, a research unit of the International Organization of Migration, in Warsaw. Her research interests include Polish migration policy, European migration policies, migration policy of the European Union, and mobility issues for the highly skilled. She is preparing her PhD thesis on the development of Polish migration policy between 1918 and 2004 under the supervision of Professor Dariusz Stola (Polish Academy of Sciences).

Imke Kruse is a researcher at the Max Planck Institute for the Study of Societies in Cologne, Germany. She received her PhD from the Free University Berlin in 2005. In 2001, she was a staff member of the German Government's Federal Commission on Immigration Reform, and in 2001–2, she participated in the Migration Task Force of the Council on Asia–Europe Cooperation (CAEC). Her research interests include international relations, the European integration process, refugee policies, legal and irregular migration and human rights.

Sandra Lavenex is Professor of International Relations and Global Governance at the University of Lucerne in Switzerland. Her research focuses on European and international migration policy, EU association relations with non-member states, and international democracy promotion. Her publications on European migration policy include two books (*Safe Third Countries* [1999]; and *The Europeanisation of Refugee Policies*, 2001), a co-edited volume (*Migration and the Externalities of European Integration* [2002], with Emek M. Uçarer), and articles in *Journal of Common Market Studies, Journal of European Public Policy, West European Politics, Cooperation & Conflict, Journal of Ethnic and Migration Studies* and *Journal of Refugee Policy*.

Georgia Mavrodi is currently a PhD candidate in the Department of Social and Political Sciences, European University Institute (Florence). She graduated in international relations and political studies at the

University of Macedonia, Thessaloniki, in 2000. She also received additional training in human rights law at the Catholic University of Nijmegen in 1999, her MA in European Studies from Humboldt University of Berlin in 2002, and her Master of Research from the European University Institute in 2004. Her professional experience includes the post of political scientist at the Refugee Reception Centre of Thessaloniki. Her research interests focus on European integration, comparative immigration and refugee policies in Europe after the Second World War, and the impact of European institutions on immigration and refugee policies in southern European countries.

Kathrin Prümm currently works as a research assistant with a focus on quality management at the University of Applied Science in Bremen, Germany, where she has also taught courses in political science. She graduated in political science from the Freie Universität Berlin in 1993 and received her PhD from the Institute for Migration Research and Intercultural Studies at the University of Osnabrück in 2003. Her research interests are mainly European politics, and particularly migration and the higher education system.

Mikael Spång received his PhD in Political Science at Lund University, Sweden, and is currently Assistant Professor in Political Science at the School of International Migration and Ethnic Relations, Malmö University, Sweden, where he teaches mainly in the area of human rights. His publications include articles and a book on democracy in Swedish and a study on dual citizenship in Sweden ('Pragmatism all the Way Down? The Politics of Dual Citizenship in Sweden', forthcoming in Thomas Faist [ed.], *The Politics of Dual Citizenship*).

Agnieszka Weinar was awarded a PhD in Political Science in 2006. She is a researcher at the Centre for Migration Research at Warsaw University. Her current work focuses on migration policy regimes, discourse on immigration in liberal democracies, immigration theory, immigrant narratives and theories of citizenship. She is the author of the forthcoming book *Europeizacja polskiej polityki wobec cudzoziemców w debatach parlamentarnych 1990–2003* (Europeanization of Polish migration policy, 1990–2003 [Warsaw: 2006]).

List of Abbreviations

AP	Accession partnership
AsylVfG	Asylverfahrensgesetz (Law on Asylum Proceedings)
AufenthG	Aufenthaltsgesetz (Law on Residency of Foreigners)
BT DS	Bundestag Drucksache (Official Bulletin of the Federal Parliament)
CAHAR	Committee of experts on the legal aspects of territorial asylum, refugees and stateless persons
CD	Council Directive
CDU	Christlich Demokratische Union Deutschlands
CEE	Central and Eastern European countries
CIREA	Centre for Information, Reflection and Exchange on Asylum
CIS	Commonwealth of Independent States
COREPER	Comité des représentants permanents
CSU	Christlich Soziale Union Deutschlands
CTF	Consultative Task Force
EC	European Community
ECHR	European Convention for the Protection of Human Rights and Fundamental Freedoms
ECJ	European Court of Justice
ECRE	European Council on Refugees and Exiles
EEC	European Economic Community
EMU	European Economic and Monetary Union
ENP	European Neighbourhood Policy
EP	European Parliament
EU	European Union
FDP	Freie Demokratische Partei Deutschlands
FPÖ	Freiheitliche Partei Österreichs
ICMPD	International Centre for Migration Policy Development
ILO	International Labour Organization
IOM	International Organization for Migration
IU	Izquierda Unida
JHA	Justice and Home Affairs
NAFTA	North American Free Trade Agreement
NGO	Non-governmental organization
NPAA	National Programme for the Adoption of the Acquis

ORA	Office for Repatriation and Aliens
OSCE	Organization for Security and Cooperation in Europe
PD	Procedures Directive
PDS	Partei des Demokratischen Sozialismus
PNV	Basque National Party
PSOE	Partido Socialista de Obreros Españoles
PP	Partido Popular
QMV	Qualified majority vote
RPP	Regional Protection Programme
SAA	Stabilization and Association Agreement
SAP	Stabilization and Association Process
SIS	Schengen Information System
SPD	Sozialdemokratische Partei Deutschlands
TCN	Third-country national
TEU	Treaty on the European Union
UK	United Kingdom
UN	United Nations
UNDP	United Nations Development Programme
UNHCR	United Nations High Commissioner for Refugees
VIS	Visa Information System

Part I
Regulating Migration in Europe

1
The Europeanization of National Policies and Politics of Immigration: Research, Questions and Concepts

Andreas Ette and Thomas Faist

Introduction

In June 2005, the European Council proposed a 'period of reflection' responding to the concerns of its citizens about the future of Europe. It was a necessary reaction to the difficulties encountered in ratifying the Treaty that was to establish a Constitution for Europe. Reflecting and stocktaking have also shaped academic scholarship on the European Union (EU)[1] during recent years. What has emerged is an increasing interest in the actual impact of the EU on its member states. Two waves of scholarship on the multi-level governance structures in the EU can be discerned. The first wave of EU studies was geared towards an understanding of the development of common political institutions and policies on the supranational European level. This first stage of European integration theory was dominated by bottom-up thinking and focused mainly on the role played by member states in the evolution of European integration. Only during the 1990s did this focus start to shift. The term 'Europeanization' characterizes the second wave of scholarship which reverses this perspective and has looked top-down.[2] The established political structures and policies on the European level are now taken for granted, only now are their effects on domestic structures and policies being analysed. This volume contributes to this new research agenda by providing a comparative analysis of the impact of the EU on the policies and politics of immigration control in its member states as well as on its neighbouring states. In particular, three main research questions structure this volume. First, the contributors ask which dimensions of domestic change – only the policy or also the politics of immigration – have been Europeanized. The second question looks into the extent of Europeanization in domestic policies and politics. Finally, the third question focuses on the differential impact of the EU on its member states and the different modes of Europeanization which help to make sense of the patterns of Europeanization.

Three main reasons motivated us to undertake this work. The first concerns recent developments on the European level. The European integration of immigration policies is about the most significant 'task expansion' of the EU to have taken place during recent years. In the late 1990s, justice and home affairs (JHA) has become 'the most active field for meetings convened under the Council of Ministers in the late 1990s' (Lavenex and Wallace 2005: 463). The Commission biannually publishes the Scoreboard which provides ample evidence for the expansion of the level of integration in immigration policy. Furthermore, the shift of immigration policy competencies from the third pillar of the EU to the first in 1997 and the recent introduction of qualified majority voting (QMV) and the co-decision procedure in 2005 significantly widened the scope of integration.[3] These recent developments make the volume a particularly timely study for the purpose of analysing the ways in which this newly supranationalized policy area has already influenced European member states.

The second motive concerns certain central characteristics intrinsic to this policy area. Immigration policy is a particularly interesting field for the study of Europeanization because it concerns the member state's sovereign discretion over the entry and residence of non-citizens in its territory. The European harmonization of immigration policy literally defines the 'finality of Europe', its outer borders and how they are controlled. Scholars of European integration have traditionally considered policies on immigration, internal security and national defence as cases in which integration would be the least likely to occur (see, for example, Lindberg and Scheingold 1970: 263). With the exception of the recent shift towards supranationalization, immigration policies have for the most part and most of the time remained under national control (Scharpf 1999; Schmidt 1999). The volume therefore contributes to our understanding of processes of Europeanization in policy areas where nation states are least likely to cede control.

Finally, the third motivation to publish this volume is the limited empirical foundation about European influences on national immigration policies. The majority of Europeanization studies carried out so far have focused on environmental and social policies (Mastenbroek 2005:

1112). Immigration policies, however, have received comparatively little attention and there is a clear need for more comprehensive and comparative data to assess the nature and the extent of the Europeanization of national immigration policies. This lack of comparative data on Europeanization is a general problem and not unique to the study of the Europeanization of immigration policies. Vink and Graziano (forthcoming) have even called for an 'empirical turn' in Europeanization research. So far, most studies of Europeanization are qualitative case studies or focus on a very limited number of countries. The few quantitative analyses available deal mainly with the differences in transposition rates of EU directives in member states (see, for example, Falkner et al. 2005; Mastenbroek 2003). The volume makes a contribution to this 'empirical turn' in Europeanization research by producing 'theoretically informed comparative case studies that gradually include new policy sectors and countries' (Haverland 2003: 204).

The remainder of this introductory chapter provides an overview of the state of research concerning the Europeanization of the policies and politics of immigration. It outlines the main research questions and presents the conceptual tools used throughout the empirical case studies included in this volume. Finally, it provides an overview of the structure of the volume and the findings of all the case studies, which point to a largely differential experience concerning the impact of the EU on its member and non-member states in this policy area.

The European integration of immigration policy

Compared to other policy areas, the regulation of entry and residence of third-country nationals has received a European dimension only recently. Andrew Geddes (2003) differentiates four periods of the slowly increasing European integration of immigration policies (for the following see also Bendel in this volume). The first period, from 1957 to 1986, was characterized by *minimal immigration policy involvement* in national immigration policies. Immigration policies fell under national control, and initiatives by the European Commission towards closer EU cooperation within the traditional Community method of decision-making were regularly declined. Nevertheless, the period witnessed significant cooperation in this policy area outside the EU's traditional structures. Examples of such cooperation include the Trevi group, which was established by European member states during the 1970s to cooperate on internal security measures, and most importantly the Schengen Agreement from 1985 concerning cooperation on the mutual abolishment of internal border controls and the development of compensating internal security measures. These intergovernmental forms of cooperation helped to shape cooperation during the second period, from 1986 until 1993. That period was characterized by *informal intergovernmentalism* during which representatives of the administration of the member states engaged in a process of closer cooperation. Examples are the Ad Hoc Working Group on Immigration which was established in 1986, and the group of coordinators who prepared the 'Palma Programme' which dealt with the security implications of the free movement measures of the Single European Act of the EU. The third period, from 1993 until 1999, was shaped by the Maastricht Treaty and its structure of *formal intergovernmental cooperation*. The three-pillar structure of the EU integrated immigration policies under the EU umbrella. It recognized immigration issues as being of common interest. The decision-making structures in the third pillar, however, ensured cooperation remained strictly intergovernmental.

For the moment, the final period is characterized by increasing *communitarization* and begins in the late 1990s with the Treaty of Amsterdam. The Treaty brought immigration policies into the Community pillar by creating a new Title IV. Furthermore, it incorporated the Schengen Agreement into the *acquis communautaire*. With its sights set on raising the level of integration, the European Council summit in Tampere in 1999 defined a five-year action programme on the central measures of a common European immigration policy. Five years later, in June 2004, the Commission published its final assessment concerning the original Tampere Programme, stating that 'substantial progress has been made in most areas of justice and home affairs'. Because of the intergovernmental decision-making procedures based on unanimity in the Council of Ministers, however, 'it was not always possible to reach agreement at the European level for the adoption of certain sensitive measures relating to policies which remain at the core of national sovereignty' (Commission of the European Communities 2004: 3–4). Major obstacles relating to the decision-making structures and the scope of integration were overcome in December 2004, when the Council decided that beginning 1 January 2005 decision-making on EU immigration policies (with the exception of legal immigration) was to change to QMV and the co-decision procedure with the European Parliament (EP), thus providing for serious supranationalization of this policy area. Finally, the recent attempts by migrants to enter the EU illegally in the two Spanish enclaves of Ceuta and Melilla in autumn 2005 very likely served to open the next 'windows of opportunity' for continuing integration of this policy area. Those incidents have once again shown the weaknesses of a migration policy with a foremost focus on migration control and too little emphasis on measures addressing the root causes of migration (see Bendel, this volume; Boswell 2003).

Overall, the last 30 years have witnessed important changes in this policy area in the direction of greater European regulation. These changes include the shift of competencies from the national to the European level and shifts in the modes of European policy-making. What began as intergovernmental cooperation among member states has become a form of 'intensive transgovernmentalism' (Lavenex and Wallace 2005). Recent years have seen further moves towards the 'traditional Community method' with powers increasingly transferred from the national to the EU level (Wallace 2005).

Academic scholarship on the European integration of JHA in general and immigration policies in particular has been sparse. In the field of European studies at least the subject has received some attention as can be seen from the regular coverage of this policy field in yearbooks of European integration (see, for example, Weidenfeld and Wessels 2005). Students of immigration policy, however, have engaged with developments at the European level comparatively late in the day. Their focus was for some time directed towards nationally distinct policy responses to immigration (see, for example, Hammar 1985a; Heckmann and Bosswick 1995; but see also Thränhardt and Miles 1995). Research on the development of supranational regimes and structures and their impacts on national immigration policies has therefore seriously lagged behind. In the 1990s, however, this situation started to change. An increasing number of studies show the awakening interest in the European integration of JHA and immigration policies. Existing studies analyse these developments either as part of the more general construction of the Justice and Home Affairs pillar (for example, Den Boer 1998; Monar and Morgan 1994) or as the development of a European immigration policy more specifically (Favell 1998; Geddes 2000; Guiraudon 2003; Koslowski 1998; Tomei 2001).

The explanation for the increase in European cooperation on immigration matters falls back on a wide range of causes and theories. In particular, two characteristic views are regularly found in the literature, which largely reflect the divide between neo-functional and intergovernmental theories on European integration more generally. The first view is rooted in international relations theories of interdependence; it argues that in an increasingly global world, states seek international solutions to domestic problems (Keohane and Nye 1977). In this line of thinking, EU cooperation on immigration matters is caused by the decreasing ability of states to control immigration because of the self-preserving nature of immigration, the constraining impact of economic imperatives and international legal norms (Faist 2000; Sassen 1999; Soysal 1994). These arguments are closely connected to those of a neo-functionalist tradition, where 'spillover' and 'unintended consequences' from other EU policies provide rationales for common EU policies on immigration. In consequence, the construction of the internal market of the EU with its free movement of goods and persons encouraged compensatory measures to maintain public order across the EU (Lavenex and Wallace 2005: 460).

The second view on the European integration on immigration policy takes a state-centric and intergovernmental perspective. Here, the starting point is the nation state which indeed has the power to manage international migration and control the national territory (Zolberg 1999). Two different arguments can be found from this perspective. The first is closely connected to liberal intergovernmentalism and argues that exogenous pressures stemming from growing international migration and crime cause convergence of national preferences and therefore establish a precondition for cooperation. From this perspective the EU provides the framework for member states to cooperate with the aim of reducing negative externalities and transaction costs (Hix 2005: 359–64; Moravcsik 1993). The second argument has a different starting point. Rather than exogenous factors, it is domestic political constraints that cause nation states to cooperate on the supranational level. Public opinion, extreme right-wing parties, economic actors, ethnic groups and constitutional courts have been singled out as factors that have led to the loss of control over the immigration agenda (Castles and Kosack 1985; Freeman 1995; Joppke 1999; Lahav 2004; Thränhardt 1993). From this point of view, the development of a common EU immigration policy is explained by the opportunity afforded to national bureaucrats to circumvent political constraints on the national level by shifting to the new venue the European level offered (Guiraudon 2000a, 2003; Huysmans 2000).

The Europeanization of national immigration policies

In contrast to the study of the European integration of immigration policies, our knowledge about the Europeanization of national immigration policies is far more limited. In the study of Europeanization in general, we already have a good conceptual understanding of what we are studying as well as about the terms and concepts we are using (Börzel 2005a; Eising 2003; Featherstone 2003). Overall, however, Europeanization still has the status of an 'attention directing device' (Olsen 2002: 943–4) and little attention has been focused on the European influence on national politics and policies of immigration. This can be explained by the fact that European competencies in this area are relatively recent and that migration policies are closely linked to national sovereignty and to fairly well-established national models. A second explanation is that the legal base of EU action was deliberately designed to minimize the scope for intervention by EU-level institutions such as the Commission, Parliament and the European Court of Justice (ECJ) into member state affairs.

While there are good reasons why the analyses of the European impact on national immigration policies have lagged, important questions remain. The past 15 years have witnessed important national reforms of immigration policies in all major European immigration countries. For example, Germany fundamentally altered its asylum policy in 1992 and introduced its first encompassing immigration Act in January 2005. The United Kingdom (UK) has produced three major immigration Acts since 1999 and the Immigration, Asylum and Nationality Act 2006 received royal assent on 30 March 2006. Similarly, the Spanish 'Alien Law' has seen three major reforms during recent years, Poland introduced major legislation in 2001 and 2003 and Turkey is discussing a new 'Law of Settlement' to replace the original Act dating back to 1934. Scholars of immigration have come up with different models to explain distinct national policies of immigration and its developments (for recent reviews see Cornelius and Rosenblum 2005; Hollifield 2000). What we know little about, however, is the extent of the international and in particular the European impact on these national immigration policy reforms. What role can the EU play in the increasing multi-level governance of migration? If a European influence on member states of the EU exists, what is the nature of that influence: do national immigration policies develop towards a similar shared model or does the Europeanization of national policies lead to greater divergence? The available literature on the Europeanization of immigration is mainly concerned with policies on refugees and asylum. What about the European impact on policies of other categories of immigrants, for example family reunification, labour migration or irregular immigration? Europeanization studies of other policy areas have provided ample evidence that Europeanization is highly differentiated between the member states. Do these findings hold true for immigration policies as well, and if so, how can we explain these differential European impacts? Finally, prior discussion on the theories of European integration of immigration policies has shown that national political constraints provided a major rationale for policy-makers to 'escape to Europe'. How does the establishment of a harmonized policy on the European level subsequently affect the domestic politics of immigration?

So far, the available literature provides us with contradictory evidence on these questions. On the one hand some scholars attest that the EU exerts great impact on national immigration policies. Eiko Thielemann (2002: 2), for example, argues that 'European integration must be regarded as a crucial catalyst' for the far-reaching changes in national asylum systems introduced during the early 1990s across Europe. On the other hand some scholars see only weak links between European and domestic policies. Maarten Vink (2002: 13) argues in his study on the Netherlands 'that many proactive efforts to bring about a common European policy, do not necessarily imply the subsequent Europeanisation of domestic politics'. And Andrew Geddes (2003: 196) shows in his comparative analysis that the EU's impact constituted only a marginal explanatory factor to account for national immigration policy reforms during the 1980s and 1990s.

These contradictory findings arise primarily because there is 'little systematic empirical research on how European developments "hit home" at the national level' (Vink 2005a: 4). Nevertheless, in recent years there has been an increasing interest in the study of European influences on domestic immigration policies and the compliance of member states with European norms in this policy area. Most available studies are overly descriptive and provide only few insights about the underlying driving forces of the European impact on its member states. For example, a number of juridical studies offer detailed information concerning the legislative absorption of Europe and the compliance with European policies (see Carlier and De Bruycker 2005; Higgins 2004). Into the same category fall a number of comparative volumes with single-country studies on immigration policies in different European member states. Their main focus, however, is aimed at national developments and not at the role of the EU in the multi-level governance of immigration (see, for example, Angenendt 1999; Brochmann and Hammar 1999). More explicit attention to the role of Europe in driving national changes in the policies and politics of immigration can be found in a number of single-country studies.

Examples include studies of the UK (Geddes 2005), the Netherlands (Vink 2005b) and Germany (Tomei 2001) as well as of non-member states like Switzerland (Fischer et al. 2002) and the analyses included in the volume by Lavenex and Uçarer (2002). From a theoretical point of view, Lavenex's analysis of the restrictive European discourse on asylum policy and how it framed national asylum and refugee policies (Lavenex 2001) is particularly significant. Other studies with a theoretical interest include Geddes's (2003) comparative analysis of the Europeanization of immigration policy in selected European countries, which provides initial indications about the extent of the domestic European impact on this policy area. Finally, mention should be made of the analysis by Grabbe (2005), who applied a rational choice approach to account for the European impact on the immigration policies in countries in Central and Eastern Europe, and the work by Thielemann (2002), who differentiated between three mechanisms of Europeanization to understand the changes in asylum policies of European member states during the 1990s.

Although recent years have witnessed a definitive interest in the Europeanization of the policies and politics of immigration, comparative and systematic research is still sparse. Most analyses are concerned with asylum and refugee policies, take little or no account of policies for other categories of migration, and focus mainly on the period prior to the Amsterdam Treaty. Theoretical approaches tend to deal primarily with the particular situation in the countries under consideration. Much attention is directed towards domestic factors that contribute to understanding the impact of the EU on a particular country or group of countries. The different types of interactions between the EU and its member and non-member states, however, have received comparatively little attention in the effort to explain the differential domestic impact of the EU.

Concentric circles of Europeanization

Building upon the shortcomings of the available literature, this volume consists of a comparative analysis of nine empirical case studies – six member and three non-member states of the EU. The case selection is presented in Figure 1.1. Overall, the analysis follows the institutional politics of emerging European immigration policy comprised of 'concentric circles' of European integration and different dates of accession to the EU. The inner core of Schengen member states is represented by Germany, Sweden, Greece and Spain. Although all four countries are

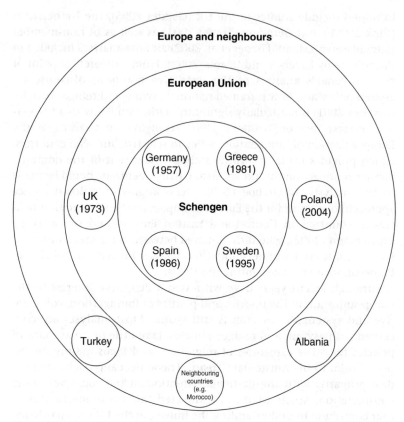

Figure 1.1   Concentric circles of the emerging European immigration policy and the selection of cases for this volume (time of accession to the EU in parentheses)

members of the EU and Schengen, each entered the EU at a different time. Germany represents one of the founding members of the EU, whereas Greece and Spain joined the EU during its southern enlargement in the 1980s, and finally Sweden, which joined the EU only in 1995. The second circle – EU member states that are not members of Schengen – comprises the UK as a traditional member state, which joined the EU in 1973, and Poland, which joined the EU in May 2004 and represents a country of the European eastern enlargement. Finally, the third circle consists of two non-member states with a long-term EU membership perspective – Turkey and Albania. This circle also includes a third case study that does not deal with a single country but rather with the European efforts to include neighbouring states in its immigration control efforts. In contrast to the studies on Albania and Turkey, however, this final chapter addresses the question to what extent and how the EU is affecting the immigration policy of countries that have no or only a very vague membership perspective (Lavenex, this volume).

In addition to the institutional politics of European immigration policy and the accession date of the respective countries, the case selection also accounts for three further aspects: first, it includes countries that have received relatively little attention in comparative projects, such as Sweden and Greece. So far, most available studies on Europeanization have tended clearly to favour some larger member states such as Germany, the UK and Italy (Mastenbroek 2005: 1112); some comparative work has been done within a certain group of states, such as the new member states (Schimmelfennig and Sedelmeier 2005). What is lacking are studies comparing traditional EU member states with new and prospective members with respect to the differential extent and modes of Europeanization in these largely different cases. Second, the case selection also takes into account one of the major findings of previous studies on the Europeanization of national immigration policies, namely its great impact on new and future member states. The volume attempts to compare the differential effects of Europe between countries representing different circles of the developing European immigration policy, and with a focus not only on major European member states but on non-member states as well. The analysis includes not only the 'externalities of European integration' (Lavenex and Uçarer 2002) but also traditional member states in order to compare and explain the differential impacts of the EU. Finally, the case selection also takes into account the largely different experiences of immigration in Europe. Here, the UK, Germany and Sweden represent those countries with the longest history of immigration after the Second World War. That history is characterized by large-scale postcolonial migration in the first case and large-scale guest worker migration in the latter two cases. All three countries therefore began early on to develop a comprehensive national immigration policy. In contrast, the experience of immigration in all other countries analysed in this volume is of more recent provenance. Spain and Greece are 'latecomers' to immigration; both share a history of emigration and both turned into immigration countries only during the 1980s. Poland's post-Second World War migration experience was dominated by low levels of international migration. The main turning point occurred after the end of the cold war when Poland began to serve as an important transit country for migrants from the former USSR heading west. Similarly, Turkey and Albania have been for the most part emigration countries since the Second World War and have begun to receive major inflows of migrants only in recent years. From the perspective of the EU, however, both states are major transit countries for migrants on their way to Europe.

Dimensions of Europeanization

This volume defines Europeanization generally as the impact of the EU on its member states. More specifically, the volume follows the work by Bulmer and Radaelli (2004: 4) who define Europeanization as consisting of

> processes of a) construction, b) diffusion and c) institutionalisation of formal and informal rules, procedures, policy paradigms, styles, 'ways of doing things' and shared beliefs and norms which are first defined and consolidated in the EU policy process and then incorporated in the logic of domestic (national and sub-national) discourse, political structures and public policies.

This definition provides a broad framework with which to understand multi-level governance interactions in Europe, and it stresses that Europeanization is clearly a two-way process – bottom-up and top-down – between the member states and the EU. It acknowledges that any comprehensive explanation of member-state responses to the EU requires an analysis of how the two processes interact (see, for example, Beyers and Trondal 2003; Börzel 2005a). For purposes of clarity, however, this volume defines Europeanization as the top-down process of member-state adaptation to the EU in order to distinguish it from European integration understood as the bottom-up process of member states projecting influence. The volume therefore follows the usual 'three-step approach': the process of Europeanization starts first with the development of a governmental system and particular policies at the European level. In the second step these political structures and European policies generate adaptational pressures for domestic policies and policy-making processes. The third stage, or end point, of this process consists of national policies and politics adapting to EU-level developments.

Following on from this definition, the contributors to this volume are mainly interested in three substantive research questions. First, we ask what is Europeanized. Second, we are concerned with the extent of Europeanization. And finally, we want to improve our understanding of why and how Europeanization occurs in these areas of policies and politics. Concerning the first question, the volume addresses two main 'dimensions of domestic change' (Börzel and Risse 2003: 59): the Europeanization of national *policies* of immigration and the Europeanization of national *politics* of immigration. In the case of policies of immigration the volume focuses on four politically defined categories of migration: (1) labour migration, (2) refugee and asylum migration, (3) secondary migration (for example, family reunification) and (4) irregular migration. Consequently, other areas of immigration policies are generally excluded – these include the free movement regulations of citizens of EU member states in the EU, as well as ethnic migrants, who are not subject to European immigration policy. Finally, policies of integration, such as anti-discrimination legislation and citizenship policies,[4] are also excluded from this volume. This concentration on immigration control policies (Hammar 1985b) takes into account the need to disaggregate migration policies to successfully explain the dynamics of policy-making (Freeman 2003).

There are three main reasons for the focus on the second dimension – the Europeanization of national politics of immigration. The first is that the bulk of studies focusing on European influences in the domestic sphere have dealt only with the domestic implementation of EU policies (Vink and Graziano forthcoming: 3). Despite some informative and important works (see for example the volume by Goetz and Hix 2001), the institutional structures and processes of national political systems have received less attention. In a related vein, Haverland (2003: 216f.) argues that 'it is likely that by changing national policies and sectoral regulatory structures the European Union also affects domestic institutional structures of representation and cleavages more generally. Policy-oriented case studies of the new generation should consider these broader effects.' The second reason is that there are difficulties assessing the domestic adjustments in policy-making processes in response to the EU. Available studies often conclude with rather fuzzy results because of the vast differences between individual policy sectors. Schmidt (forthcoming) argues that studies on the Europeanization of politics need to take into account the 'micro pattern' of policy-making concerning individual policies. The volume follows this advice and contributes to this research approach. Finally, the third factor has already been noted. National political constraints have been singled out as a major driving force for European integration in this policy area. It is thus of great interest to analyse whether the national politics of immigration have changed subsequently. As shall be seen, in this volume the politics of immigration has a rather broad meaning. It ranges from basic characteristics of national policy-making processes to changes in the political or public discourse on immigration and the changing beliefs of policy-makers on immigration.

The extent of Europeanization

The second research question raised in the case studies concerns the actual extent of Europeanization. Here, the two dimensions differentiated above are taken up again. The contributors examine the extent of Europeanization with respect to the national policies and politics of immigration. To assess the degree of the Europeanization the contributors to this volume apply the typology by Radaelli (2003) who differentiates between four types of change: inertia, absorption, transformation and retrenchment:

1. *Inertia* describes a situation of lack of change. This may happen when a member state assesses that EU policies are too dissimilar to domestic practice. On the other hand, inertia can also describe cases where EU policies are similar to national policies and do not cause national changes to be transposed. Inertia may take the forms of delays in the transposition of directives, resistance to EU-induced change, or notes by national governments on the transposition of certain European directives stating minimal changes as for example in the case of lowest-denominator directives. In the analyses included in this volume, inertia has been observed, for example, in the UK where, notwithstanding the timely transposition of certain directives, the actual changes to Britain's own immigration policy have been minimal. Other examples include Germany, where recent years are best characterized as a period of inertia with a whole range of European immigration policies not yet implemented.
2. *Absorption* describes a type of change in which the domestic policies or politics adapt to European requirements. The domestic structures of politics and policy provide a mixture of resiliency and flexibility: they can absorb certain non-fundamental changes, without real modification of the essential structures or changes in

policy or politics. In all the analyses included in this volume, absorption is the most common type of change. It aptly characterizes the experience with European immigration policy of member states like Sweden. Although some EU policies like the Schengen Agreement caused more substantial change, most European directives have been easily absorbed into the existing Swedish approach to immigration control. Another example is Greece where early European policies on asylum were easily absorbed into the original Greek approach during the 1990s. The process flowed smoothly and without significant domestic political conflict because the restrictive European asylum measures have been supported by the national government and have the additional advantage of being seen as 'modern'.

3. *Transformation* is similar to what Hall (1993) labels 'third order' or paradigmatic change. It occurs when the fundamental logic of the domestic policy or political behaviour changes. It is obvious that only a few cases exist where the European impact on a particular member state would cause such far-reaching developments. In a policy area that was long dominated by unanimity voting in the European Council and which despite the recent moves towards QMV in certain areas is still dominated by cooperation based on intergovernmental thinking, member states will be attentive that European decisions will not overturn already established national 'ways of doing things'. Nevertheless, even in the case of immigration policy examples of transformative change exist. A first example – although outside of the scope of this volume – is the anti-discrimination directive of the EU. Here, a particular constellation of circumstances – European opposition to the extreme right-wing successes of the FPÖ in Austria and the engagement of an array of concerned interest groups – allowed the EU to pass this directive which in many European countries fundamentally changes the logic of policies on the integration of immigrants (Geddes and Guiraudon 2004). In the case of the politics and policies of immigration control, transformative domestic changes can be found as well. The best example among the cases included in this volume is Poland, where the fundamental logic of its new immigration policy has followed the role model of European neighbours and the requirements by the EU. But not only has Polish policy experienced transformative changes, but the politics and here in particular the elite discourse and the beliefs of Polish politicians have also come to closely resemble the European discourse.

4. Finally, *retrenchment* implies that national policies and politics become less 'European' than they were. In the case of the Europeanization of the politics and policies of immigration only a few cases of retrenchment exist, but even a couple of case studies provide ample evidence for the importance of national interests in immigration policy. In countries where the preferences of the national government are in contradiction to the development of European immigration policy, retrenchment is a possible outcome. The most obvious case in point here is the introduction and continuation of the Spanish quota policy on irregular migration.

Beyond this typology, the extent of change caused by the EU can be defined further by a clear focus on policy outputs instead of policy outcomes. The focus is therefore on legislative changes on the national level. Less attention is focused on the subnational levels, on the implementation of these policies and on the results of policies. Finally, the case studies included in this volume focus more on already established policies on the European level and their domestic impacts. Measures that have been discussed at the European level but where no political agreement could be reached receive less attention. This brings the volume closer in line with Europeanization research in other policy areas as well as with studies on the compliance of nation states with European norms.

Modes of Europeanization

The third major research question which structures this volume and each individual chapter concerns the 'how' question and the differences between the European impact on the different dimensions – policies and politics – as well as the different countries under consideration. The literature on the Europeanization of domestic policies and political processes indicates a 'differential' impact of European requirements on domestic policies (see, for example, Héritier et al. 2001). Theoretical concepts that attempt to account for these varying patterns of Europeanization focus mainly on the 'goodness of fit' between the European-level policies and politics and the domestic level and on a number of mainly domestic intervening variables (for an overview see Mastenbroek 2005; Risse 2001). One of the main findings of this volume is that – at least for the policies of immigration – the mode of Europeanization is the crucial explanatory variable, rather the 'goodness of fit'. The volume draws upon the work by

Scharpf (1999, 2000) and Wallace (2005) to differentiate between two fundamental modes of Europeanization to account for the differential impact of the EU on the policies of its member and non-member states. Both modes – prescriptive and discursive Europeanization – are 'types of interaction' (Scharpf 2000), 'steering modes' (Knill and Lenschow 2005) or 'governance techniques' (Fletcher 2003) which characterize ideal-typical patterns of governance in the multi-level European immigration policy.[5]

Overall, both modes differ along the degree of coercive pressure the EU can exert on a particular state to change its policies. The first mode – prescriptive Europeanization – is concerned with national reregulation in cases where the EU provides institutional models for domestic compliance. Prescriptive Europeanization is a form of coercive governance, defined as legally binding European legislation which leaves little or no discretion to the national implementer. Member states are required to make sure that these supranational policies are put into practice. In this mode the EU exerts high coercive pressure on a member state. In contrast, the second mode – discursive Europeanization – operates largely without pressure. There is no legally binding prescription of institutional models for domestic compliance; rather, these models offer non-binding suggestions for national policy-makers to guide the search for regulatory solutions to certain policy problems. Here, the EU serves mainly as an arena for the exchange of political ideas and promotes information exchange in transnational networks. This pattern of governance is often used to prepare the ground for policies that subsequently define institutional models for domestic compliance. The best known example in this respect is the open method of coordination.

Main results

Following this broadly defined research framework set out in the preceding sections the comparative country chapters in this volume all follow roughly the same structure. After providing some general information about each country's experience with immigration and its relations towards the EU, the chapters offer analyses of the impact of European immigration policy on, first, the national policies of immigration and, second, the national politics of immigration. The third part of the analysis considers the main driving forces and explanatory factors for the particular pattern of Europeanization.

The remainder of this introductory chapter provides a broad overview of the main results of the volume, with special attention to two main conclusions. The first finding concerns the differential outcomes of the European impact on the national immigration policies in different member states. Whereas in traditional member states discursive modes of Europeanization lead to greater national policy changes, the extent of change decreases with the trend towards more prescriptive modes of interaction between the EU and its member states. In newer member states, in contrast, this pattern is reversed. Here, the extent of Europeanization is higher in cases characterized by prescriptive modes of interaction compared to discursive modes which result in only moderate policy change. The second conclusion concerns the comparison of Europeanization of the two dimensions analysed throughout the volume – policy and politics. Overall, the different case studies show that the European impact is far greater on the national policies than on the national politics of immigration. Furthermore, the volume reveals that Europeanization in the two dimensions follows largely different logics. Whereas the extent of Europeanization of the policies of immigration are best explained by the mode of Europeanization, the extent of the Europeanization of the politics of immigration is better explained by the compatibility between national and European structures of policy-making.

As to the extent of Europeanization of the domestic immigration policies, the volume shows great differences between the countries analysed. This differential extent of Europeanization is best understood as a continuum ranging from inertia or minor changes in domestic policies at one end of the spectrum to transformative and comprehensive changes at the other. All of the six member states of the EU studied can be situated on this continuum, with the UK at one end, with minor changes, and Poland at the other, with great alterations of its policy. In between are countries such as Germany and Sweden, which are closer to the British pole, as well as Greece and Spain, which are closer to the experience of Poland. Furthermore, the case studies overall show the reciprocal relationship between the mode and the extent of Europeanization, with discursive modes of interaction leading to greater national policy change in the case of traditional member states and prescriptive modes resulting in a greater extent of Europeanization in the case of new member states.

Compared with the other countries analysed in this volume, the UK is the case that displays the least EU influence on the original British approach to immigration control. The analysis of the British case shows overall minor national policy changes caused by the EU since the end of the 1990s (see Andreas Ette and Jürgen Gerdes in this volume). But the British case is not only the one with the least extent of Europeanization, it also provides evidence for the importance of the pattern of governance in accounting for the outcome of the European impact. During the 1990s and for some years prior, the interaction between the UK and the EU on immigration and asylum matters was based on discursive modes of interaction. This changed with the Amsterdam Treaty and the increasing supranationalization of this policy area. The British case provides a first indication of the importance of the modes of Europeanization to account for the European impact on national immigration policies. Overall, Britain's immigration and asylum policy experienced greater impact and harmonization with European policy approaches during the 1990s than after the Amsterdam Treaty. Examples from the early 1990s include the changes to British asylum policy that came about as a result of, for example, European initiatives that led to the Dublin Convention and the London Resolutions. In contrast, the years after 1999 have seen minimal national policy changes resulting from EU initiatives. The sole exception is policies on human trafficking and smuggling, for which the UK adopted the European policy framework – no original British policy had been developed in advance. In the case of all other European policies, the European requirements have introduced only minor changes, or the British governments decided to opt out of particular European measures.

The relationship between the extent and mode of Europeanization is even more obvious in the German case (see Stefan Alscher and Kathrin Prümm, this volume). Germany was generally seen as the 'model student' of European integration, actively participating in the process of European integration in general and showing particular interest in a common European immigration policy. In line with this image, European activities during the 1990s profoundly altered Germany's immigration policy. In particular, the fundamental change of Germany's asylum policy associated with the change in its basic law can be directly attributed to European involvement. The Amsterdam Treaty, however, marks a turning point for Germany's involvement in the common European immigration policy as Germany changed 'from a vanguard to a laggard' (Hellmann et al. 2005). In contrast to the earlier period, European developments after 1999 have not, overall, significantly affected Germany's immigration policy. And a recent draft bill announced by the German government in January 2006 to transpose several European directives is not expected to introduce serious policy changes either.

At the other end of the spectrum is Poland, a new member state which joined the EU in the course of the eastern enlargement only in 2004. Generally, those countries that joined the club only recently have experienced the most comprehensive Europeanization of their domestic immigration policy. Agata Gorny, Anna Kicinger and Agnieszka Weinar (this volume) provide a detailed analysis of the European impact before and after 1997 and the associated modes of Europeanization in both time periods. Again, the mode of Europeanization seems an important predictor for the extent of policy change caused by the EU. Unlike the situation in the traditional member states, however, the impact of the EU is greatest in the case of prescriptive Europeanization. Nevertheless, the need to establish an immigration policy in due course after the collapse of the Eastern Bloc allowed the EU to impact on Poland's immigration policy already before more coercive measures had been in place. In consequence, the EU's impact on Poland's immigration policy has been considerable already from the early 1990s but has been especially powerful after 1997, when negotiations on EU accession were launched. During the early 1990s, the European impact was felt in particular in the establishment of an asylum system as Poland joined the Geneva Convention on refugees and the European Convention for the Protection of Human Rights and Fundamental Freedoms. Those developments were finally given expression in the 1997 Alien Act and introduced a range of measures that had been discussed on the European level at that time including, for example, temporary residence permits, carrier sanctions and the safe third country concept. The European impact actually intensified after 1997 and the amendments of the Alien Act in 2001 and 2003 transposed many European proposals into Polish immigration policy. 'Governance by conditionality', a particular form of prescriptive Europeanization, has characterized the interaction between the EU and Poland during the accession negotiations. In the course of these negotiations, and with strong aspirations to join the EU, Poland has willingly accepted the requirements on immigration policy.

Finally, the Greek case shows similarities with the Polish situation. Georgia Mavrodi's chapter in this volume shows how different modes of Europeanization have influenced immigration policy in Greece. In the Greek case the greater importance of prescriptive compared to discursive modes of Europeanization is obvious in the conditionality mechanisms in the run-up to Greece's joining the Schengen Agreement, as well as in the expected impact of recent European directives on immigration policy on Greek domestic policy. To become a party to the Schengen system Greece had to implement specific legal provisions concerning border controls, visa policy and the fight against clandestine immigration. The Europeanization of Greece's immigration policy was in this sense a precondition to joining common European institutions and is therefore – and in parallel to the Polish experience – best understood as a form of conditionality. The importance of prescriptive modes of governance for the Europeanization of Greece's immigration policy is also obvious in the transposition of the directives passed on the European level after the Amsterdam Treaty came into force. Although the directives on asylum have not yet been implemented it is expected that they will introduce fundamental changes to the recent policy approach. Overall, the obligation to adapt to EU immigration legislation is therefore expected to lead to increased Europeanization of Greek immigration and asylum legislation. Notwithstanding the importance of prescriptive modes of governance for the great impact of the EU on Greece's immigration policy, discursive forms also play a role. This is of no surprise in a country 'where European political and social developments have often been considered as synonymous with modernization' (Mavrodi, this volume). Nevertheless, the changes introduced by prescriptive modes of interaction had greater impact on the development of immigration policy in the Greek case.

The assessment of the extent of Europeanization of immigration policies in countries such as Turkey (Ahmet İçduygu in this volume) and Albania (Imke Kruse in this volume) shows differences as well. The situation in both countries can be likened to that in Poland between 1997 and 2004 – highly coercive and prescriptive modes of Europeanization governed by conditionality. Both Turkey and Albania have a keen interest in joining the EU, and they are likely to accept European demands when it comes to changing their immigration policy. Finally, in countries that have no or only a very vague EU membership prospect (such as Morocco or Ukraine) the mode of Europeanization changes again. In those countries the 'EU lacks the carrot of accession in order to yield cooperation' (Lavenex in this volume). In consequence, different types of interaction come into play. Lavenex identifies three: positive conditionality linked with intergovernmental negotiations (for example, in the case of readmission agreements), policy transfer through transgovernmental networking and the mobilization of overarching international organizations such as the International Organization for Migration and the UNHCR. Overall, the impact of the EU on third countries such as Ukraine or Morocco, as well as to a lesser extent on Turkey and Albania, is weaker than, say, in the Polish case. In those cases, the EU can exert less pressure to comply with European policies. Furthermore, the incentives to comply are reduced because the rewards of compliance are smaller and more precarious than, for example, in the Polish case where EU accession was a more likely prospect. In consequence, Europeanization is far less encompassing and focuses only on those aspects of a country's immigration policy that serves European interests of immigration control.

The second conclusion of this volume is that the European impact is far greater on the national policies than on the national politics of immigration, as indicated by the evidence provided by the analyses in the chapters that follow. The explanation for this conclusion falls back on two different factors which are both able to account for this difference. The first factor focuses on general characteristics of immigration policies with regard to the importance of different actors in the policy-making and decision-making processes and general findings of the impact of the EU on national politics. Despite recent arguments about the importance of interest groups and the judiciary in immigration policy-making (see, for example, Freeman 2006; Guiraudon 2000b), immigration politics as well as other policy areas in JHA are usually regarded as elite-dominated and characterized as a policy sector with strong executive dominance and only minor access by the legislatures, political parties and interest groups (Hammar 1985a; Statham and Geddes 2006). During recent years, this pattern of executive dominance has even increased. The tightness of the migration–security–nexus, the continuing securitization of immigration and the mingling of external and internal security issues with immigration have strengthened the grasp of the executive in this policy area (Faist 2005). Given these general findings on the impact of the EU on national politics, fundamental shifts in this dimension are unlikely. Those studies mainly conclude that the European impact on national politics results in a strengthening of the executive as opposed to the legislatures (see for example Andersen and Burns 1996; Börzel and Sprungk forthcoming). Therefore, there is a good fit between general patterns of the politics of immigration on the one hand and the European impact on national politics on the other. In consequence, a maintaining or even strengthening of this pattern can be expected, while any fundamental changes are unlikely.

The second explanation for the comparatively weak impact of the EU on national politics is based on nationally specific institutional arrangements which are clearly visible in the politics but not so obvious in the policies dimension. National institutional frameworks for politics are much harder to Europeanize than more contingent regulatory approaches in the policy dimension (see for example Maurer et al. 2003). The results of the individual country chapters in this volume all indicate that the extent of Europeanization in the politics compared to the policy dimension is small, and that there has been generally little impact on the national politics of immigration. A first example is Sweden (Mikael Spång this volume) with its traditionally strong, policy-shaping parliament. Here, the Europeanization of policy-making processes has clearly strengthened the executive, with parliamentary committees facing great difficulties in influencing the government on European issues. Similar problems are reported for the process of transposition. The implementation of EU directives in Swedish law is generally prepared by expert commissions and working groups in the ministries rather than in parliament, which contributes to a further weakening of this institution. Another example supporting the same trend is provided by Margit Fauser's analysis (this volume) of the Spanish situation. In a country with a strong executive the European impact actually reinforces classical features of the Spanish political system. When the 'EU pushes and the government pulls for a more restrictive policy' the parliamentary opposition as well as interest groups have great difficulties getting their voices heard.

Despite these findings which show the reinforcement of traditional national patterns of policy-making, the contributions in this volume report a number of cases where the EU provides for new configurations in the national politics of immigration. A first example is the UK which is traditionally seen as a country where a strong executive and weak judicial control has enabled a very tough immigration control regime. Overall, the analysis shows that the politics of immigration in the UK have not been altered by Britain's participation in the developing European immigration policy. Nevertheless, the British adoption of the European Convention on Human Rights (ECHR) could in the long term significantly alter these established ways of doing things. Indeed, the analysis provides initial evidence towards such a development. The most remarkable results, however, can again be seen in the new member states such as Poland, as well as in potential future members of the EU such as Turkey or Albania. In the Polish case, the institutional framework of immigration policy-making has not changed in substance for more than 15 years. Even in Poland we find a clear executive dominance over immigration policy-making. Neither the parliament nor interest groups have real access to the policy-making process.

Europeanization has changed this institutional framework only slightly, in a proposal to establish a central government organ dealing with migration policy. Instead, the beliefs and elite discourse of politicians in Poland have been Europeanized to a large extent. The perception of uncontrolled immigration as a threat and the 'fortress Europe' approach have been effectively transferred to the Polish ground notwithstanding the small numbers of immigrants in Poland.

We began this introductory chapter with the observation that the recent crisis of the EU provides a chance to pause and assess the progress of European integration. All the contributions in this volume have collected detailed information about the European impact on policies and politics of immigration up to the end of the first five-year period of the Tampere Action Plan. Together, they provide striking evidence for the importance of the EU for understanding national political reactions to immigration and the changing multi-level governance of migration in Europe. The empirical and theoretical insights of this volume open the box towards an even fuller understanding of the interactions between the EU and its member states.

Notes

1   For the sake of simplicity, this volume refers to the EU, even if the term 'European Community' would be more accurate, for example for events before the entry into force of the Treaty on European Union in 1993.
2   The term 'EU-ization' compared to 'Europeanization' would be more accurate to describe the impact of the EU on its member and non-member states. However, we go along with the widely used term 'Europeanization' also because of linguistic simplicity.
3   For the differentiation between level and scope see, for example, Börzel (2005b).
4   On citizenship policies, see Faist (2006).
5   The modes of Europeanization discussed here are in clear contrast to the discussion on the 'mechanisms of Europeanization'. Whereas mechanisms generally refer to the domestic processes that link the European level and national change, the modes of Europeanization describe the patterns of governance which link the EU with a particular member state (see Knill and Lehmkuhl 1999).

References

Andersen, S. S. and T. R. Burns (1996) 'The European Union and the Erosion of Parliamentary Democracy: a Study of Post-parliamentary Governance'. In S. S. Andersen and K. A. Eliassen (eds), *The European Union: How Democratic Is It?* London: Sage.

Angenendt, S. (ed.) (1999) *Asylum and Migration Policies in the European Union*. Bonn: Europa Union Verlag.

Beyers, J. and J. Trondal (2003) 'How Nation-States "Hit" Europe – Ambiguity and Representation in the European Union'. *European Integration online Papers (EIoP)*, Vol. 7, No. 5.

Börzel, T. A. (2005a) 'Europeanization: How the European Union Interacts with its Member States'. In S. Bulmer and C. Lequesne (eds), *The Member States of the European Union*. Oxford: Oxford University Press.

Börzel, T. A. (2005b) 'Mind the Gap! European Integration between Level and Scope'. *Journal of European Public Policy*, Vol. 12, No. 2: 217–36.

Börzel, T. A. and T. Risse (2003) 'Conceptualizing the Domestic Impact of Europe'. In K. Featherstone and C. M. Radaelli (eds), *The Politics of Europeanization*. Oxford: Oxford University Press.

Börzel, T. A. and C. Sprungk (forthcoming) 'Undermining Democratic Governance in the Member States? The Europeanisation of National Decision-Making'. In R. Holzhacker and E. Albaek (eds), *Democratic Governance and European Integration*. Aldershot: Edward Elgar.

Boswell, C. (2003) 'The "External Dimension" of EU Cooperation in Immigration and Asylum'. *International Affairs*, Vol. 73, No. 3: 619–38.

Brochmann, G. and T. Hammar (eds) (1999) *Mechanisms of Immigration Control: a Comparative Analysis of European Regulation Policies*. Oxford and New York: Berg.

Bulmer, S. J. and C. M. Radaelli (2004) 'The Europeanisation of National Policy?' *Queen's Papers on Europeanisation*, Vol. 1/2004.

Carlier, J.-Y. and P. De Bruycker (eds) (2005) *Immigration and Asylum Law of the EU: Current Debates*. Brussels: Bruylant.

Castles, S. and G. Kosack (1985) *Immigrant Workers and Class Structure in Western Europe*. New York: Oxford University Press.

Commission of the European Communities (2004) 'Area of Freedom, Security and Justice: Assessment of the Tampere Programme and Future Orientations'. COM(2004) 4002 final. Brussels.

Cornelius, W. A. and M. R. Rosenblum (2005) 'Immigration and Politics'. *Annual Review of Political Science*, Vol. 8: 99–119.

Den Boer, M. (1998) 'Justice and Home Affairs'. In W. Wallace (ed.), *Policy-making in the European Union*. Oxford: Oxford University Press.

Eising, R. (2003) 'Europäisierung und Integration. Konzepte in der EU-Forschung'. In M. Jachtenfuchs and B. Kohler-Koch (eds), *Europäische Integration*. Opladen: Leske & Budrich.

Faist, T. (2000) *The Volume and Dynamics of International Migration and Transnational Social Spaces*. Oxford: Oxford University Press.

Faist, T. (2005) 'The Migration–Security Nexus: International Migration and Security before and after 9/11'. In Y. M. Bodemann and G. Yurdakul (eds), *Migration, Citizenship, Ethnos: Incorporation Regimes in Germany, Western Europe and North America*. London: Palgrave Macmillan.

Faist, T. (ed.) (2006) *Dual Citizenship in Europe: from Nationhood to Societal Integration*. Avebury, UK: Ashgate.

Falkner, G., O. Treib, M. Hartlapp and S. Leiber (2005) *Complying with Europe. EU Harmonisation and Soft Law in the Member States*. Cambridge: Cambridge University Press.

Favell, A. (1998) 'The Europeanisation of Immigration Politics'. *European Integration online Papers (EIoP)*, Vol. 2, No. 10.

Featherstone, K. (2003) 'Introduction: in the Name of "Europe"'. In K. Featherstone and C. M. Radaelli (eds), *The Politics of Europeanization*. Oxford: Oxford University Press.

Fischer, A., S. Nicolet, and P. Sciarini (2002) 'Europeanisation of a Non-EU Country: the Case of Swiss Immigration Policy'. *West European Politics*, Vol. 25, No. 4: 143–70.

Fletcher, M. (2003) 'EU Governance Techniques in the Creation of a Common European Policy on Immigration and Asylum'. *European Public Law*, Vol. 9, No. 4: 533–62.

Freeman, G. P. (1995) 'Modes of Immigration Politics in Liberal Democratic States'. *International Migration Review*, Vol. 29, No. 4: 881–902.

Freeman, G. P. (2003) 'Political Science and Immigration: Policy Types and Modes of Politics'. R. F. Harney Lecture Series, University of Toronto.

Freeman, G. P. (2006) 'National Models, Policy Types, and the Politics of Immigration in Liberal Democracies'. *West European Politics*, Vol. 29, No. 2: 227–47.

Geddes, A. (2000) *Immigration and European Integration: towards Fortress Europe?* Manchester: Manchester University Press.

Geddes, A. (2003) *The Politics of Migration and Immigration in Europe*. London: Sage.

Geddes, A. (2005) 'Getting the Best of Both Worlds? Britain, the EU and Migration Policy'. *International Affairs*, Vol. 81, No. 4: 723–40.

Geddes, A. and V. Guiraudon (2004) 'Britain, France, and EU Anti-Discrimination Policy: the Emergence of an EU Policy Paradigm'. *West European Politics*, Vol. 27, No. 2: 334–53.

Goetz, K. H. and S. Hix (eds) (2001) *Europeanised Politics? European Integration and National Political Systems*. London: Frank Cass.

Grabbe, H. (2005) 'Regulating the Flow of People across Europe'. In F. Schimmelfennig and U. Sedelmeier (eds), *The Europeanization of Central and Eastern Europe*. Ithaca, NY: Cornell University Press.

Guiraudon, V. (2000a) 'European Integration and Migration Policy: Vertical Policy-making as Venue Shopping'. *Journal of Common Market Studies*, Vol. 38, No. 2: 251–71.

Guiraudon, V. (2000b) 'The Marshallian Triptych Reordered: the Role of Courts and Bureaucracies in Furthering Migrants' Social Rights'. In M. Bommes and A. Geddes (eds), *Immigration and Welfare. Challenging the Borders of the Welfare State*. London: Routledge.

Guiraudon, V. (2003) 'The Constitution of a European Immigration Policy Domain: a Political Sociology Approach'. *Journal of European Public Policy*, Vol. 10, No. 2: 263–82.

Hall, P. (1993) 'Policy Paradigms, Social Learning, and the State: the Case of Economic Policymaking in Britain'. *Comparative Politics*, Vol. 25, No. 3: 275–96.

Hammar, T. (1985a) *European Immigration Policy: a Comparative Study*. Cambridge: Cambridge University Press.

Hammar, T. (1985b) 'Introduction'. In T. Hammar (ed.), *European Immigration Policy: a Comparative Study*. Cambridge: Cambridge University Press.

Haverland, M. (2003) 'The Impact of the European Union on Environmental Policies'. In K. Featherstone and C. M. Radaelli (eds), *The Politics of Europeanisation*. Oxford: Oxford University Press.

Heckmann, F. and W. Bosswick (eds) (1995) *Migration Policies: a Comparative Perspective*. Stuttgart: Enke.

Hellmann, G., R. Baumann, M. Bösche, B. Herborth and W. Wagner (2005) 'De-Europeanization by Default? Germany's EU Policy in Defense and Asylum'. *Foreign Policy Analysis*, Vol. 1: 143–64.

Héritier, A., D. Kerwer, C. Knill, D. Lehmkuhl, M. Teutsch and A.-C. Douillet (eds) (2001) *Differential Europe: the European Union Impact on National Policymaking*. Lanham: Rowman & Littlefield.

Higgins, I. (ed.) (2004) *Migration and Asylum Law and Policy in the European Union. FIDE 2004 National Reports*. Cambridge: Cambridge University Press.

Hix, S. (2005) *The Political System of the European Union*, 2nd edn. Houndmills: Palgrave.

Hollifield, J. F. (2000) 'The Politics of International Migration: How Can We "Bring the State Back in"?'. In C. B. Brettell and J. F. Hollifield (eds), *Migration Theory: Talking across Disciplines*. New York: Routledge.

Huysmans, J. (2000) 'The European Union and the Securitization of Migration'. *Journal of Common Market Studies*, Vol. 38, No. 5: 751–77.

Joppke, C. (1999) *Immigration and the Nation-State: the United States, Germany and Great Britain*. New York: Oxford University Press.

Keohane, R. O. and J. S. Nye (1977) *Power and Interdependence: World Politics in Transition*. Boston: Little, Brown.

Knill, C. and D. Lehmkuhl (1999) 'How Europe Matters: Different Mechanisms of Europeanization'. *European Integration online Papers (EIoP)*, Vol. 3, No. 7.

Knill, C. and A. Lenschow (2005) 'Coercion, Competition and Communication: Different Approaches of European Governance and their Impact on National Institutions'. *Journal of Common Market Studies*, Vol. 43, No. 3: 581–604.

Koslowski, R. (1998) 'European Union Migration Regimes, Established and Emergent'. In C. Joppke (ed.), *Challenge to the Nation-State*. Oxford: Oxford University Press.

Lahav, G. (2004) *Immigration and Politics in the New Europe: Reinventing Borders*. Cambridge: Cambridge University Press.

Lavenex, S. (2001) 'The Europeanization of Refugee Policies: Normative Challenges and Institutional Legacies'. *Journal of Common Market Studies*, Vol. 39: 851–74.

Lavenex, S. and E. M. Uçarer (eds) (2002) *Migration and the Externalities of European Integration*. Lanham: Lexington Books.

Lavenex, S. and W. Wallace (2005) 'Justice and Home Affairs: towards a "European Public Order"?' In H. Wallace, W. Wallace and M. A. Pollack (eds), *Policy-Making in the European Union*. Oxford: Oxford University Press.

Lindberg, L. N. and S. A. Scheingold (1970) *Europe's Would-Be Polity: Patterns of Change in the European Community*. Englewood Cliffs, NJ: Prentice-Hall.

Mastenbroek, E. (2003) 'Surviving the Deadline: the Transposition of EU Directives in the Netherlands'. *European Union Politics*, Vol. 4, No. 4: 371–95.

Mastenbroek, E. (2005) 'EU Compliance: Still a "Black Hole"?'. *Journal of European Public Policy*, Vol. 12, No. 6: 1103–20.

Maurer, A., J. Mitag and W. Wessels (2003) 'National Systems' Adaptation to the EU System: Trends, Offers and Constraints'. In B. Kohler-Koch (ed.), *Linking EU and National Governance*. Oxford: Oxford University Press.

Monar, J. and R. Morgan (eds) (1994) *The Third Pillar of the European Union: Cooperation in the Fields of Justice and Home Affairs*. Brussels: European Interuniversity Press.

Moravcsik, A. (1993) 'Preferences and Power in the European Community: a Liberal Intergovernmentalist Approach'. *Journal of Common Market Studies*, Vol. 31, No. 4: 473–524.

Olsen, J. P. (2002) 'The Many Faces of Europeanization'. *Journal of Common Market Studies*, Vol. 40, No. 5: 921–52.

Radaelli, C. M. (2003) 'The Europeanization of Public Policy'. In K. Featherstone and C. M. Radaelli (eds), *The Politics of Europeanization*. Oxford: Oxford University Press.

Risse, T. (2001) 'Europeanisation and Domestic Change: Introduction'. In M. Green Cowles, J. Caporaso and T. Risse (eds), *Transforming Europe: Europeanization and Domestic Change*. Ithaca, NY: Cornell University Press.

Sassen, S. (1999) *Guests and Aliens*. New York: The New Press.

Scharpf, F. W. (1999) *Regieren in Europa: effektiv und demokratisch?* Frankfurt am Main: Campus Verlag.

Scharpf, F. W. (2000) *Interaktionsformen. Akteurzentrierter Institutionalismus in der Politikforschung*. Opladen: Leske und Budrich.

Schimmelfennig, F. and U. Sedelmeier (eds) (2005) *The Europeanization of Central and Eastern Europe*. Ithaca, NY: Cornell University Press.

Schmidt, M. G. (1999) 'Die Europäisierung der öffentlichen Aufgaben'. In T. Ellwein and E. Holtmann (eds), *50 Jahre Bundesrepublik Deutschland*. Opladen: Westdeutscher Verlag.

Schmidt, V. A. (forthcoming) 'Procedural Democracy in the EU: the Europeanization of National and Sectoral Policymaking Processes'. *Journal of European Public Policy*.

Soysal, Y. N. (1994) *Limits of Citizenship: Migrants and Postnational Membership in Europe*. Chicago: University of Chicago Press.

Statham, P. and A. Geddes (2006) 'Elites and the "Organised Public": Who Drives British Immigration Politics and in Which Direction?' *West European Politics*, Vol. 29, No. 2: 248–69.

Thielemann, E. R. (2002) 'The "Soft" Europeanisation of Migration Policy: European Integration and Domestic Policy Change'. ECPR Joint Session of Workshops, Turin, 22–27 March.

Thränhardt, D. (1993) 'Die Ursprünge von Rassismus und Fremdenfeindlichkeit in der Konkurrenzdemokratie. Ein Vergleich der Entwicklungen in England, Frankreich und Deutschland'. *Leviathan*, Vol. 3: 336–57.

Thränhardt, D. and R. Miles (eds) (1995) *Migration and European Integration: the Dynamics of Inclusion and Exclusion*. London: Pinter.

Tomei, V. (ed.) (2001) *Europäisierung nationaler Migrationspolitik. Eine Studie zur Veränderung von Regieren in Europa*. Stuttgart: Lucius & Lucius.

Vink, M. P. (2002) 'Negative and Positive Integration in European Immigration Policies'. *European Integration online Papers (EIoP)*, Vol. 6, No. 13.

Vink, M. P. (2005a) 'European Integration and Domestic Immigration Policies. An Immigration Policy for Europe?', Florence, 13–15 March, 2005.

Vink, M. P. (2005b) *European Integration and Domestic Immigration Policies*. Basingstoke: Palgrave Macmillan.

Vink, M. P. and P. Graziano (forthcoming) 'Challenges of a New Research Agenda'. In M. P. Vink and P. Graziano (eds), *Europeanization: New Research Agendas*. Basingstoke: Palgrave Macmillan.

Wallace, H. (2005) 'An Institutional Anatomy and Five Policy Modes'. In H. Wallace, W. Wallace and M. A. Pollack (eds), *Policy-Making in the European Union*. Oxford: Oxford University Press.

Weidenfeld, W. and W. Wessels (eds) (2005) *Jahrbuch der Europäischen Integration 2005*. Baden-Baden: Nomos.

Zolberg, A. R. (1999) 'Matters of State: Theorizing Immigration Policy'. In C. Hirschman, P. Kasinitz and J. DeWind (eds), *The Handbook of International Migration: the American Experience*. New York: Russell Sage Foundation.

2

Everything under Control? The European Union's Policies and Politics of Immigration

Petra Bendel

In 2005, in the two Spanish exclaves of Ceuta and Melilla, hundreds of African immigrants tried to climb the fences of 'Fortress Europe' and several died from the injuries they sustained in the attempt. These incidents represented what was obviously just the tip of the iceberg of a much broader immigration movement, and made it perfectly clear to the broad European public that the European Union (EU) was quite far from having migration 'under control'. Indeed, these incidents catapulted immigration policies back to the top of the EU's agenda (Council of the European Union 2005a).

In order to (re-)gain control, the Commission and the Council of Ministers were quick to suggest a whole package of tools. Some of them were rather traditional and focused on the control aspect – in the sense of impeding the entry of broader immigration movements through visa regulations or border checks. Others went further, but were not really innovative either, seeming to have been taken out of the Commission's drawer where they had been waiting for years for their time to come. These suggestions comprised, for instance, a 'close co-operation with the countries of origin', or preventive measures – the fight against poverty, against human rights abuses, against authoritarian regimes and other push factors well known to be present in sub-Saharan Africa. So Ceuta and Melilla might have opened up, in 2005 and 2006, a real 'window of opportunity' for a pre-existing, but still more comprehensive idea of immigration management. This window, which had already been opened at least halfway after the Amsterdam Treaty and the Tampere Conclusions in 1999, had been closed after the terrorist attacks of 9/11 and after the conservative change in the Council of Ministers in and around 2001. Other ideas were taken out of the member states' drawers, too: such was the case with the so-called

Regional Protection Programmes which had been introduced into the Council of Ministers under different names (Protection Zones, Centres) and by different member states, but had until then been rejected.

It remains to be seen whether this package of measures, which implies a stronger relationship between immigration, trade and development, can be effectively pushed through the 'Ceuta window' and go effectively beyond the strict control aspect. If so, we would see as a result a comprehensive immigration management system that takes into account the complexity of immigration matters in the EU.

The aim here first is to assess if this new approach on the part of the EU, which will be developed under the new institutional conditions of the Programme of The Hague, might imply innovative strategies for a common asylum and immigration policy and whether the new co-decision procedures can help to change the character of the EU's immigration policy. Beyond that first assessment I then aim to analyse the respective instruments that the EU is planning for the years to come and to evaluate what the prospects for the contents of future common immigration policies might be.

Decision-making in EU immigration policies

Asylum and immigration policies have long since become unthinkable without the EU. Beginning with the establishment of EU citizenship in the Treaty of Maastricht (1992–93) and followed by the introduction of an entire chapter on asylum and immigration policies in the Treaty of Amsterdam (1997, in force 1999), the Community gained competence in this delicate area – an area that has traditionally been strongly linked to aspects of national sovereignty. European law on visa and on most asylum and refugee issues is now binding and justifiable and it is superior to national legislation in most of the member states. Only the UK, Ireland and Denmark have opted out of the common immigration, asylum and civil law policies. For the other member states, national veto power in the EU institutions was gradually reduced and the competencies of the European Parliament were gradually extended. According to article 67 (2) of the EC Treaty (Nice) and The Hague Programme, the Council has even recently decided to change the decision-making rules, introducing qualified majority voting (QMV) in 2005.

The introduction of QMV by The Hague Programme certainly challenges what has been labelled a 'two-level game' of the JHA Ministers in the Council who, more often than not, exploited the absence of public opinion and the practical exclusion of the European Parliament and the Court of Justice in Brussels to push forward decisions they might not have got through in domestic politics, while selling the negotiated directives in their member states as an 'EU decision'. Another way of regarding that game was 'policy venue shopping' (Guiraudon 2000). But as we have seen, democratic procedures and controls are being progressively introduced even in this sensitive area. Nevertheless, it remains to be seen whether this change in procedures also implies a simultaneous change in the traditionally restrictive and reactive contents of these policies, as some scholars expect. We should also bear in mind that the European Parliament is cited as being 'under considerable pressure to take a "realistic attitude" towards the protection of human rights in JHA policies'(Maurer and Parkes 2005: 10).

In spite of the above-mentioned changes in procedures, communitarization is still far from being complete since the member states have certainly retained (and will surely continue to retain) important discretions for themselves: in legal migration and integration policy some member states have insisted on preserving their domestic competencies and have refused to transmit them towards supranational authorities. In particular Germany and its *Länder* have been the most rigid defenders of maintaining domestic discretion with respect to labour migration issues, arguing that their labour market is too vulnerable to attract foreign labour. The Hague Programme that regulates JHA until 2010, therefore, retains unanimous voting as well as restricted parliamentary rights in this special part of immigration policy. Access to work for third-country nationals is, admittedly, a contentious issue and therefore the prerogative of member states which, according to the European Commission itself, can only be 'put in place progressively'.

The contents of common immigration policies and their development: the role of control

How can the contents of communitarized policies be sketched in more detail? If we accept, as I have argued (Bendel 2005), that immigration policy can and should follow at least five different (and often enough even contradictory) aims, such as: (1) the restriction and control of immigration, (2) the protection of refugees, (3) the prevention of refugee movements, (4) the integration of migrants and (5) the attraction of special groups of immigrants (for instance, the highly skilled), then we have to admit that migration policies in the EU have, so far, concentrated on only one overarching aspect: restriction and control.

By measures of immigration control I understand all those measures that refer to the selection, admission and deportation of third-country nationals, as well as those rules that control third-country nationals once they visit or take up residence in the EU member states; thus I do not limit the discussion to the mere admittance or non-admittance of third-country nationals to the territory of EU member states. We may then distinguish between external controls, such as entry restrictions and border controls, as well as visa schemes and carrier liabilities, legislation against illegal trafficking and certain preventive measures abroad such as so-called 'safe havens', as they are now and again discussed at EU level. But I also include some of the EU's instruments on internal migration control such as remigration and repatriation incentives. Nonetheless, I do not share the broad definition of migration control as a simple equivalent of migration management (Brochman and Hammar 1999).

Certainly these overarching aspects of security and (border) control did not develop in the course of immigration policy, but had already been present at the very birth of intergovernmental cooperation on migration issues like the Trevi Group (Terrorism, Radicalism, Extremism and Violence) or at least since Schengen II (Tomei 2001) and were later on inspired by the aim of restricting the 'waves' of asylum in the 1990s. These policies certainly showed a tendency to undermine social and economic aspects and were characterized by a mostly reactive rather than proactive understanding of migration (among others: Maurer and Parkes 2006). The fact that the process remained vastly intergovernmental sometimes led to a low degree of judicial binding and formalization of directives which, more often than not, limited themselves to minimum standards, thereby leaving just enough space for the member states to model their own understanding of migration issues (Maurer and Parkes 2006). The common denominator normally referred precisely to the control aspects. These were of course even more strongly emphasized when it came to terror prevention and, subsequently, to the so-called 'securitization' of JHA.

Nevertheless, it should also be kept in mind that control and security issues had been temporarily enriched by a more comprehensive and multidimensional vision of immigration that would have made more allowance for issues like protection, prevention, inclusion and even the attraction of (certain) migrants. This had been the case with the Tampere Conclusions of 1999. These guidelines, which are sometimes neglected by those scholars who focus their studies on the securitization of migration policies and leave out this important interlude, were the obvious expression of a real change of paradigms on the Commission's level. At least the Commission had realized that EU member states could enter into global competition only if they disposed of adequate human capital and if they were ready to address their demographic problems, mitigating them at least partly by enforcing replacement migration. These changes had led to regarding migration as a chance, instead of a threat, for the recipient countries, and the Commission maintains this view up to the present day. This is what I would like to call a real shift of paradigms in immigration issues, at least on the level of the Commission's proposals.

Although the Tampere guidelines, considered as a milestone in developing a common policy on immigration, had in fact represented a very promising programme, (internal) security and control aspects of migration policies were reinforced both in national and in EU migration policy after 9/11, and even more strongly after the terrorist attacks in Madrid in March 2004 and in London in May 2005.[1] This was surely also an effect of the more conservative political changes in the European countries' governments and, subsequently, in the Council of Ministers. Analysis can certainly show that the EU's directive proposals in almost every aspect of migration policy have undergone a most rigid change after 2001: windows of opportunity for a more liberal and comprehensive idea of migration that would include prevention and inclusion measures were definitively closed after that date. Ideas changed clearly in favour of those political actors who defended a more security- and control-related idea of migration policies. Without doubt, 9/11 was a clue; it was a real 'focusing event' for the enforcement of the control aspect in migration policies, policies that had their own well-known 'political entrepreneurs' backing them.

The Hague Programme, approved by the European Council in November 2004 as the EU's agenda for the five-year course up to 2010, put forth this position once again: the combating of terrorism was mentioned there as the first and central task for the common policies in JHA. Within immigration and asylum policies the security and control aspect is central in the form of border checks and the 'fight against illegal immigration' and it is found in many other guidelines issued by the European Council. In order to guarantee more security, the European Council invites the European organs and member states 'to continue their efforts to integrate biometric identifiers in travel documents, visas, residence permits, EU citizens' passports and information systems without delay and to prepare for the development of minimum standards for national identity cards'. The exchange of law-enforcement information is another important element of common policies envisaged in The Hague Programme. Although control and sur-veillance of external borders are, of course, still a national discretion, a specialized border assistance programme provided by the European Agency for the Management of Operational Cooperation at the External Borders was established. Moreover, the European Council invites the member states to study the feasibility of a European border guard.

Given the continuing 'blur' between internal and external security (Maurer and Parkes 2005: 4), the control and security aspect has 'spilled over' across the different migration policies, and has penetrated subjects such as foreign and developmental policies, including greater interventionism in human rights issues or preventing terrorism at its source. In this way a number of issues are addressed, including some that have long been neglected with regard to migration policies, since immigration has traditionally been regarded as a subject of JHA.

Following some very vague comments in The Hague Programme on assistance for the countries of origin, but above all those expressed at an informal meeting of the EU Heads of State and Government in Hampton Court,[2] the British Presidency took 'out of the drawer' in November 2005[3] precisely some of the more multidimensional approaches towards migration issues,[4] although still under the head-line of security. It linked JHA to General Affairs and External Relations, to Developmental policy, to the European Neighbourhood Policy and to Employment. The Austrian Presidency put JHA within External Relations. In this sense, the Strategy for Africa as well as the more complex view of control measures for migration would possibly not have been pushed forward had it not been a reaction to the incidents in Ceuta and Melilla at the end of 2005.[5]

Preventive measures have thus regained place and space in migration policies – although not without the aspects of security and control – which had long been tapped by other issues. The Commission has already developed a detailed thematic programme for cooperation with third countries in the areas of migration and asylum (Commission of the European Communities 2005a), which includes humanitarian aid, stability and macro-financial assistance as well as pre-accession assis-tance, support to the European neighbourhood as well as development and economic cooperation.

Some of the other tools sketched out by the Austrian and Finnish Presidencies in 2006 were along more traditional lines: they want a common asylum procedure to be established and a uniform status guaranteed for those immigrants who are granted asylum and subsidiary protection. They then insist on addressing illegal immigration and trafficking as priorities and put particular emphasis on border control and similar measures. Apart from some instruments fostered in particular by the British Presidency, then, it would not be unreasonable to conclude that the most recent guidelines, too, are above all oriented to a sense of control.

Indeed, the number of 'illegal' immigrants who enter the EU is quite high, estimated at around half a million per year. The Council adopted some time ago a plan to combat illegal immigration and trafficking, including visa policies and border management, but also readmission, repatriation and human trafficking. We will take a more detailed look at these policies as well as at those developed for asylum-seekers and refugees and the new preventive measures suggested more recently.

Visa policies and borders: the classical policies of control

While the Schengen Accord removed border controls between the EU's member states, the Schengen Convention, incorporated meanwhile into EU law, forms the basis for external border controls. On the external control level European Council Regulations' (EC 539/2001) visa guidelines have been passed for a roster of countries of origin, a list which is reviewed once a year. The common visa policy also includes regulations on the security of documents and it requires, of course, information exchange. Thus, the European 'Schengen Information System' (SIS I and II) as well as a Visa Information System (VIS) were adopted; an electronic system for the identification of asylum-seekers' fingerprints was introduced (EURODAC, in order to determine which country is responsible for an asylum claim under the Dublin II Convention); as well as FADO, an image archiving system in order to combat 'illegal' immigration. Their common aim consists in collecting and exchanging data on asylum-seekers and on arrest warrants, missing persons or stolen objects. The Hague Programme also calls for the SIS II, VIS and EURODAC systems to be linked, and the Council is planning to prepare a legal and technical platform for SIS II, which will be operational in 2007.[6] Biometric identifiers (iris scanning, fingerprints, facial recognition) – a subject of hot debate among human rights activists – are going to be introduced. The Commission has recommended overturning a Council decision on the access to consultation of VIS by the member states and by Europol for the purposes of the prevention, detection and investigation of terrorist offences and other serious criminal offences (Commission of the European Communities 2005b). This proposal has also been criticized by human rights organizations for its violations of the principle of purpose limitation (VIS is not a law enforcement instrument, but one for the application of European visa policy), as well as by the European Data Protection Supervisor.

Although control and surveillance of external borders still fall, in principle, under national discretion, the European Border Agency (Frontex) was established in 2005 as a coordinating agency. Its task lies in supporting national authorities in training and risk assessment and in monitoring borders between member states. Another measure is the imposition of standard external border controls, as a Commission's proposal sketches it. This measure is already subject to the newly introduced co-decision method of the Council and the European Parliament. At the same time, veto power in the Council of the European Union has already been abolished. Therefore, this is a test case for the above-mentioned question as to whether the change in procedures is also followed by a change in content towards a more liberal idea of immigration.

> A detailed analysis of the current state of the negotiations within the Council, and between the Council and EP, shows that the EP has had some success in getting a number of its more modest amendments accepted. But more radical changes have either been rejected by the Council or not tabled at all by the EP. (Peers 2005: 1)

Looking at the concrete operational measures, it is clear that they contain a strong control aspect: Frontex is expected to 'implement border management measures in the Mediterranean region', to 'present a Risk Analysis report on Africa', to launch a feasibility study on 'reinforcing monitoring and surveillance on the southern maritime border of the EU, namely in the Mediterranean Sea, and on a Mediterranean Coastal Patrols Network involving EU Member States and North African countries'. A surveillance system covering the entire southern maritime border of the EU and the Mediterranean Sea is planned. Surveillance will not, however, be enough. This raises the question of which other policies are envisaged in order to restrict further undocumented immigration, and whether they will be introduced as the member states' individual responsibility or as a common responsibility.

Policies on undocumented migration: towards control convergence?

Under the Tampere guidelines, several measures addressing 'illegal' migration have already been undertaken, such as the introduction of carriers' liability. But the combating of illegal migration is now considered to represent a key priority for the EU in the coming years (Frattini 2005). Recent events – not only those in Ceuta and Melilla but also many other incidents such as those from Lampedusa – have shown that migration pressure from sub-Saharan Africa is still rising, and a multidimensional approach to address these challenges is obviously necessary. The most important measures in combating undocumented migration in the past were the communication and action plan on human trafficking delivered by the Commission in 2005. The Commission also proposes common rules concerning return, removal, the use of coercive measures, temporary custody and re-entry, and it establishes the rule that illegal stays should be ended by means of a fair and transparent procedure. Furthermore, a network – ICONET – is designed for the rapid exchange of information required by the member states' Migration Management Services in their fight against illegal immigration. The network is intended to enable member states to transmit early warning messages. It could also possibly be used by the so-called immigration liaison officers who are being sent into the countries of origin or countries of transit. These officers shall advise their respective governments on possible policies towards the countries of origin, provide relevant information to the transportation companies, and so on.

Return policies: the new challenge for internal control

With regard to return policies, the *acquis* had, so far, been rather modest and is just recently being developed. Instruments introduced in this area can surely be of common utility, since return has come to represent quite an expensive package of tools.

Persons legally residing in a member state, whether for economic migration reasons or as recognized refugees, may wish to return to their countries of origin, but may face financial or legal (for instance, pension) problems that must be addressed. Other difficulties arise when refugees or asylum-seekers have to return. A Green Paper dating from 2002 had already set up the framework for cooperation. The Commission (2005a) has launched some innovative ideas on the situations of refugees, on making use of migrant workers' remittances and on promoting brain circulation instead of brain drain.

By contrast, the recently proposed 'Returns Directive' (Commission 2005c) focuses solely on illegally resident third-country nationals, in connection with joint operations for return and other issues, and has been criticized because it is said to be not always consistent with international standards (ECRE 2006: 5). Criticism includes 'the absence of a mandatory right of appeal against removal with suspensive effect, and the imposition of a re-entry ban that could amount to a double penalty with potentially far-reaching consequences for the principle of non-refoulement' (Human Rights Watch 2006). A Return Fund is also being established in order to improve the return management.

At the same time, the EU is trying to establish additional readmission agreements with several countries of origin. These agreements, which existed in 2001 with Hong Kong and in 2002 with Sri Lanka and Macau, were signed with Albania and Russia in April and October of 2005 respectively. They include an obligation for states to take back their own nationals who have entered or stayed illegally in the EU member states, and also nationals of non-contracting parties who have illegally entered or stayed in their territories. Talks with other states are ongoing (Peers 2005).

Asylum-seekers and refugees: the common system in its second phase of control

Tools regarding asylum-seekers and refugees have presented, in the view of many NGOs, a collection of member states' 'worst practices, with some of the proposed standards set so low as to permit fundamental breaches of international refugee and human rights law' (ECRE 2006: 2). It is well known that the exclusionary tendency in asylum policies, symbolized by concepts such as 'safe countries of origin' or 'safe third countries' (both German exports) and by common asylum directives, was gradually extended. The Asylum Procedures Directive, agreed by the European Council in April 2004, was criticized by the European Parliament which called for around 100 amendments.

The European Parliament (Opinion of 27 of September 2005), the UNHCR and a number of NGOs also debated the Directive on minimum standards on procedures in member states for granting and withdrawing refugee status (2000/0238 CNS) (called in short 'the Procedures Directive', or just 'PD'), the aim of which was to establish a minimum of equivalent procedures in member states for examining applications for persons who legitimately seek protection in the Community. Of course, the objective is to guarantee equivalent treatment in all the member states, but also to limit 'secondary movements

of applicants for asylum between Member States where such movement would be caused by differences in legal frameworks' (Council of
the European Union 2005d: (6)), that is evidently in the EU's internal
control. The debate around the PD centres on whether some of the
directive's provisions are truly compatible with the 1951 Geneva
Convention on the status of refugees and the European Convention on
Human Rights (ECHR). Above all, human rights organizations fear that
the directive could not possibly guarantee a sufficiently fair examination of each asylum application and thus would fall below ECHR standards, including the principle of non-refoulement. Some NGOs have
called in particular for the scrapping of the draft list of the so-called
'safe countries of origin' as part of the directive. They also maintain
that it risks breaching fundamental rights, restricting access to asylum
procedures and that not all the designated states are entirely safe for
return (compare, for instance, Statewatch 2004).

Together these instruments build an entire framework of asylum policies. These policies referred to 'burden-sharing' between the member
states, and to common asylum procedures that have been established
and are being implemented by the member states. At the moment, the
second phase in the construction of a common asylum system is on
its way, according to The Hague Programme. In February 2006, EU
Commissioner Franco Frattini presented new common EU roles on
asylum in the form of a Communication. Its main ideas are to achieve a
single asylum procedure in the whole EU which takes into consideration both the Asylum Procedures Directive and the Qualification
Directive and establishes a Single Procedure where all possible grounds
for protection are considered in just one procedure. Another aim lies in
establishing an asylum cooperation network to steer its activities, to
pool expertise and resources and to develop joint approaches to procedural and information-gathering aspects of decision-making. In addition, the Commission plans a new information system on the countries
of origin. At the same time, it plans to set up expert teams that help to
facilitate information and reaction to what are called 'particular pressures', that is, to sudden arrivals of large numbers of migrants at its
external borders (comp. MEMO 06/82 17/02/2006, Press Release of the
European Commission).

New windows? Migration and development: 'preventive control'?

Migration and development is surely the most difficult, complex and
comprehensive aspect within the field. Some of the Commission's
ideas, developed in its 'Thematic programme for the cooperation with

third countries in the areas of migration and asylum' (Commission of the European Communities 2005a), are found to be quite promising.

As usual, the Commission has incorporated and underlined features in its 2005 Priority Actions (Commission of the European Communities 2005a). Interestingly enough, the Commission states,

> ... that until recently the external dimension of the migration policy has been prevalently built around the objective of better managing the migratory flows with a view to reducing the migratory pressure on the Union. Although this remains a valid goal, the additional challenge today lies in the development of policies which recognise the need for migrant workers to make our economies function in those sectors where the EU is facing labour and skills shortages and, at the same time, which maximise both for the migrants and for their countries of origin the benefits triggered by the migration. This presupposes an approach which goes beyond the questions of border control and fight against illegal migration, to incorporate other dimensions of the migratory phenomenon, in particular development and employment. (Commission of the European Communities 2005a: 9)

This proposed programme will be the second test for the contents resulting from the Parliament's co-decision procedures in migration policies after the above-mentioned questions of border control.

Regional protection programmes: 'remote control'?

As is well known, most refugees do not cross the Mediterranean Sea, but rather remain in their own area of origin. It is therefore certainly important to improve their protection in the places of refuge, to convert those places into real 'safe havens'. This idea is, of course, driven by human rights concerns, but it is certainly not only altruistic. It has also been considered as a sort of 'remote control' of immigration movements. Regional Protection Programmes as they were hailed by the Council for JHA in October 2005 regard refugee camps as an important step in improving refugees' access to protection and to durable solutions for those in need of international protection. The first of these programmes were initiated in Ukraine and in Tanzania. It is true to say that these (modestly funded) programmes must be part of 'a wider strategy for the region that is principled, holistic, comprehensive and aimed at ensuring that refugee protection standards are upheld and implemented' (ECRE 2006: 5). Nevertheless, human rights organizations continue to warn that the principle of non-refoulement must not be violated and that proper individual assessments of immigrants' asylum claims must be guaranteed. In addition, there must be safeguards to ensure that human rights are not being violated in the safe third countries where the protection programmes are going to be implemented.

Outlook: any open window in 'Fortress Europe'?

The measures proposed by the European Council and by the Commission as new answers directly or indirectly related to the Ceuta and Melilla crisis range from developmental aid to the combat of 'illegal' immigration. Given the window of opportunity opened up by the Ceuta and Melilla crisis, and given the Hampton Court guidelines developed in the aftermath of that crisis which linked external and internal policies on migration, pre-existing and comprehensive policy solutions might finally re-emerge in that field. These policy solutions took an approach that had long been missing in much of the Commission's proposals and the EU's practical policies – addressing the root causes of migration. They might seem much more viable than in the past, but are, of course, not at all guaranteed by the new institutional possibilities that give allowance to the European Parliament's co-decision.

The fight against irregular or, in EU terms, 'illegal' immigration, suits most of the member states, especially those that have their own EU external borders, but also those that know of the pre-existent immigrant networks and their pull force. It is therefore quite possible that this control aspect will rapidly gain support. This might also be true for the concepts of the much cited, but until now minimal cooperation with the countries of origin that has long concentrated on the support for border control and the Regional Protection Programmes, which have been introduced on a continuous basis. Developed first by the Blair government and reintroduced to the agenda (where it was harshly attacked by some member states), and some years later by the then German Minister for Home Affairs, Otto Schily, initial opposition from a number of countries against these concepts has been given up in the meantime. It could be that 'salami tactics' have already done their job here.

Help for third countries is, of course, not to be rejected per se. Neither is help for third countries in the case of training of border controls, support for border control equipment, and related issues. But at the moment we are facing the fact that wherever third countries reinforce their border controls, human trafficking creeps towards other countries: where Morocco intensifies its controls at the Spanish (that is, the EU-) border, immigrants risk their lives setting out from Mauretania towards the Canary Islands. At the same time, an entire industry in human smuggling and human trafficking blossoms. Traffickers know, or at least pretend to know, the 'safe' ways immigrants may take. They might provide them not only with knowledge, but also with material support such as life jackets, mobile phones and GPS systems.

On the other hand, the Commission advocates the promotion of well-managed labour migration within the EU, arguing that legal alternatives must be opened. Given Germany's reservations in particular on that subject and its persistent veto position within the Council of Ministers, it is unlikely that there will be a common approach to managing economic immigration in the next few years. This is particularly regrettable in the case of the fight against illegal employment, being without any doubt a strong pull factor for immigration. It is also increasingly difficult to go on fighting illegal immigration when legal channels to EU territory remain scarce. Legal alternatives – although surely not a panacea against illegal migration – would certainly imply more 'control' over migration than building higher fences in border controls, travel documents, and so on. They would help to build up a genuine migration management that takes into consideration not only the relationship between external control and internal management, but also the EU's legitimate self-interest in replacement migration. The EU cannot – and this is a truism – cope with its urgent demographic and socio-economic challenges, but it can at least create legal alternatives that are part of a whole package of solutions. The European Commission has played, and goes on playing, the role of the political entrepreneur in this field.

Notes

1 Bigo (2001); Guiraudon and Joppke (2001); Lavenex (2001); Bendel (2002); Faist (2002); Maurer and Parkes (2005); Fauser (2006).
2 The EU Heads of State and Government met at Hampton Court on 27 October 2005, calling for a comprehensive approach to tackle migration issues. Both security and developmental aspects of migration were addressed. The Commission published a Communication to the Council proposing priority actions for responding to the challenges of migration (Commission of the European Communities 2005a).

3   In order to meet the expectations of its citizens the European Union must respond to the security threats of terrorism and organised crime, and to the challenge of managing migration flows. If the EU is to be effective in doing so it needs to work with countries outside the EU. In an increasingly interconnected world this will become ever more important. The EU should therefore make JHA a central priority in its external relations and ensure a co-ordinated and coherent approach. The EU's attempts to create an area of freedom, security and justice can only be successful if they are underpinned by a partnership with third countries to strengthen the rule of law and promote human rights and the respect for international obligations. (Council of the European Union 2005b: I.1).

4   'The Council recalls the Conclusions of the Tampere European Council on 15 and 16 October 1999, which stressed the need for a comprehensive approach to migration and asylum and which designated partnership with third countries a key element for the success of such an approach ...' (Council of the European Union 2005a: 1).

5   'The European Council, against the background of the EU's Strategy for Africa and the Strategy for the external dimension of Justice and Home Affairs, *as well as recent events in the Mediterranean region,* agrees to initiate priority actions with a focus on Africa and the Mediterranean countries' (Council of the European Union 2005c: 9, italics added).

6   A treaty agreed outside the Schengen Treaty and the Schengen *acquis* is the so-called Schengen III Treaty, signed by only seven states (Austria, Belgium, France, Germany, Luxembourg, the Netherlands and Spain). These countries have joined in order to realize the so-called 'principle of availability', which would allow the exchange of information among law enforcement agencies. It touches upon immigration policy in that it includes the exchange of DNA and fingerprint data and the fight against 'illegal' migration and joint deportation, using 'contact points' in order to coordinate actions (see also Statewatch 2005).

References

Bendel, P. (2002) 'Zurück in die Festung. Europäische Einwanderungs- und Flüchtlingspolitik nach dem Sevilla-Gipfel'. *Gesellschaft, Wirtschaft, Politik*, Vol. 3: 283–94.

Bendel, P. (2005) 'Immigration Policy in the European Union: Still Bringing up the Walls for Fortress Europe?' *Migration Letters*, Vol. 2, No. 1: 21–32.

Bigo, D. (2001) 'Migration and Security'. In V. Guiraudon and C. Joppke (eds), *Controlling a New Migration World*. London: Routledge.

Brochmann, G. and T. Hammar (eds) (1999) *Mechanisms of Immigration Control. A Comparative Analysis of European Regulation Policies*. Oxford, New York: Berg.

Commission of the European Communities (2005a) *Communication from the Commission to the Council and the European Parliament. Priority Actions for Responding to the Challenges of Migration: First Follow-up to Hampton Court*. COM (2005) 621 final. Brussels.

Commission of the European Communities (2005b) *Proposal for a Council Decision Concerning Access for Consultation of the Visa Information System (VIS) by the Authorities of Member States Responsible for Internal Security and by Europol for the Purposes of the Prevention, Detection and Investigation of Terrorist Offences and of Other Serious Criminal Offences.* COM (2005) 600 final, COM 2005/0232 (CNS). Brussels.

Commission of the European Communities (2005c) *Proposal for a Directive on Common Standards and Procedures in Member States for Returning Illegally Staying Third-country Nationals.* COM 2005/291 final. Brussels.

Council of the European Union (2005a) *Cover Note from Presidency to Delegations.* Brussels European Council 15/16 December 2005, Presidency Conclusions, Brussels, 17 December 2005, 15914/05, CONCL 3.

Council of the European Union (2005b) *Note from Presidency to Coreper. A Strategy for the External Dimension of JHA: Global Freedom, Security and Justice.* 14366/05 Limite JAI 417/RELEX 628. Brussels.

Council of the European Union (2005c) *Note from Presidency to Permanent Representatives Committee, Draft Council Conclusions on Migration and External Relations.* 14310/05, Limite, ASIM 50, DEVGEN 210, RELEX 623, Brussels.

Council of the European Union (2005d) *Council Directive 2005/85/EC of 1 December 2005 on Minimum Standards on Procedures in Member States for Granting and Withdrawing Refugee Status.* OJ L 326/13. Brussels.

ECRE (European Council on Refugees and Exiles). (2006) *Memorandum to the Austrian Presidency: Cooperation, the Key to Refugee Protection.* AD1/1/2006/EXT/RW. http://www.ecre.org (last accessed on 14 March 2006).

Faist, T. (2002) '"Extension du domain de la lutte": International Migration and Security before and after September 11, 2001'. *International Migration Review,* Vol. 35, No. 1: 7–14.

Fauser, M. (2006) 'Transnational Migration – a National Security Risk? Securitization of Migration Policies in Germany, Spain and the United Kingdom'. Centrum Stosunkòw Miedzynarodowych/Center for International Relations, 2/06, Warsaw.

Frattini, F. (2005) Vice President of the European Commission responsible for Justice, Freedom and Security. 'Legal Migration and the Follow-up to the Green Paper and on the Fight against Illegal Immigration'. Harvard University, 7 November 2005. http://europa.eu.int/rapid/pressReleasesAction.do?reference=SPEECH/05/666&form at=HTML&aged=0&language=en&guiLanguage=en (last accessed on 14 March 2006).

Guiraudon, V. (2000) 'European Integration and Migration Policy: Vertical Policymaking as Venue Shopping'. *Journal of Common Market Studies,* Vol. 38, No. 2: 251–71.

Guiraudon, V. and C. Joppke (eds) (2001) *Controlling a New Migration World.* London: Routledge.

Human Rights Watch (2006) European Union. http://hrw.org/english/docs/2006/01/18/ eu12240.htm (last accessed on 14 March 2006).

Lavenex, S. (2001) 'The Europeanization of Refugee Policies: Normative Challenges and Institutional Legacies'. *Journal of Common Market Studies,* Vol. 39: 851–74.

Maurer, Andreas and Roderick Parkes (2005) 'Democracy and European Justice and Home Affairs Policies under the Shadow of September 11'. Working Paper FG1, 2005/11, December, SWP Berlin.

Maurer, A. and R. Parkes (2006) 'Asylum Policy and Democracy in the European Union from Amsterdam toward the Hague Programme'. Working Paper FG1, 2006/01, SWP Berlin.

Peers, S. (2005) 'Revising EU Border Control Rules: a Missed Opportunity?' Statewatch Analysis, 6 June, Essex. http://www.statewatch.org/news/2005/ jul/17schengen-III.htm (last accessed on 8 February 2006).

Statewatch (2004) 'EU Divided over List of "Safe Countries of Origin" – Statewatch calls for the list to be scrapped'.

Statewatch (2005) 'Some Remarks on Schengen III'. http://www.statewatch.org/ news/ 2005/jul/17schengen-III.htm (last accessed on 8 February 2006).

Tomei, V. (2001) 'Europäisierung nationaler Migrationspolitik. Eine Studie zur Veränderung von Regieren in Europa'. Stuttgart, Forum Migration 6 (europäisches Forum für migrationsstudien [efms]).

3
The Europeanization of What? Migration, Asylum and the Politics of European Integration

Andrew Geddes

Introduction

While the notion that 'Europe matters' is commonplace in contemporary debates about migration and asylum, little has been said about how the European Union's specific institutional and policy content might actually affect politics and policy in member states (and non-member states, too). Does the EU's distinct institutional setting mean that it is distinct from other regional or international organizations? Does the EU's capacity to turn treaties between states into laws that bind those states create the potential for far-reaching effects on the domestic migration and asylum politics of its members? Are we seeing policy convergence between member states as a result of EU action? Does the content of EU action on migration and asylum mean, perhaps, that there is something distinctly *European* about the measures that have been introduced by the EU and its member states? These issues concern the motives for, and the impacts of, European integration, as well as relations between EU action and that taken in other parts of the world. These questions must be examined closely if the contemporary politics of migration in Europe and the scope for their 'Europeanization' are to be understood. To do so we must go beyond the assumption that there is some simple linear process by which EU competencies are straightforwardly translated into domestic political change in the member states. Such an understanding would misread European integration and the ways in which a whole host of intervening factors structure the relationship between 'Europe' and its member states, while also forgetting that what 'Europe' does is actually inspired to a great extent by what its member states want it to do.

This chapter explores these dynamics by bringing together work on European and EU migration with that on Europeanization. The argument is developed in four stages. First, the relationship between European integration and Europeanization is examined and attempts are made to specify some characteristics of European integration that may then influence the ways in which economic and political integration affects member states' migration and asylum policies. Next, definitions of Europeanization are analysed and the relationship between EU action and domestic change in member states is discussed. Migration and European integration are simultaneously societal and international issues and as such require conceptual and theoretical links to be made across these levels (Heisler 1992). The aim here is to avoid simple top-down approaches and, instead, look at the kinds of intervening variables that affect the relationship between EU migration and asylum policy and domestic politics and that may induce policy convergence, divergence or, indeed, inertia. The chapter then provides an assessment of the ways in which EU impact on member states can be evaluated, with an emphasis on linking the scope for impact to the definition of migration and asylum as policy issues at EU level. The argument is made that the effects of EU action are thus likely to be differential, that is, to have more effect on those countries most exposed to 'unwanted' migration flows such as asylum-seeking and irregular migration. Finally, the issue of the *European* content of EU action is considered: is EU action distinct from that undertaken by other similar states in other parts of the world? If there are similarities between EU action and, for example, that undertaken by Australia or the USA, then this would suggest that more general political dynamics are at play.

These arguments make use of two analytical distinctions, which should be specified from the outset. First, a distinction is made between EU processes (which are distinct and linked to a unique supranational organization) and the content of policy (which may be less distinct when placed in a broader international setting). Second, a distinction is made between the Europeanization of policy as an analytical challenge and the politics of Europeanization as a political–strategic choice by member states.

European integration and Europeanization: ontology and post-ontology

The role of the EU in migration and asylum is consequential for two main reasons. First, at a general level, it can be said that: 'Europe's degree of integration, level of political community, and pooling of sovereignty far outstrip those seen anywhere else. If there is any place in the world where the nation state would seem to be in retreat, it is in Europe' (Checkel 2005). Second, and more specifically, there is an emerging EU migration and asylum policy that builds on the development of intra-EU migration policy that has been going on since the 1960s. Within this EU framework there has been a strong emphasis on measures that tackle those forms of migration defined as 'unwanted' by state policies, such as asylum and irregular migration, with a concomitant focus on border controls and security. There has been much less attention paid to legal migration channels which remain for now national competencies.

The study of Europeanization presupposes, of course, a process of European integration (the development of patterns of European cooperation and integration) that went before it. Europeanization studies can thus be understood as the post-ontological offspring of an earlier generation of studies that explored the motives for European integration and, for example, the relative influence of intergovernmental and supranational dynamics as the EC/EU was built and consolidated (Puchala 1972; Caporaso 1996).

An exploration of the ontological phase of EU development would mean charting the negotiation of various treaties and the subsequent institutionalization of EU-level policy competencies. Before examining the impacts that European integration then has on member states, understood as Europeanization, it is important first to pay some attention to core features of the EU as a unique form of supranational governance. Unique because there is no other international organization like it; supranational because it possesses the capacity to turn treaties agreed by states into laws that bind those states; and governance because the development of European integration needs to be located alongside broader patterns of multi-level politics in Europe and debates about the relationship between new patterns of governance and the state (Bache 2003).

For the purposes of the analysis of Europeanization that follows, three core elements of the EU setting can be identified. First, core EU objectives have tended to centre on economic integration from the creation of the Common Market in the 1950s, the establishment of the single market in the late 1980s and 1990s and the move to Economic and Monetary Union (EMU) from the 1990s. Free movement for workers was a key intention but one that has been difficult to attain in practice because of national sensitivities about migration. This has recently been evident in the restrictions imposed on migration from Central and Eastern Europe after the May 2004 accession of ten new member states, including eight Central and East European countries, but also in the complex migratory dynamics that enlargement helps create and sustain (Favell and Hansen 2002; Wallace 2002). The more overtly political dimension of European integration has tended to lag, but there was highly significant movement into areas of 'high politics' that more clearly and directly impinge on the sovereign authority of states from the 1990s onward (Hoffmann 1966). This was particularly apparent in the Maastricht Treaty which, after it came into force in November 1993, created an intergovernmental Justice and Home Affairs (JHA) 'pillar' dealing with, among other things, immigration and asylum (Geddes 2000). A substantial body of work has subsequently developed that explores the ways in which responses to migration and asylum have been 'securitized', with migration constructed as threats that can strike at the very heart of the political identity of a given community (Wæver et al. 1993; Huysmans 2006). An ostensibly liberalizing logic of economic integration has been accompanied by security logics that are clearly evident in the post-cold war setting to which the Maastricht Treaty and subsequent migration and asylum developments have been to a considerable extent a response. The more substantial realization of this occurred when the Amsterdam Treaty added to the EU's objectives the aim of creating an area of freedom, security and justice (Monar 2001). In many ways the development of EU migration and asylum competencies has occurred since Amsterdam and other landmarks, such as the basic elements of an EU common migration and asylum policy outlined by the heads of government in the Finnish city of Tampere in October 1999. These were: partnership with countries of origin; a common asylum system; fair treatment for third-country nationals; and management of migration flows (European Council 1999).

The significance of Amsterdam and Tampere is that they provided a legal basis and a political direction, but the issues of migration and asylum had been 'framed' as security concerns in the context of post-cold war European migration politics. EU action has since tended to have a strong focus on 'unwanted' migration flows such as asylum-seeking and irregular migration and on the strengthening of border capacity in EU states and neighbouring states. The issue of asylum casts an interesting light on the significant EU developments in this area because it signifies a regional response to the dilemmas posed by asylum-seeking migration. There were a series of developments initially within the intergovernmental JHA pillar created by Maastricht, but these were not legally binding on member states. Most significant in terms of establishing a template for future action was the Dublin Convention which came into force in 1997 and, after Amsterdam, was re-elaborated as a legally binding EU regulation in 2003. The 'Dublin' principle is that asylum is to be a one-stop process and that a claim can be made in only one EU member state. Since Amsterdam, the EU has also elaborated other aspects of a common asylum system covering the definition of refugee status, conditions for the reception of asylum-seekers and a database on rejected claims (EURODAC). In February 2006, the Commission set out a work programme for the three main EU asylum objectives: a single procedure covering all possible grounds for asylum to be considered in one application; a common approach to the information used to make decisions; the sharing of information with, in the long term, a common database; and an agreed procedure for dealing with asylum pressure points (such as border areas that may face sudden large influxes of refugees) and funds made available for emergency measures. An asylum cooperation network will also be established for the exchange of information and the development of a common set of best practice criteria (Commission of the European Communities 2006).

In such terms recent EU action can be seen as emphasizing the external face of Europeanization and relations with sending and transit states and paying less attention to economic migration, although a policy plan on legal migration was proposed in late 2005 as a follow-up to the Commission Green Paper of late 2004 (Commission of the European Communities 2004). The Hague Programme, which outlines migration and asylum priorities for the period 2004–9, stated that 'Legal migration will play an important role in enhancing the knowledge-based economy in Europe, in advancing economic development, and thus contributing to the implementation of the Lisbon strategy' (Council of the European Union 2004). In December 2005 the Commission published a 'road map' for 2006–9 and identified the measures that it proposes to take: proposals concerning entry, residence and movement for third-country nationals (TCNs) in employment with a general framework directive defining the rights of all immigrant workers entering the EU; four specific directives addressing conditions of entry and residence for four categories of migrants: the highly skilled, seasonal workers, intra-corporate transferees and remunerated trainees (Commission of the European Communities 2005b). The Commission also noted that this framework directive will not deal with procedure or the numbers to be admitted, but will impinge on related activities such as the development of a common agenda for integration (NB not a common policy) (Commission of the European Communities 2005a).

The development of policy as described provides an important component of any discussion of what it is that might be Europeanized. Other elements of the EU setting are also germane. These include the EU's existence as an incomplete and partial polity, which is likely to remain the case. The EU is a partial polity in the sense that it is far from the federal superstate of Eurosceptic nightmares because its policy scope remains quite limited as, too, are its financial resources (just over 1 per cent of the combined national income of the member states). European integration is also 'incomplete' in the sense that patterns of European cooperation and integration vary significantly across policy sectors. While free movement for workers who were citizens of a member state was extensively supranationalized during the 1960s, migration and asylum were latecomers to the scene in the 1980s and 1990s through Schengen (1985), the Single European Act (1986), the Maastricht Treaty (1992) and the Amsterdam Treaty (1997) (Geddes 2000). Even then there has been a slow and halting movement towards supranational integration from the Amsterdam Treaty onward, with a reliance on intergovernmental cooperation and reluctance to empower supranational institutions such as the European Commission, European Parliament and European Court of Justice.

Migration is, of course, also linked to other important components of European integration such as single market integration, welfare entitlements, social rights and citizenship. As we discuss below, migration in its various forms (to work, to seek refuge, to study, to join with family members) is made visible as a social and political process not only at the territorial borders of states, but also at key organizational borders at which access to work, welfare and other important social institutions such as citizenship are determined. European integration has implications, too, for these borders of work, welfare and citizenship. While labour markets are highly diverse in terms of their organizational characteristics, welfare states retain a strong national organizational focus. EU measures in the area of welfare and social rights have been largely concerned with ensuring the portability of entitlements for those that move within the EU (Eichenhofer 1997; Bommes and Geddes 2000).

The third background factor is the way in which attempts have been made to conceptualize the EU's developing migration and asylum role. The balance of these has been decisively towards what could be called an intergovernmental account of EU action that stresses the motives of state actors in seeking to Europeanize. The accounts have tended to stress a politics of Europeanization as a political–strategic choice and as a means to avoid the Europeanization of policy where unwanted or unintended effects of EU action could intrude on the decision-making of key domestic migration policy actors (for example, interior ministries). States have thus sought to 'escape to Europe' to avoid domestic constraints on their ability to regulate migration (Freeman 1998; Guiraudon 2001). The aim was to avoid a Europeanization of policy that could have meant empowering supranational institutions such as the Commission, European Parliament and the European Court of Justice. A politics of Europeanization rather than a Europeanization of policy was designed to create a tightly defined policy domain at the European level populated largely by interior ministry officials that would pursue the core underlying objective of controlling 'unwanted' forms of migration while seeking to ensure that this core objective was translated into action in those member states and surrounding states that were seen as most 'challenging' in terms of their ability (or perceived lack of it) to effectively control their borders and regulate migration.

European integration has only recently appeared on the radar screen for those interested in international migration. There was an understandable initial tendency to focus on the shift to Europe – the ontological issues identified earlier – rather than on the potential impacts of EU migration and asylum policy on the member states understood as Europeanization. Moreover, the analytical focus of much of the work on international migration has tended to be on particular European countries of immigration with – either implicitly or explicitly – an institutionalist approach that emphasizes the close links between approaches to international migration and national sovereignty and well-established national models (Hansen 2002). The institutionalist literature also suggests that these are likely to be resistant to change (Hall 1993; Pierson 1996, 2004). Indeed, this has important implications for EU capacity to penetrate modes of migration governance in EU member states. The field of migration studies itself has also been prone to a certain degree of what Wimmer and Glick Schiller (2002) call 'methodological nationalism', in which a profusion of country studies deal with the specificities of that case rather than broader generalizations about the politics of immigration in Europe. One advantage of the debate about European integration and Europeanization is that it encourages comparative analysis that looks across cases and explores points of convergence and divergence rather than assuming locked national trajectories.

Europeanization: definitions and scope

Following from the discussion of the ontological stage of EU development we are now better placed to consider some of the post-ontological issues associated with Europeanization. We shall begin by exploring definitions of Europeanization. Next, we shall analyse the scope for European integration to change the preferences and identities of domestic migration policy actors such as interior ministry officials. In this analysis the point is made that simple top-down approaches to Europeanization should be avoided and that it is necessary to identify the kinds of variables that intervene in the relationship between EU and domestic politics and that may lead to policy convergence, divergence or inertia as a response to EU action.

Since the 1990s a new generation of EU scholarship has shifted its focus to the impacts of European integration. Following Radaelli (2004), Europeanization can be seen as an analytical problem rather than as a solution, that is, as something to be explained rather than the thing that does the explaining and as a way of organizing existing concepts rather than a catch-all explanation. There are also 'many faces' of Europeanization, as Olsen (2002) put it. In this vein, the present analysis focuses on the scope for the penetration of domestic systems of migration and asylum governance in EU member states by the EU as a form of international governance (see Lavenex, this volume, for analysis of the impacts on non-EU member states).

As a more specific variant of these general patterns we can then consider the impact of European integration on domestic structures of governance. A useful definition of Europeanization for this purpose has been offered by Radaelli (2000: 4) as

> the construction, diffusion and institutionalization of formal and informal rules, procedures, policy paradigms, styles, 'ways of doing things' and shared beliefs and norms which are first defined and consolidated in the EU policy process and then incorporated in the logic of domestic (national and sub-national) discourse, political structures and public policies.

We can supplement this by noting that this is an iterative process as member states may seek to shape interaction between the domestic and EU level. They may influence emergent policy paradigms by 'uploading' preferred policies in order to minimize the costs of subsequent 'downloading' (Börzel 2002). It is also possible that cross-national influences such as European integration can also exert their influence by becoming domestic political issues and thus leading to 'an unexpected "closing of the research circle" with the effect that our understanding of global issues can be illuminated by comparative micro-level inquiries' (Gourevitch 1986).

What kinds of linkages exist between the EU and domestic politics? One relevant issue here is the way in which the institutionalization of cooperation between EU states may change the preferences and identities of those actors involved in this process. Could European integration mean, for instance, that interior ministry officials, as a result of frequent interaction, set aside narrow national interests and 'become European'? There are two ways of thinking about this question of European socialization. First, institutional linkages between domestic and EU politics may be only a 'thin' constraint on national actors in the migration/asylum field and in accordance with what March and Olsen would call a 'logic of consequentialism', which offers an interest-based approach to institutional change. Alternatively, European integration may have a 'thicker' effect by operating through a logic of appropriateness that changes the interests and identities of actors. The issue here is whether and with what effects national actors operating at the EU level can 'go native' and be socialized into EU 'ways of doing things' with the result that they become European rather than national representatives. Socialization can be defined 'as a process of inducting actors into the norms and rules of a given community. Its outcome is sustained compliance based on the internalization of these new rules' (Dawson and Prewitt 1969; Checkel 2005). Beyers (2005) distinguishes between Type 1 socialization with a key role played by the domestic political contexts, as well as other factors such as career structures for senior officials that remain nationally based. Type II 'thicker' socialization occurs when agents 'go beyond role playing and ... accept community or organizational norms as the right thing to do' (Checkel 2005). Research suggests that the impact of EU socialization is weak (Beyers 2005; Hooghe 2005; Lewis 2005) and that EU dynamics are secondary to those operating at the national level (Zürn and Checkel 2005). These include career structures and the continued primacy of domestic politics. While research evidence tends to suggest Type I socialization prevails, Lewis's analysis of the national representations at the EU level (COREPER) suggests that a rigid distinction between logics of consequences and of appropriateness can neglect the ways in which 'national and supranational identifications can become entwined', or as March and Olsen (1998) put it: 'political actors ... calculate consequences and follow rules, and the relationship between the two is often subtle'.

Radaelli (2000, 2004) cautions against construing Europeanization as a simple top-down process from which effects on domestic politics in the member states can be read off. Simply put, just because the EU says that member states must do something does not necessarily mean that they do it. There may be convergence, there may be divergence or there may be inertia, or there may be all of these things simultaneously across policy areas and member states. Similarly the relationship between EU action and domestic change may be causal, but it may also be coincidental. So, while it does seem plausible to identify Europeanization as a potential source of domestic change in EU member states, there are other possible sources of change and thus alternative or complementary explanations. To get an idea of what these might be it is useful to attempt to specify the intervening variables that may affect the relationship between EU action and domestic political change. A distinction can be made between three types of borders that play a key intervening role in the relationship between EU migration and asylum policies and domestic policy contexts in EU member states (Geddes 2005):

1. *Territorial borders* are those points at which migration is traditionally made visible and where decisions about who can enter and who cannot are emblematic of the sovereign authority of states. Research has shown that these borders have shifted, in the sense of receiving states trying to exert and implement stricter controls in sending and transit states (Guild 2001) and involving an increased range of private and non-state actors while doing so (Guiraudon and Lahav 2000). A great deal of EU effort has been expended seeking to secure territorial borders in those member states seen as exposed to potentially large migration flows, as well as in non-member states such as those in the EU's 'neighbourhood' (Commission of the European Communities 2003). But territorial forms of borders are not the only variables that intervene in the relationship between EU migration and asylum policy and the domestic contexts in the member states.

2. *Organizational borders* are equally important as these are the sites at which access to key social and political institutions such as the labour market, the welfare state and social entitlements as well as

the formal status of national citizenship are determined. Borders of welfare, social rights and citizenship still tend to be within states, while labour markets tend to be more complex and may transcend national borders (for example, the information and communications technology sector) or be closely linked to patterns of welfare support and social provision (such as domestic work). It is also worth reminding ourselves that migrants do not move generally; they move specifically into certain types of occupations in certain parts of receiving states (and from certain parts of sending countries, too, it should be added). To this can be added the 'fuzziness' of key forms of social organization at their boundaries and the associated presence of a 'twilight zone' of informality and irregularity within which many migrants exist. The point here is that irregular migration and informal employment by migrant workers are at least as much an issue of fuzzy organizational boundaries within states as of the strength of external frontier controls (Reyneri 1998; Baldwin-Edwards 1999).

3. *Conceptual borders* though more nebulous are no less important because notions of entitlement, belonging and identity may function as significant boundaries between domestic systems of governance and the scope for European integration to penetrate that system. The analysis of traditions of citizenship and nationhood in France and Germany (Brubaker 1992), for example, used a Weberian metaphor to emphasize the importance of world images created by ideas 'that have like switchmen, determined the tracks along which action has been pushed by the dynamic of interests' (Weber 1948). Conceptual borders of belonging and identity can reinforce territorial and organizational borders and have tended in the area of migration and asylum to have a strong national focus. To illustrate, the boundaries of welfare entitlement demarcate a community of legitimate receivers of welfare state benefits in a way that has an organizational dimension (formal entitlement) reinforced by an ideational dimension (who deserves, who is entitled) (Bommes and Geddes 2000).

These different types of borders intervene in the relationship between EU migration and asylum policy and domestic contexts in member states. They also help make the point that Europeanization should not be seen as a straightforward top-down process of policy change. Moreover, EU action may be one source of change, but there are others as well. From the borders specified above, there could be a range of international, domestic and subnational factors that could impinge on strategies of territorial management, on the borders of work, welfare and citizenship and on the boundaries of belonging, entitlement and identity. How then can we identify the effects of European integration?

Assessing the impact of EU action

Trying to specify the effects of European integration has become a core research challenge for those working in the area of EU studies. Any assessment of policy change is subject to the vagaries of time, because what might seem quite momentous at one point may seem less significant a few years later and, similarly, what may seem insignificant now may actually turn out to have been a considerable shift. In the areas of migration and asylum, these effects could be assessed on a country-by-country basis or in relation to particular types of migration. It has been argued that the impacts of European integration can be evaluated in relation to whether these effects are direct/intended or indirect/unintended and whether Europeanization is voluntary in the sense of being embraced by key domestic actors or coercive in the sense of being imposed on them (Bache 2003; Bache and Jordan 2006). This approach highlights a variety of potential effects of European integration on migration and asylum policy that will be dependent on (i) the type of instrument adopted by the EU and (ii) the ways in which specific EU measures are refracted through the territorial, organizational and conceptual borders that mediate the EU's influence. In this regard it is especially worth noting that the EU can employ a range of 'harder' and 'softer' measures such as legally binding directives that must be implemented or Action Plans that specify action to be taken but do not have the force of law. As mentioned earlier, there is a range of other factors that may also induce domestic change in a way that is unrelated to EU action. Even if there is change and this does seem to result from EU measures it is necessary to try to show that the EU action was strongly related to this domestic change rather than coincidental.

An influential school of thought on Europeanization has focused on 'fit' and 'misfit' between the EU and domestic processes and subsequent pressures for domestic political change as a result of European integration. The EU may 'fit' with domestic policy frameworks or there may be some 'misfit' that can lead to adaptational pressures (Green-Cowles et al. 2001). If there is a low level of misfit then it has been argued that member states are likely to absorb the effects of European integration. Alternatively there may be a process of accommodation when change occurs as a result of European integration but without fundamentally changing domestic arrangements. More dramatic shifts may occur if there is a fundamental misfit between EU measures and domestic arrangements with the scope for European integration to effect a domestic transformation in the policy area in question. Alternatively, member states may fail to implement or only partially implement agreed measures with the result that inertia rather than change is the outcome (Börzel and Risse 2000). Whether there is absorption, accommodation, transformation or inertia will be strongly related to domestic structures in the member states and their ability/ willingness to respond to EU pressures.

This focus on fit and misfit has been criticized by those who argue that while levels of fit may be relevant it is also useful to bear in mind that there are different kinds of EU output that can have different kinds of effect. Thus, there may be direct, legal effects but also other kinds of effect such as the impact of EU membership, financial resources, policies, norms and ideas on domestic political opportunity structures and patterns of mobilization. European outputs may well be strongest when they require institutional compliance such as when an EU directive is issued. They may have weaker effects if they change domestic political opportunity structures by, for example, offering new sources of financial support or new opportunities for mobilization, and they are likely to be weaker when they provide scope for new policy ideas to enter into domestic debate. These are analytical rather than empirical distinctions and may occur simultaneously, so for example, institutional compliance can reorder domestic opportunities and provide some scope for policy reframing (Knill and Lehmkuhl 2002). EU policy impact may thus be as shown in Table 3.1. EU action may also mix these methods. So, for example, the legally binding anti-discrimination directives of 2000 were accompanied by an Action Plan that was designed to affect domestic opportunity structures and beliefs and expectations.

Table 3.1 Impacts of European integration on domestic governance structures

Strength of impact	Result of impact
Strongest	Very prescriptive and demand change in accordance with specified parameters
Intermediate	Change domestic opportunity structures
Weakest	Change domestic beliefs and expectations

The Europeanization literature encourages us to consider the types of measures, the relationship between these measures and domestic political structures and the variables that can intervene in the relationship between the EU and its member states. A substantial body of work on European integration also suggests these effects are more likely to be absorbed by or accommodated within existing domestic arrangements rather than being transformatory (Green-Cowles et al. 2001; Bache and Jordan 2006). That said, in the area of migration and asylum where policy frameworks in member states that were newer immigration countries were underdeveloped, then the effects of EU action may be more substantial. Writing about Spain, Cornelius argued that the development of migration policy in the late 1980s and early 1990s was almost entirely related to EU membership, while Arango makes a distinction between the EU's impact on Spanish external border controls and what he calls the 'Pandora's box' of internal controls and state–society relations (Cornelius 1994; Arango 2000). Similar distinctions between the EU emphasis on external frontiers and the rather more complex domestic politics of migration have been made about Italy as well (Sciortino 1999; Zincone 1999).

Analyses of Central and East European accession states have also identified the onus placed on new member states to adapt to the formal requirements of the EU *acquis* before they could join the club (Lavenex 1999; Lavenex and Uçarer 2002). The research evidence tends to suggest that the particular focus of EU action is on those forms of migration defined as 'unwanted' and that this has prompted measures to strengthen border controls with a particular focus on those states seen as vulnerable or as weak links. However, the distinction made earlier between territorial, organizational and conceptual borders can highlight the rather more complex institutional settings in member states. Seen in this light, EU migration and asylum policy may be refracted into domestic contexts in situations where there are labour markets with formal and informal components, differing modes of welfare state organization and traditions of citizenship and social rights, and divergent ideas about belonging, entitlement and identity. An analytical focus on territory alone would miss some of these dynamics. A focus on the politics of Europeanization would also show how those EU member states that are longer established as countries of immigration have used the EU as an external venue within which they have sought to attain domestic policy objectives in a new setting where there is a special burden on those states most vulnerable to flows of 'unwanted' migrants. This returns to two distinctions made earlier in this chapter: between the Europeanization of policy and the politics of Europeanization and between the process and content of EU politics and policy-making on migration and asylum. It is to this issue of policy content that we now turn.

How European is EU action?

The final issue that this chapter addresses is the extent to which EU action on migration and asylum is distinctly European. While a thorough overview of the global politics of migration would be beyond the scope of this chapter (and its author's abilities), it can be useful to consider the extent to which the kinds of responses that have developed in Europe to migration and asylum differ from those that we see in similar states confronting similar dilemmas. Although there is much that is distinct about the EU in terms of the process of EU action in its institutional setting, there are also some points of commonality with responses seen in the USA and Australia. Two can be identified. First, the consequences of the liberal paradox and boundary build-up whereby openness to certain forms of mobility such as those by goods, capital and labour has been accompanied by moves to reinforce state borders against those forms of migration defined as unwanted. The second point of similarity is the externalization of policy with an increased emphasis placed by economically developed receiving states on migration control measures in sending and/or transit states.

The issues at play here seem to be the identity of EU states as liberal states and their relationship to wanted and unwanted migration flows and the forms of 'international migration relations' that develop between states. Mitchell (1989) explored links between migration, international relations and foreign policy and noted that:

- Relations between states have important effects on migration flows
- Migration policy may influence national foreign policies
- Domestic laws may have an 'international political projection' because internal policy changes can have international repercussions
- The state is conceptualized 'as a network of interdependent political and economic structures, but with some autonomy in relation to each other' (Zolberg et al. 1986: 158).

There may then be more general forms of convergence on boundary build-up and externalization that derive from more general patterns of migration policy and politics and that need not be specifically and uniquely linked to the EU as a particular expression of international governance. The concept of policy convergence is thus broader than

Europeanization. Knill (2005: 768) maintains that convergence can be understood as: 'Any increase in the similarity between one or more characteristics of a certain policy (e.g. policy objectives, policy instruments, policy settings) across a given set of political jurisdictions (supranational institutions, states, regions, local authorities) over a given period of time'. Convergence may also take such different forms as decreased variation, laggards catching up with leaders, the change of country rankings in specific policy areas and the measurement of domestic change in relation to some kind of exemplary model such as an EU standard. Convergence could be caused by 'trigger factors' such as security fears or demographic changes or when there are facilitating factors such as basic institutional similarities between countries. As we shall discuss more fully later, there do seem to be some similar border and migration management strategies in other parts of the world where liberal states seek to manage what Hollifield (2003) has identified as the 'liberal paradox' – economic forces press for openness and political forces for closure. There are explanations in the migration literature for broader patterns of convergence such as Freeman's (1995) account of modes of immigration politics in liberal states that draws from work on the politics of regulation to postulate interest-based dynamics leading to open and inclusive migration politics in liberal states. Others have pointed to the effects of the 'embedded liberalism' of the post-war international order and highlighted the role of courts in opening 'social and political spaces' for migrants (Hollifield 1992; Guiraudon 1998).

The first point of commonality seems to be the process of boundary build-up where openness to certain forms of mobility such as that by goods, capital and services is not matched by any similar commitment to free movement for people. Indeed, there does seem to be some similarity between the boundary build-up evident at the US–Mexico border and border control measures currently being undertaken by the EU at its borders with non-member states to its south and east (Cornelius 2001; Nevins 2002). In his analysis of the US–Mexico border, Mike Davis (2002: 3) wrote that 'economic globalisation and free trade, per the model of NAFTA, tends to strengthen, not weaken, the institutional apparatus of borders, and to deepen the existential and juridical divides between "legal" and "illegal" beings'. Nevins (2002) analyses the simultaneous 'militarisation' and 'NAFTA-isation' of the US–Mexico border as part of a war of sorts ... against 'illegal' or unauthorized immigrants. Yet at the same time, these same countries are increasingly opening their boundaries to flows of capital, finance, manufactured goods and services. Such apparently contradictory roles speak to the growing gatekeeper role played by states. This role entails maximizing the perceived benefits of globalisation while 'protecting' against the perceived detriments of increasing transnational flows – especially of unauthorized immigrants. States' efforts to repel unauthorized immigrants are most intense along those international boundaries that separate widely divergent levels of socio-economic development. (Nevins 2002: 7)

A problem for the EU is that it is an ongoing project and its borders have shifted recently and will shift again in the near future.

The second point of commonality is the attempt to externalize migration control measures. There is a link here to the earlier consideration of the intergovernmental motive for the development of EU action on migration and asylum. EU states 'escape' to Europe to resolve some collective action dilemmas raised by interdependence between them. Then, in order to offset some of the costs of border reinforcement in those states vulnerable to migration flows on the southern and eastern borders of the Union, there have also been attempts to externalize EU action by incorporating neighbouring states that may be sending and/or transit states within the framework of EU controls. This could be understood as a process of policy diffusion whereby there is a 'socially mediated spread of policies across countries and within political systems' (Knill 2005: 766). One area where this has been particularly evident is the debate about asylum and the controversial issue of extraterritorial processing of asylum claims. The point is that there may be a wider process of policy diffusion at work here because the content of EU debate has drawn from elements of the Australian response to asylum and the so-called 'Pacific solution' (Maley 2003; Rajaram 2003).

Conclusion

This chapter has explored one particular 'face' of Europeanization, namely the EU's capacity to penetrate domestic systems of governance. The aim was to specify the relationship between European integration and Europeanization, to define and consider the scope for Europeanization, to identify the kinds of variables that can intervene in the relationship between EU and domestic politics and to assess the extent to which EU action is distinctly European in the sense of differing from that pursued by similar states in other parts of the world confronting similar dilemmas. The distinction has been made between the *Europeanization of policy* as an analytical challenge and the *politics of Europeanization* as a political–strategic choice and between the *process* of EU action and its *content*. By making these distinctions we are better placed to examine the conceptual, analytical and political dynamics of the Europeanization of migration and asylum.

The basic question asked in the title of this chapter was 'The Europeanization of what?' An attempt has been made to show that EU competencies have grown and that any consideration of European migration policy and politics must consider the EU's role. That said, it would be wrong to see the EU as a straightforward driver of domestic change. To do so would neglect some rather fundamental features of the EU as a partial and incomplete polity, as well as the intervening variables that can structure the relationship between EU action and domestic change. Moreover, the consideration of the underlying politics of Europeanization also demonstrates that EU action may to a considerable extent actually be driven by the policy preference of the member states, so rather than being an imposition on them it may actually be a political–strategic choice by them.

Borders of territory, key organizational borders of work, welfare and citizenship and conceptual borders of belonging, entitlement and identity were specified as central to the scope for EU action to affect domestic responses to migration and asylum. Of particular relevance to future EU development is the continued focus in EU action on the reinforcement of external borders. By emphasizing the importance of organizational and conceptual borders this chapter has sought also to highlight the domestic social and political processes that give meaning to migration. In the same way that the politics of Europeanization is incomplete if it addresses solely these borders of territory, then so the analysis of the Europeanization of policy is incomplete if it fails to address the relationship between migration and 'internal' organizational and conceptual borders.

The 'Europeanization of what?' question was also posed to raise the issue of the extent to which the content of EU action differs from that evident in other parts of the world. There are, of course, very specific types of border dynamic within the EU, but if the analysis is extended to consider migration and asylum responses in similar states confronting similar dilemmas then it is possible to identify processes of boundary build-up and externalization that seem to be more common aspects of the response to migration and asylum than a focus on Europeanization alone would permit. Indeed, these processes seem more closely linked to the identity of liberal democratic states and new forms of international migration relations than to the specific features of the EU. The EU could be a specific regionalized example of a more general set of responses to migration flows and the attempt to sift 'wanted' from 'unwanted' migrants that seems to preoccupy economically developed migrant receiving states.

References

Arango, J. (2000) 'Becoming a Country of Immigration at the End of the Twentieth Century'. In R. King, G. Lazaridis and C. Tsardanidis (eds), *Eldorado or Fortress: Immigration in Southern Europe*. London: Macmillan.

Bache, I. (2003) 'Europeanisation: a Governance Approach'. Paper presented at the biennial meeting of the European Union Studies Association, Nashville, 27–29 March.

Bache, I. and A. Jordan (2006) *The Europeanisation of British Politics*. London: Palgrave Macmillan.

Baldwin-Edwards, M. (1999) 'Where Free Markets Reign: Alien in the Twilight Zone'. *South European Society and Politics*, Vol. 3, No. 3: 1–15.

Beyers, J. (2005) 'Multiple Embeddedness and Socialization in Europe'. *International Organization*, Vol. 59, No. 3: 899–936.

Bommes, M. and A. Geddes (eds) (2000) *Immigration and Welfare: Challenging the Borders of the Welfare State*. London: Routledge.

Börzel, T. (2002) 'Pace-setting, Fence-sitting and Foot-dragging: Member States Responses to Europeanisation'. *Journal of Common Market Studies*, Vol. 40, No. 2: 193–214.

Börzel, T. and T. Risse (2000) 'When Europe Hits Home: Europeanization and Domestic Change'. *European Integration On-Line Papers*, Vol. 4.

Brubaker, R. (1992) *Citizenship and Nationhood in France and Germany*. Cambridge, Mass.: Cambridge University Press.

Caporaso, J. (1996) 'Forms of State in the European Union: Westphalian, Regulatory and Post-modern'. *Journal of Common Market Studies*, Vol. 34, No. 1: 29–52.

Checkel, J. (2005) 'International Institutions and Socialization in Europe: Introduction and Framework'. *International Organization*, Vol. 59, No. 3: 801–26.

Commission of the European Communities (2003) *Commission Communication to the Council and the European Parliament. Wider Europe – Neighbourhood: a New Framework for Relations with our Eastern and Southern Neighbours*. Brussels: Commission of the European Communities, COM (2003) 104 final.

Commission of the European Communities (2004) *Green Paper. A Common Approach to Managing Economic Migration*. Brussels: Commission of the European Communities, COM (2004) 811 final.

Commission of the European Communities (2005a) *Commission Communication to the Council and the European Parliament. A Common Agenda for Integration.* Brussels: Commission of the European Communities, COM (2005) 389 final.

Commission of the European Communities (2005b) *Policy Plan on Legal Migration.* Brussels: Commission of the European Communities, 21 December.

Commission of the European Communities (2006) *Commission Communication to the Council and the European Parliament. Strengthened Practical Co-operation. New Structures, New Approaches: Improving the Quality of Decision-Making in the European Asylum System.* Brussels: Commission of the European Communities, SEC (2006) 67 final.

Cornelius, W. (1994) 'Spain: the Uneasy Transition from Labor Exporter to Labor Importer'. In W. Cornelius, P. Martin and J. Hollifield (eds), *Controlling Immigration: a Global Perspective.* Stanford, Calif.: Stanford University Press.

Cornelius, W. (2001) 'Death at the Border: Efficacy and Unintended Consequences of US Immigration Control Policy'. *Population and Development Review*, Vol. 27, No. 4: 661–85.

Council of the European Union (2004) *The Hague Programme: Strengthening Freedom, Security and Justice in the European Union.* Brussels: Council of the European Union, 16054/04 JAI559.

Davis, M. (2002) 'Foreword'. In J. Nevins (ed.), *Operation Gatekeeper: the Rise of the 'Illegal Alien' and the Making of the US–Mexico Boundary.* New York: Routledge.

Dawson, R. and K. Prewitt (1969) *Political Socialization.* Boston: Little Brown.

Eichenhofer, E. (ed.) (1997). *The Social Security of Migrants in the European Union of Tomorrow.* Osnabrück: Universitätsverslag.

European Council (1999) *Tampere European Council Presidency Conclusions.* Tampere, Finland, 15–16 October.

Favell, A. and R. Hansen (2002) 'Markets against Politics: Migration, Enlargement and the Idea of Europe'. *Journal of Ethnic and Migration Studies*, Vol. 28, No. 4: 581–601.

Freeman, G. (1995) 'Modes of Immigration Politics in Liberal States'. *International Migration Review*, Vol. 29, No. 4: 881–913.

Freeman, G. (1998) 'The Decline of Sovereignty: Politics and Immigration Restriction in Liberal States'. In C. Joppke (ed.), *Challenge to the Nation State: Immigration in Western Europe and the United States.* Oxford: Oxford University Press.

Geddes, A. (2000) *Immigration and European Integration: Towards Fortress Europe?* Manchester: Manchester University Press.

Geddes, A. (2005) 'Europe's Border Relationships and International Migration Relations'. *Journal of Common Market Studies*, Vol. 43, No. 4: 787–806.

Gourevitch, P. (1986) *Politics in Hard Times: Comparative Responses to International Economic Crises.* Ithaca, NY: Cornell University Press.

Green-Cowles, M., J. Caporaso and T. Risse (2001) *Transforming Europe: Europeanization and Domestic Change.* Ithaca, NY: Cornell University Press.

Guild, E. (2001) 'Moving the Borders of Europe'. Nijmegen: Inaugural lecture, Catholic University of Nijmegen, 8 May.

Guiraudon, V. (1998) *International Human Rights Norms and their Interpretation: the Protection of Aliens in Europe.* San Domenico di Fiesole: European University Institute.

Guiraudon, V. (2001) 'European Integration and Migration Policy: Vertical Policy-making as Venue Shopping'. *Journal of Common Market Studies*, Vol. 27, No. 2: 334–53.

Guiraudon, V. and G. Lahav (2000) 'A Reappraisal of the State Sovereignty Debate: the Case of Migration Control'. *Comparative Political Studies*, Vol. 33, No. 2: 163–95.

Hall, P. (1993) 'Policy Paradigms, Social Learning and the State: the Case of Economic Policy-making in Britain'. *Comparative Politics*, Vol. 25, No. 3: 275–94.

Hansen, R. (2002) 'Globalization, Embedded Realism and Path Dependence: the Other Immigrants to Europe'. *Comparative Political Studies*, Vol. 35, No. 3: 259–83.

Heisler, M. (1992) 'Migration, International Relations and the New Europe: Theoretical Perspectives from Institutional Political Sociology'. *International Migration Review*, Vol. 26, No. 2: 596–622.

Hoffmann, S. (1966) 'Obstinate or Obsolete: the Fate of the Nation State and the Case of Western Europe'. *Daedalus*, Vol. 95, No. 3: 862–915.

Hollifield, J. (1992) *Immigrants, States and Markets: the Political Economy of Migration in Europe*. Cambridge: Harvard University Press.

Hollifield, J. (2003) 'The Emerging Migration State'. Princeton, NJ: Princeton University Center for Migration Development Working Paper No. 03–09.

Hooghe, L. (2005) 'Several Roads Lead to International Norms, but Few via International Socialization: a Case Study of the European Commission'. *International Organization*, Vol. 59, No. 3: 861–998.

Huysmans, J. (2006) *The Politics of Insecurity: Fear, Migration and Asylum in the European Union*. London: Routledge.

Knill, C. (2005) 'Introduction: Cross-national Policy Convergence: Concepts, Approaches and Explanatory Factors'. *Journal of European Public Policy*, Vol. 12, No. 5: 764–74.

Knill, C. and D. Lehmkuhl (2002) 'The National Impact of European Union Regulatory Policy: Three Europeanization Mechanisms'. *European Journal of Political Research*, Vol. 41, No. 2: 255–80.

Lavenex, S. (1999) *Safe Third Countries: Extending the EU Asylum and Immigration Policies to Central and Eastern Europe*. Budapest: Central European University Press.

Lavenex, S. and E. Uçarer (2002) *Migration and the Externalities of European Integration*. Lanham, Md: Lexington Books.

Lewis, J. (2005) 'The Janus Face of Brussels: Socialization and Everyday Decision-making in the European Union'. *International Organization*, Vol. 59, No. 3: 937–71.

Maley, W. (2003) 'Asylum Seekers in Australia's International Relations'. *Australian Journal of International Affairs*, Vol. 57, No. 1: 187–202.

March, J. and J. Olsen (1998) 'The Institutional Dynamics of International Political Orders'. *International Organization*, Vol. 52, No. 4: 937–71.

Mitchell, C. (1989) 'International Migration, International Relations and Foreign Policy'. *International Migration Review*, Vol. 23, No. 3: 681–708.

Monar, J. (2001) 'The Dynamics of Justice and Home Affairs: Laboratories, Driving Factors and Costs'. *Journal of Common Market Studies*, Vol. 39, No. 4: 747–64.

Nevins, J. (2002) *Operation Gatekeeper: the Rise of the 'Illegal Alien' and the Making of the US–Mexico Boundary*. New York: Routledge.

Olsen, J. (2002) 'The Many Faces of Europeanisation'. *Journal of Common Market Studies*, Vol. 40, No. 5: 921–52.

Pierson, P. (1996) 'The Path to European Integration: a Historical Institutionalist Analysis'. *Comparative Political Studies*, Vol. 29, No. 2: 123–63.

Pierson, P. (2004) *Politics in Time: History, Institutions and Social Analysis.* Princeton, NJ: Princeton University Press.

Puchala, D. (1972) 'Of Blind Men, Elephants and International Integration'. *Journal of Common Market Studies*, Vol. 10, No. 3: 267–82.

Radaelli, C. (2000) 'Whither Europeanization: Concept Stretching and Substantive Change'. *European Integration On-Line Papers*, Vol. 4, No. 8.

Radaelli, C. (2004) 'Europeanisation: Solution or Problem?' *European Integration On-Line Papers*, Vol. 8, No. 16.

Rajaram, P. K. (2003) '"Making Place": the "Pacific Solution" and Australian Emplacement in the Pacific and on Refugee Bodies'. *Singapore Journal of Tropical Geography*, Vol. 24, No. 3: 290–306.

Reyneri, E. (1998) 'The Role of the Underground Economy in Irregular Migration to Italy: Cause or Effect?' *Journal of Ethnic and Migration Studies*, Vol. 24, No. 2: 313–31.

Sciortino, G. (1999) 'Planning in the Dark: the Evolution of Italian Immigration Control'. In G. Brochmann and T. Hammar (eds), *Mechanisms of Immigration Control: a Comparative Analysis of European Regulation Policies*, Oxford: Berg, pp. 233–59.

Wæver, O., B. Buzan, M. Kelstrup and P. Lemaitre (1993) *Migration and the New Security Agenda in Europe.* London: Pinter.

Wallace, C. (2002) 'Opening and Closing Borders: Migration and Mobility in East-Central Europe'. *Journal of Ethnic and Migration Studies*, Vol. 28, No. 4: 603–25.

Weber, M. (1948) *From Max Weber: Essays in Sociology.* Edited, translated and with an introduction by H. H. Gerth and C. Wright Mills. London: Routledge & Kegan Paul.

Wimmer, A. and N. Glick Schiller (2002) 'Methodological Nationalism and Beyond: Nation-state Building, Migration and the Social Sciences'. *Global Networks*, Vol. 2, No. 4: 301–34.

Zincone, G. (1999) 'Illegality, Enlightenment and Ambiguity: a Hot Italian Recipe'. *South European Society and Politics*, Vol. 3, No. 3: 43–81.

Zolberg, A., A. Suhrke and S. Aguayo (1986) 'International Factors in the Formation of Refugee Movements'. *International Migration Review*, Vol. 20, No. 2: 151–69.

Zürn, M. and J. Checkel (2005) 'Getting Socialized to Build Bridges: Constructivism and Rationalism, Europe and the Nation State'. *International Organization*, Vol. 59 (Fall): 1045–79.

Part II

The European Impact on National Policies and Politics of Immigration – Core Member States

4
From Model to Average Student: the Europeanization of Migration Policy and Politics in Germany

Kathrin Prümm and Stefan Alscher

Introduction

Germany is often regarded as the model student or *Musterknabe* of European integration. Even though this may have been the case for several decades, trends and patterns since the Amsterdam Treaty show a more differentiated picture between absorption on the one hand and partial reluctance on the other. While most of the European regulations are transferred into national law without any controversial debates, the German government and actors on the subnational level (*Länder*) have become increasingly resistant to further integration in the field of migration policy. It is important to mention that the generally small degree of misfit between European and German regulations is also linked to Germany's role as an agenda-setter on the level of the European Union (EU).

Germany[1] participated in the process of European integration from the very beginning. The first years of Germany's integration into the European Coal and Steel Community and the European Economic Community were characterized by its (self-) containment and integration into 'Western' structures in the context of the post-war period. During the following decades the German government mainly played the role of the front-runner in the integration process, thanks in part to a strong pro-integrationist consensus among German elites. On many occasions, Germany – together with France – was labelled the 'motor' or 'locomotive' of European integration, especially during the strong Franco-German cooperation of the Kohl and Mitterrand era. Since the late 1990s, however, the German position in the European concert has changed slightly. Although still located on the pro-integrationist side among EU member states, the federal government and especially the subnational actors of the *Länder* have become somewhat reluctant with regard to certain aspects of European integration, not only in the field of migration policy. The growing power of the *Länder* in the decision-making process has made them reluctant to pass competencies to the EU level (Hellmann et al. 2005: 153). Indeed, on several occasions the German *Länder* insisted on the principle of subsidiarity.

Where migration policies are concerned, it is important to bear in mind that Germany has been one of the principal receiving countries of immigration flows in recent decades. 'Germany is not an immigration country' has been the often cited official motto of all German federal governments – regardless of their political orientation – until the late 1990s, even though this statement did not at all reflect reality. The German self-perception as a non-immigration country even gave rise to the false estimation that there was no German immigration policy at all (Geddes 2003: 90). Only after the centre-left coalition of Social Democrats and Greens came to power in 1998 did the reality of Germany as an immigration country finally receive official recognition. Since then, German migration policy has been focused mainly on two objectives: maintaining the already long-established policy of reducing the inflow of unwanted migration, that is, of asylum-seekers, refugees and undocumented migrants, while at the same time entering the global competition in attracting highly skilled workers and specialists. While the first objective is also strongly reflected in German migration policy on the EU level, the second remains attached to the nation state, as the German position is to maintain labour migration as a field of exclusively national competence.

Where the politics of immigration is concerned, it is important to note that political actors are used to decision-making processes in a multi-level system (Monar 2003: 313). In several fields of policy-making, the representation of the German *Länder* on the federal level (Bundesrat) has a decisive role in the legislative process. If the interests of the *Länder* are affected, a law becomes binding only when both chambers of parliament (Bundestag and Bundesrat) approve it. As a general rule, German politics are characterized by a consensus-oriented model with significant influence and inclusion of interest groups, which is another similarity with the EU.

This chapter focuses on the Europeanization of immigration policy and politics in Germany in the aftermath of the Amsterdam Treaty of 1997. The main question is to what extent immigration policy rules and regulations, which are first defined in the supranational policy process and then incorporated in the domestic political structures, challenge German immigration policy and politics. The concept of the goodness of fit will be used to analyse the impact of European regulations on German policy. Goodness of fit refers in general to the extent of disagreement between the supranational and the national level and is linked to the hypothesis that the greater the misfit the stronger the pressure for adaptation to the domestic level (Börzel 2003). Characteristics such as inertia, retrenchment, absorption, accommodation and transformation (Radaelli 2003) are used as instruments to measure and specify the range of impact resulting from varying levels of goodness of fit (see Ette and Faist in this volume). The argument will be made in this chapter that with respect to immigration policy and politics Germany represents a case of high compatibility with low misfit and consequentially minimal change. Therefore, the process of Europeanization can be characterized primarily as a process of absorption.

The chapter is divided into five parts. We begin with a brief historical review of immigration to Germany, including some remarks on the mode of Europeanization prior to the Treaty of Amsterdam. The second part analyses the Europeanization of the German politics of immigration, while the third focuses on the policy level and an overview of central directives and regulations after the Treaty of Amsterdam. This is followed by an analysis of the extent of Europeanization of immigration policy in the fourth part. In the fifth section we attempt to explain the German case through an examination of its historical roots and some particularities of the German political system.

German immigration policy in retrospective

To understand the process of Europeanization in the aftermath of the Amsterdam Treaty, it is necessary to review the most important changes that occurred in the material and procedural outcomes of that period. But before going into details of these recent developments, a brief overview of the history of immigration to Germany during the last half century is in order.

The groundwork of migration processes to Germany was laid by the massive recruitment of guest workers (*Gastarbeiter*) in the 1950s and 1960s. Regulated by government agencies in cooperation with employers' associations and labour unions, the agreements with Mediterranean countries led to an influx of several million foreign workers until the recruitment was halted in 1973 (*Anwerbestopp*). Even though the guest worker programme was envisaged to encourage only temporary immigration, many of the foreign workers decided to remain in Germany, especially after the recruitment programme was brought to an end. Migration in the following years was then characterized mainly by family reunification – spouses and children of the foreign workers – who were constitutionally protected through the Basic Law.

The Basic Law also played a central role in the influx of asylum-seekers in the late 1980s and early 1990s. For historical reasons the German Constitution was founded on universal human rights obligations concerning political persecution, in addition to the international law on the rights of refugees. In times of political turmoil, this relatively liberal asylum law led to a sharp increase in asylum migration: as data from the federal statistical office show, Germany attracted more than 1.4 million asylum-seekers between 1988 and 1993. According to Joppke (1999: 85), the law guaranteeing asylum-seekers from all over the world the right to judicial review invalidated 'the sovereign right of the state to deny access to its territory'. To deal with this dilemma, a grand coalition of the oppositional SPD and the governing coalition of CDU/CSU and FDP reached an agreement in 1992 that would restrict and regulate future policy, the so-called 'asylum compromise' (Giesler and Wasser 1993: 225). As a central instrument, the amendment (clause 16a) of article 16 of the Basic Law was implemented. The amendment stipulates that the right to asylum shall not be granted in cases of applicants arriving in Germany via a safe third state, a concept that severely limits individual rights vis-à-vis the provenance and the routing of the immigrating person and provides shelter only to those who did not cross into Germany from a state regarded as 'safe' (Giesler and Wasser 1993).

The coalition on the amendment to the Basic Law and its judicial confirmation by the Constitutional Court in 1996 established an informal new policy paradigm, which included an agreement on the necessity of restricting and directing immigration flows (Sachverständigenrat für Zuwanderung und Integration 2004: 138) as a policy goal for the majority of the political actors (BT DS 14/7387). It took a few more years, however – until the change of government in 1998 – for this informal policy paradigm to become official policy. From the cessation of guest worker recruitment in 1973 until the time of the new immigration law, German immigration legislation for third-country nationals was based on the principle of outlawing residence for foreigners except in special cases for which an exception had been granted (Frings and Knöse 2005: 11). In practice, special residence permits were issued in several cases, for example, for seasonal workers, contingency workers, Jewish migrants from the former Soviet Union – and above all in the case of family reunification.

Looked at in terms of processes of Europeanization, there is no doubt that developments on the EU level facilitated the restrictive reform of the asylum law in Germany. The Schengen Agreements reframed asylum and migration policies in such a way that security questions rather than human rights concerns stood in the foreground. The German government made use of the opportunity to argue that a reform of the Basic Law was necessary in order to fulfil European demands (Hellmann et al. 2005: 152). European cooperation on asylum strengthened rather than weakened German capacity to regulate access to state territory through measures such as recognition of 'safe third countries', 'safe countries of origin' and fast-track procedures for 'manifestly unfounded applications' (Geddes 2003: 85–6). The implementation of the safe third-country concept and, ironically, the idea of the supranational burden-sharing – that is, a so-called 'escape to Europe' – has been accepted as a means to regain sovereignty (Freeman 1998; Geddes 2003; Guiraudon 2000). This 'escape' addresses the deficiencies of immigration policy, allows a rebuilding of the capacity of nation states in areas of 'lost control', strengthens the sovereignty of the states and may help to control unwanted migratory movements such as illegal migration or trafficking (Boswell 2002). Moreover, it has been argued that the 'escape to Europe' enables member states to avoid legal and political restrictions (Geddes 2003; Guiraudon 1998; Hollifield 2000). Based on the foregoing, the period prior to the Amsterdam Treaty can thus be described through the mode of discursive Europeanization. Political actors in Germany used developments on the EU level in order to prepare the ground for a domestic policy change.

European impact on the German politics of immigration

In the following section, the European impact on the politics of immigration in Germany before and after the Amsterdam Treaty will be described. Here we consider changes in the institutional structures, party politics and – our primary focus – the lengthy procedure involved with the recent Immigration Act of 2005, especially the role of Europeanization during the process of political bargaining around this law.

The inclusion of German administration into European structures and the creation of special EU units and 'task forces' in government agencies are clear examples of the so-called top-down processes of Europeanization, even though bureaucracy tends to be resistant to these kinds of changes. But the impact of Europeanization was not felt in the administration alone. In 1994, after the Treaty of Maastricht, a new Committee on European Union Affairs was institutionalized in the German parliament, endowed with special powers and constitutionally anchored in the German Basic Law. This committee is the central forum for the decision-making process on European policy. Unlike other commissions, it is able to submit binding opinions directly to the federal government. It is responsible for all fundamental questions concerning European integration, institutional reforms of the EU, the amendment of community treaties, enlargement and cooperation with the European Parliament. It also takes part in the discussion of draft legislation.

Political bargaining on immigration policy is based on the paradigm of directing immigration with the instruments of European integration. In any case, the communitarization of asylum policy and control of external borders were relatively unquestioned in Germany (Geddes 2003). Likewise, the significant steps toward Union-level cooperation, which were taken at the Tampere European Council in October 1999, were accepted with virtually no parliamentary dispute; only the PDS voted against them (BT DS 14/2703). Though it may not be obvious at first sight, this informal coalition has not changed substantively. With respect to the common asylum system in general, no oppositional standpoint was expressed: in the debate on certain proposals, for example, the oppositional FDP either voted in favour of the government or else failed to appear, which is uncommon in the German political system. The grand coalition supporting Europeanized immigration policy for all practical purposes still exists.

The impact of European immigration policy after the Treaty of Amsterdam reverberated during the six-year negotiation process over the Immigration Act, which finally came into force in 2005. In discussions of the government's draft law, questions were raised concerning the compliance with some of the proposals of the European Commission and their expected effects on German immigration legislation. The drawn-out legislative process for the new Act was reflective of the weight immigration policy carries among the German public, reinforced by permanent election campaigns and the institutional counterbalance of the German political system. Whereas normally the state parliament is concerned only with the implementation of European legislation in matters that fall in its jurisdiction, the implementation of these directives which were included in the new draft law now became part of the entire process of negotiating around the Act. The new Immigration Act was already under consideration when the first proposals of the commission on a common asylum system were submitted. Once the proposals entered the national legislation procedure around the Immigration Act, the national political counterbalance, that is, the state parliament, also became an important veto factor in the negotiations. In the case of the individual proposals presented above, it is possible to identify, by evaluating the debates overall – including some undiscussed proposals – a few central issues that were discussed in the committees and expert hearings. The issue of the status of third-country nationals and the open question of non-state persecution are but two examples. The debates concerning international burden-sharing took place in the parliament as part of the discussion of the draft bill and were also evaluated by the Committee on Human Rights. In one part of the proceedings, for example, the Council proposal on the qualification and status of third-country nationals and stateless persons as refugees (CD 2004/83/EC) became a central focus of the parliamentary fight between the oppositional CDU/CSU and the two governing parties (SPD and Greens), and was accepted in the end by the Committee on Human Rights[2] which recommended its acceptance.

The Council proposal on minimum standards for procedures in member states for granting or withdrawing refugee status (COM/2002/326 final) was one of the requested amendments intended to address several mismatches with the German legislation. It was again the CDU which submitted an application in the federal parliament, asking for an initiative on a revision of the proposal, arguing that the German airport protocol, the safe country principle and the principle of unfounded appeal were endangered. It was also pointed out that the concept of a harmonized asylum policy was accepted in general by the party (BT DS 14/5759). In its critique, the oppositional CDU referred to the asylum compromise of 1992 as a general agreement which would be affected by the proposal. An expert hearing was initiated by the German government in which several experts brought forward their arguments on the special consequences of that proposal and on its material and procedural outcome. In the end, the proposal was accepted by the governing parties of the SPD, the Greens and also, rather atypically for the German political system, the oppositional FDP, all of whom had denied the CDU's proposition on another revised version. The factor for such a vote was that the proposed changes would not affect the desired outcome of a restricted and directed immigration, and would at the same time meet the designated political aim of a harmonized European immigration policy (Santel and Weber 2000). When the oppositional CDU/CSU regained power in the upper chamber of the parliament (Bundesrat), their opposition to some of the proposals carried more and more weight during negotiations.

To understand the arguments concerning the proclaimed European policy, it is helpful to distinguish between an expected material outcome and a procedural change. Whereas the material outcome of the Europeanized legislature has become a part of the political discussion, the procedure of a European policy and the question of its impact have not been questioned. Although the veto players used all political instruments at their disposal to hamper the successful outcome of the draft bill and its material outcome, the political debates did not encounter procedural arguments, that is, the diffusion of supranational policies on the domestic level. German immigration policy is still based on the tacit political agreement to restrict and direct immigration into Germany. Only its instruments, such as the endangerment of the concept of the safe third country, were questioned. However, the so-called 'escape to Europe' itself has never been questioned by any political party. In other words, German immigration policy is based on an informal grand coalition which accepted European integration, whereas the shape of its impact, the degree of Europeanization, is still a matter of political debate.

The European impact on German policies of immigration

The communitarization of European immigration policies became a serious issue only after the Amsterdam Treaty of 1997. The outcome of that treaty must be seen as a paradigm shift in the forthcoming integration process, passing the third pillar of justice and home affairs into the community structures and the shift of the policy areas dealing with visa regimes, asylum and immigration into the first communitarized pillar (see Bendel in this volume).

At first glance, Germany's activities on integration during the Amsterdam negotiations were not new since Germany has been one of the front-runners of the communitarization of immigration and asylum policy during the negotiations on the Amsterdam Treaty (Geddes 2000: 115; Müller 2003). Nevertheless, Amsterdam can be regarded as a turning point in the German position as far as further integration in the field of asylum and migration policy is concerned.

During the preparations for the summit, the German delegation changed its position on a central point: the introduction of the qualified majority vote (QMV) in the field of asylum and refugee policy. Germany still supported the introduction of the QMV during the Maastricht summit, but changed to a new position blockading the QMV and clinging to unanimity during the Amsterdam summit. This change of position had its roots in the growing competencies of the *Länder*, who feared a loss of political influence and additional financial obligations, especially in the context of the debate on burden-sharing in the field of asylum and refugee policy (Hellmann et al. 2005: 153). Finally, a five-year transition period was agreed upon by the member states.

Since the Tampere European Council in 1999 the process of Europeanization of immigration can be evaluated by the number of European regulations and directives concerning immigration policies, for example a common asylum system and a common system on combating illegal migration, which have been submitted in the ensuing period. It was again Germany who favoured the development of the communitarized immigration system, but fell short of achieving the goal of a uniform asylum system instead of a common asylum system, which was adopted after others that dealt with cooperation on undocumented migration, refugee flows and trafficking (Santel and Weber 2000). The Tampere Conclusions also reaffirmed the Union's obligation to respect the right of the individual to seek asylum. The aim of the Amsterdam Treaty was renewed at the meetings in Laeken in 2001, Seville in 2002 and Thessaloniki in 2003. These aims referred to strengthening measures to combat illegal migration, trafficking and smuggling, targeting illegal residence and repatriation of irregular residents.

The political instruments in the first pillar (see Ette and Faist in this volume) that transfer binding decisions from supranational to domestic law – regulations and directives – are presented in this chapter. Depending on their judicial character and their content, the implementation into German legislation naturally followed different proceedings. Whereas regulations have the status of immediately applicable law, directives serve the purpose of setting targets. Their implementation in the national legislation can be delayed if necessary (Müller 2003). As shown below, some of them were implemented without any noticeable effects on German policy, while others created new legal foundations without important effects. Nevertheless some of these measures constituted serious problems for the German policy framework. All in all, the expansion of entitlement rights of refugees created material problems, but severe misfits were noticeable only in the case of the endangered 'safe third country' concept (Deutscher Bundestag, Innenauschuss-Protokoll No. 15/18, 02.07.2003). The EU regulation implied a screening of individual cases, which had been partially abolished by the 'asylum compromise' of 1992/93.

In-between the summit of Amsterdam in 1997 and its entry into force in 1999 a change of government occurred in 1998. The governing parties of the Christian Democratic CDU/CSU and the liberal FDP lost the elections after having been in power for 16 years. The election defeat of this coalition led to a change in immigration policy, an issue that had been on the oppositional agenda for many years. One of the first measures proclaimed by the new Minister of the Interior in 1998 was to replace the so-called 'muddling-through' type of immigration control policy (Thränhardt 1999: 45) with a so-called 'new and modern' immigration policy (Bade and Bommes 2000: 163). The new element of this policy was the recognition of Germany as an 'immigration country' and the design of a selective migration policy, based mainly on qualifications of potential migrants, while maintaining the restrictive tendency towards unwanted migration flows. The realization of the different European measures and the matter of their impact on the German law became a substantial part of the proclaimed policy change. But even though the official approach and discourse towards immigration have changed, the new government displayed at least reluctance concerning further integration in some areas of this policy field. This became especially obvious during the European Convention in Strasbourg, when a 'grand coalition' of the former Minister of the Exterior Joschka Fischer (Greens), ex-Governor Erwin Teufel (CDU) and SPD delegate Jürgen Meyer wrote a joint letter to the president of the Convention, Giscard d'Estaing, demanding a national veto on questions of asylum and refugee policy (Hellmann et al. 2005: 154). This position may be explained by pressure from the *Länder* on the one hand and by the traditional restrictive approach in German migration policies – irrespective of the political colour of the government – on the other. German politicians were afraid that the restrictive policies implemented on the national level, particularly those of the early 1990s, might get watered down by European regulations.

We turn now to an examination of a number of directives and regulations and their implementation on the German level, assessing the possible consequences these measures might have for German policy. Although the main focus will be on asylum and refugee policy, other areas such as secondary migration, the combat against undocumented migration and the field of visa and border control policy will also be discussed. To analyse the degree of the goodness of fit, that is, the amount of congruence between the supranational and the domestic immigration policy, special emphasis will be given to those points that pose challenges to German immigration control policy.

Asylum policy

One of the measures that did not seriously affect German immigration policy was the proposal of 2001 for a Council Directive on minimum standards in the reception of asylum-seekers by member states (CD 2003/9/EC). The proposal required member states to grant reasonable standards of living to all asylum-seekers, guaranteeing comparable living conditions including health care or subsistence, while at the same time limiting the right to move. These standards were already defined by the German *Asylbewerberleistungsgesetz* (Law on social benefits for asylum applicants). It is plausible therefore to assume that the aim of this directive was to prevent secondary migration movements, or so-called asylum shopping. On the presumption that Germany was still one of the main destinations of migrants in the EU, the prevention of asylum shopping corresponds with the German policy idea of burden-sharing.

A Council Directive focusing on temporary protection of refugees and burden-sharing, minimum standards for granting temporary protection in the event of mass influx of displaced persons, and a burden-sharing procedure between the member states was finally approved by the Council in July 2001 (CD 2001/55/EC). The material outcome of this directive affected the German asylum system insofar as neither access to the labour market and the possibility of family reunion nor the right to apply for asylum were granted before. The directive was implemented via the new Immigration Act in 2005. Whereas the material misfit is based upon an enlargement of the rights granted to refugees, the procedural outcome of this directive, the decision-making on the European level, necessarily impacts upon German sovereignty in a normative manner as the state clearly loses its sovereign control over its territory.

In 2001 the Commission submitted a proposal for a Council Directive on minimum standards for the qualification and status of third-country nationals and stateless persons as refugees or as persons who otherwise need international protection (COM/2001/519). In 2004 the Council reached an agreement on an amended version: protection can be denied in the case of asylum-seekers whose safety can otherwise be guaranteed by other parties or international organizations such as the UNHCR (CD 2004/83/EC). Providing subsidiary shelter in addition to cases covered under the Geneva Convention and to cases of non-state persecution, this directive widened the concept of German asylum policy and became a point at issue in the debate on the German Immigration Act. The concept of state persecution as a necessary condition for granting minimum residence permission caused serious problems for the German jurisdiction because it had in the past obviously led to a lack of protection, for example in the case of stateless refugees. However, with the new Immigration Act in 2005, persecution by non-state actors was implemented for the first time (§ 60.1c AufenthG). With reference to the quantity of refugees concerned, it had been estimated prior to implementation that the acceptance of the non-governmental persecution category would not have major consequences in terms of the number of accepted refugees; merely the rights of claimants were going to be changed (Hailbronner 2005). Again, the misfit between the directive and the German law consists of the strong limitation of rights granted to the refugees.

Concerning asylum determination procedures, in 2000 the Commission submitted a proposal on minimum standards for procedures for granting or withdrawing refugee status (COM(2000) 578 final), which aimed to force the new member states to implement standards for the appeal provisions, but allowed other countries eventually to moderate their comparably high standards. In detail, the concepts of safe third countries and safe countries of origin were implemented throughout the EU. In any case, what appears to be a downward adaptation of the exceptionally liberal German law at first glance in fact caused serious problems to the German legal system. As shown above, article 16a of the German Basic Law denies the right for individual case review. The new European law grants the refugee the individual right for his or her case to be reassessed. Also a right to appeal at the ECHR was provided (see article 27, 33 26a, 34a AsylVfG, article 16a GG). In addition, the proposal provided the individual refugee with the right to legal advice in case of rejection. A revised proposal was accepted by the Council in 2004, leading to a revised version of the German concept and the acceptance of the individual appeal at the ECHR.

Apparently this directive contradicts article 16a of the German Basic Law which accepts the idea of potentially safe countries as a normative concept. The base of German asylum policy – the possibility for the state to decide which country can be defined as safe and the obligation to send refugees back immediately without assessing their individual case and without granting the right to appeal to the ECHR – has been seriously challenged by this directive. Nevertheless, the effect of the new regulation on German immigration has been seen as marginal since Germany is, after the enlargement of the Union, surrounded by Dublin II states only (except Switzerland). This means that the concept of the safe third state is losing its importance for German asylum policy (Hailbronner 2005). The determination of the state responsible for examination of the asylum application (Dublin II Convention, EC No. 343/2003) came into force in 2003. The EURODAC fingerprint system provides an instrument for defining responsibility, criteria and mechanisms for determining which member state is responsible for an asylum application submitted by a third-country national in one of the member states (EC No. 2725/2000). The force of the agreement, that each state allowing access to the EU is responsible for asylum examination, gives incentives to member states to adopt a restrictive policy (Nissen 2004). Again, the aim of this directive was to prevent secondary migration.

Secondary migration

The Commission submitted three different proposals on family re-unification in 1999, 2000 and 2002, conceding the right to family migration to a spouse and minor children. Member states may request that the applications concerning family reunification of minor children must be submitted before the age of 15 years. After that age, entry and residence of the person concerned may be authorized on grounds other than family reunion. The question of the minimum age for children to be allowed to join their parents was hotly discussed on the national level during the negotiation of the new Immigration Act. In the end, the German position was even stricter than the European legislation: children have to be under 16 years of age and to prove that they can be integrated into German society (Sachverständigenrat, Jahresgutachten 2005).

Undocumented migration

The Council Directive on mutual recognition of decisions on expulsion of third-country nationals (CD 2001/40/EC) requires member states to recognize the expulsion decisions made by another member state. The 2005 Immigration Act implemented this directive behind schedule (§ 58 Abs. 2 Nr. 3 AufenthG). Another directive concerning undocumented migration (CD 2001/51/EC) supplements the provisions of article 26 of the Schengen Implementation Agreement, harmonizing the financial penalties in case of carriers breaching their obligations. This directive, which directly targets carriers transporting people without travel documents, was implemented in 2005 with the new Immigration Act (§63 AufenthG).

The Council Directive 2002/90/EC defining facilitations on unauthorized entry, transit and residence has not yet been implemented in the German legislature, but will be transposed to national law by a recently announced bill. Following Renner (2005), no substantial protection exists against trafficking of women, since article 27 I was overruled on 5 December 2004, even though there are some effective instruments against trafficking already in place in German law. Although trafficking is illegal (§ 95f AufenthG), a loophole has been identified allowing the possibility of entry into Germany via a tourist visa (Renner 2005).

Border control and visa policy

In 2000 the Council adopted a proposal for a regulation determining the list of third-country nationals who must be in possession of visas when crossing external borders (CR EC/574/1999). This proposal was amended and a common list of countries finally approved by the Council in 2001. In 2004, the Visa Information System was established by the Commission as a database intended to help counter visa deception and improve exchanges of information between member states on visa applications and decisions. In general, the misfit between supranational and domestic law was especially low in the area of border control and common visa policy as the German government has been – and still is – one of the front-runners in this policy field. This became quite obvious during the preparation of the eastern enlargement when the German government insisted on strict control policies along the new eastern border between the new Central and Eastern European member states of the EU and its eastern neighbours.

Recent developments

Several EU regulations and directives have still not been transferred into German law. In January 2006, the German government announced a new bill which aims at the transposition of a total of 11 directives related to the areas of laws on aliens, freedom of movement, immigration policy, undocumented migration and asylum policy. Only parts of some of these directives have been transferred into German law with the Immigration Act of 2005. The main focus of the new bill under discussion will be the prevention of forced marriages, prostitution and human trafficking. According to the federal government, most of the directives require only slight alterations to the German law. The pro-immigrant NGO Pro Asyl objects that some of these changes will be more restrictive than the content of the directives, while positive changes such as the qualification directive (CD/2004/83/EC) would be transferred only partially (Pro Asyl 2006). A point of contention is likely to be the raising of the minimum age for spouses of foreigners residing in Germany to 21 years. Politicians from the governing SPD and the three oppositional parties (Greens, Left-Party and FDP) have already announced their opposition to the introduction of a fixed minimum age for spouses, while the CDU/CDU is supporting this measure (*Migration und Bevölkerung* 2006).

The overall conclusion from this analysis of the transposition of EU directives into German law is that the mode of Europeanization after the Amsterdam Treaty is best described as a prescriptive mode. German political actors had to make sure that European policies were transferred into national laws, even though some of the directives showed some degree of misfit with German regulations.

The extent of change in policy and politics

We turn now to consider the extent of change in policy and politics through Europeanization. In evaluating and measuring change, it is useful to recall the paradigm on immigration policy as the regaining of border control and managing immigration at the base of European integration. Concerning the quality and quantity of changes and the goodness of fit, one has to bear in mind the differentiation between the procedures and the material outcome. Whereas some of the procedures change, as for example in the case of the safe third-country concept, the material outcome by this measure might be negligible. In other cases, as in the Council Directive on minimum standards for granting temporary protection in the event of mass influx of displaced persons, the German government transferred a major decision on the control of its territory to the supranational level. The material outcome of additional rights for refugees should also be noted, which the European Parliament has already demanded before the forthcoming ratification of the Maastricht Treaty and the abolition of borders (BT-DS 12/4052). Though true for only some of the directives, it must be mentioned that Europeanization led to the strengthening of the opportunity structures of oppositional political actors: those who argued for additional rights as well as those who argued for a strengthening of control and security measures – a phenomenon which again strengthened the informal paradigm of the 'escape to Europe'.

In assessing the nature of the EU's presented policy measures in terms of the degree of misfit, we can conclude that some of the European directives matched German law precisely and provoked no political debate, whereas others seemed to pose a conflict between the outcome of the law and German immigration policy itself. In these cases, the presumed quantitative outcome was questioned, as for example in the case of the Dublin Convention. Mutual consensus was easily found in those cases where the quantitative change was deemed to be negligible. In other cases of suspected non-compliance of the proposals with the German legislation, forced adaptation to the supranational legislation resulted from an increase of rights granted to refugees, whereas the measures to combat illegal migration created new German legislation. The proposals on illegal migration, however, brought in completely new legislation, which did not conflict with German policy but had the effect of strengthening the political executive.

When we consider the compliance of European policy and existing German policy in terms of the pressure to change, the process can be defined all in all as a process of absorption with low institutional change in the dimension of politics. In cases where the extent of change can be defined as minor, and the paradigm on immigration policy is not a determining factor, political agreement reached through a consensus of the main political actors is more likely. With reference to the framework outlined above, we can decipher adaptation of national institutions to European measures, but also a strengthening of the opportunity structures of oppositional political actors. Europeanization itself can be understood as a process which is accepted by all political actors. The level of its expected impact, however, is understood as being determined more or less through a normal process of political bargaining (Knill 2005: 159): Even while explaining their oppositional standpoints, the parties were always eager to assert their commitment to the principles of a common immigration policy and its implementation. Put simply, the Europeanization of German immigration policy was accepted by all parties in the German parliament. An exception to this common consensus is the growing reluctance of subnational actors of the *Länder*, who are apt to blockade further integration if they fear a loss of competencies or sense that there may be intolerable financial burdens.

Finally, the impact of Europeanization on immigration policy in Germany is not fully understood without looking at the Commission proposals and the supply of the directives as a bottom-up process. Although Europeanization is clearly defined as a top-down process, an approach that in this volume informs the analytical perspective on the integration process, it should also be recalled that the member states are not passive players in the process of Europeanization. The quantity and the quality of the supranational policy outcome and the quality of the impact must be seen as influenced by the member states. Monar (2003) labelled these processes as 'downloading' and 'uploading' dimensions, noting that in terms of the 'uploading' or bottom-up process, Germany was especially successful in the transfer of Schengen into the community structures and in the efforts of harmonizing border control policies, above all in the context of EU enlargement.

Conclusion: Factors driving Europeanization of domestic policies and politics of immigration in Germany

To analyse the character of the Europeanization of German immigration policy and politics one has to bear in mind two factors. First, the nearly half-century-long process of European integration (Eising 2003: 407f.) has over time consolidated a manifest acceptance of European integration by central political actors. This acceptance is also seen as a function of German history on the one hand and the similarities between the European and the German federal system as semi-sovereign states (Katzenstein 2000) on the other.

After defeat in the Second World War, it was German integration in a European Union that held out the promise of increasing influence of the devastated nation state on the relevant political actors and thus became firmly fixed on Germany's foreign affairs agenda. In addition, German elites were convinced at the same time that the power of the German state had to be bounded. West European integration seemed to be an appropriate measure. The transformation of the German federal system on the European level afforded integration in international institutions through minimal adaptation of domestic political structures (Jachtenfuchs 2000: 87; Monar 2003). Even while German politicians proclaim the presence of German interests in Europe, no substantive change in the aftermath of German reunification has occurred. A strong limitation to German autonomy is still accepted by the German government (Jachtenfuchs 2000). This position was more or less the same during the negotiations on the Amsterdam Treaty, as

Jachtenfuchs demonstrates by showing that the preferences of the German government concerning an increasing federation were comparatively strong. The only exception, as mentioned earlier, was the change of position concerning the introduction of the QMV on asylum and refugee policy.

European integration itself is also the result of several negotiations between the member states. In this respect the member states are the relevant actors with respect to the material outcome of European regulations and the quality of fit (Auel 2005: 310). Germany was a constituent part of the European integration process throughout. As early as 26 July 1950 the German federal parliament adopted a non-party resolution concerning European policy which formed the basis of European policy for the following decades, a resolution that was opposed only by the members of the Communist Party. The German parliament supports a 'European federation' to create a European Economic Union on the basis of economic unanimity (Jachtenfuchs 2000: 86). Irrespective of the political agenda of any single party, the German coalition favouring the establishment of a European federation, aware of the implied loss of sovereignty as a member state among others, constituted an unquestioned (prior to 1989) consensus. Germany's early membership in the intergovernmental agreement of Schengen from 1985 was already a step in promoting a supranational asylum system. With the amendment to the German Basic Law in 1993, supranational policy-making was introduced into German law, and 'brought Europe in', thereby facilitating a paradigm change in domestic asylum policy.

The German government has been a primary actor in the process of supranational development, forcing institutional and policy transformations, always eager to erect a functioning single European market, based on the removal of borders and promoting the harmonization of visa policies and asylum laws (Geddes 2000). But even though Germany has been and is generally still seen as one of the drivers of the integration, it has shifted recently 'from a vanguard to a laggard' (Hellmann et al. 2005: 150). The move from nearly complete absorption to partial reluctance and 'laggardness' can be explained mainly by two factors. Along the politics dimension, the *Länder* – endowed with more political weight since the Maastricht Treaty – were afraid of giving up competencies and feared growing financial burdens implied by the admission and integration of asylum-seekers and refugees. Along the dimension of policy, German policy-makers have been interested in maintaining the restrictive policies that have been implemented in the early 1990s, fearing that a further Europeanization in this field could lead to a watering down of these regulations.

Notes

1 For the sake of simplicity, the term 'Germany' means West Germany until unification in October 1990, and unified Germany after 1990.
2 See 'Stellungnahme des Ausschusses für Menschenrechte: Deutscher Bundestag Stenografischer Bericht 42. Sitzung 07.05.2003, Plenarprotokoll 15/42. http://dip.bundestag.de/btp.15/15042.pdf (last accessed 19 September 2006).

References

Auel, K. (2005) 'Europäisierung nationaler Politik'. In H.-J. and M. L. Bieling (eds), *Theorien der europäischen Integration*. Wiesbaden: Verlag für Sozialwissenschaften, pp. 293–320.

Bade, K. and M. Bommes (2000) 'Migration und politische Kultur im Nicht-Einwanderungsland'. In K. Bade and R. Münz (eds), *Migrationsreport 2000: Fakten, Analysen, Perspektiven*. Frankfurt am Main, New York: Campus Verlag, pp. 163–204.

Börzel, T. (2003) *How the European Union Interacts with its Member States*. Political Sciences Series 93, Institute for Advanced Studies, Vienna. http://www.ihs.ac.at/publications/pol/pw_93.pdf (last accessed 19 September 2006).

Börzel, T. and T. Risse (2003) 'Conceptualizing the Domestic Impact of Europe'. In K. Featherstone und C. Radaelli (eds), *The Politics of Europeanization*. Oxford: Oxford University Press, pp. 55–78.

Boswell, C. (2002) 'EU Immigration and Asylum Policy: From Tampere to Laeken and Beyond'. Briefing Paper News Series No. 30, The Royal Institute of International Affairs, February 2002. http://www.chathamhouse.org.uk/pdf/briefing_papers/BP per cent2030.pdf (last accessed on 19 December 2005).

Eising, R. (2003) 'Europäisierung und Integration. Konzepte der EU-Forschung'. In M. Jachtenfuchs and B. Kohler-Koch (eds), *Europäische Integration*. Opladen: Leske und Budrich, pp. 387–416.

Freeman, G. (1998) 'The Decline of Sovereignty: Politics and Immigration Restriction in Liberal States'. In C. Joppke (ed.), *Challenge to the Nation State: Immigration in Western Europe and the United States*. Oxford: Oxford University Press.

Frings, D. and Peter Knösel (eds) (2005) *Das neue Ausländerrecht. Alle Gesetze und Verordnungen zum Zuwanderungsgesetz*. Frankfurt am Main: Fachhochschulverlag.

Geddes, A. (2000) *Immigration and European Integration: Towards Fortress Europe?* Manchester: Manchester University Press.

Geddes, A. (2003) *The Politics of Migration and Immigration in Europe*. London, Thousand Oaks, New Dehli: Sage Publications.

Giesler, V. and D. Wasser (1993) *Das neue Asylrecht: Die neuen Gesetzestexte und internationalen Abkommen mit Erläuterungen*. Cologne: Bundesanzeiger.

Guiraudon, V. (1998) 'International Human Rights Norms and their Incorporation: the Protection of Aliens in Europe'. European Institute/European Forum Working Paper 98/04, European University Institute, Florence.

Guiraudon, V. (2000) 'European Integration and Migration Policy: Vertical Policy-making as Venue Shopping'. *Journal of Common Market Studies*, Vol. 38, No. 2: 251–71.

Hailbronner, K. (2005) *Ausländer- und Asylrecht.* Heidelberg: C. F. Müller.
Hellmann, G., R. Baumann, M. Bösche, B. Herborth and W. Wagner (2005) 'De-Europeanization by Default? Germany's EU Policy in Defense and Asylum'. *Foreign Policy Analysis,* Vol. 1: 143–64.
Hollifield, J. (2000) 'Immigration and the Politics of Rights: the French Case in Comparative Perspective'. In M. Bommes and Andrew Geddes (eds), *Immigration and Welfare: Challenging the Borders of the Welfare State.* London: Routledge.
Jachtenfuchs, M. (2000) 'Deutsche Europapolitik: Vom abstrakten zum konkreten Föderalismus'. In M. Knodt and B. Kohler-Koch (eds), *Deutschland zwischen Europäisierung und Selbstbehauptung.* Frankfurt am Main: Campus, pp. 85–109.
Joppke, C. (1999) *Immigration and the Nation-State: the United States, Germany and Great Britain.* New York: Oxford University Press.
Katzenstein, P. J. (2000) 'Gezähmte Macht: Deutschland in Europa'. In M. Knodt and Beate Kohler-Koch (eds), *Deutschland zwischen Europäisierung und Selbstbehauptung.* Frankfurt am Main: Campus, pp. 57–84.
Knill, C. (2005) 'Die EU und die Mitgliedsstaaten'. In K. Holzinger et al. (eds), *Die Europäische Union. Theorien und Analysekonzepte.* Paderborn, Munich: Schöningh, pp. 153–80.
Migration und Bevölkerung (2006) 'Deutschland: Verschärfung des Ausländerrechts durch Umsetzung von EU-Richtlinien'. 1/2006 (February).
Monar, J. (2003) 'Justice and Home Affairs: Europeanization as a Government-Controlled Process'. In K. Dyson and K. Goetz (eds), *Germany, Europe and the Politics of Constraint.* Oxford: Oxford University Press, pp. 309–23.
Müller, T. (2003) *Die Innen- und Justizpolitik der Europäischen Union. Eine Analyse der Integrationsentwicklung.* Opladen: Leske und Budrich.
Nissen, J. (2004) *Five years of EU Migration and Asylum Policymaking under the Amsterdam and Tampere Mandates.* Brussels: MPG.
Pro Asyl (2006) *Mehr Abschottung, mehr Haft, weniger Integration.* Pro Asyl leaflet 31.01.2006. http://www.proasyl.de/fileadmin/proasyl/fm_redakteure/Archiv/Stellungnahmen/Stellungnahme_PA_nderungsgesetz_neu.pdf (last accessed on 4 June 2006).
Radaelli, C. M. (2003) 'The Europeanization of Public Policy'. In K. Featherstone and C. M. Radaelli (eds), *The Politics of Europeanization.* Oxford: Oxford University Press.
Renner, G. (2005) 'Kampf der illegalen Einreise und dem illegalen Aufenthalt'. *Migrationsrecht Net,* 18 June. http://www.migrationsrecht.net./gesetzgebung-auslaenderrecht (last accessed 19 September 2006).
Sachverständigenrat für Zuwanderung und Integration (2004) *Migration und Integration – Erfahrungen natzen, neues wagen. Jahresgutachten 2004.* Berlin, Nuremberg: Sachverständigenrat für Zuwanderung und Integration, Bundesamt für Migration und Flüchtlinge.
Santel, B. and A. Weber (2000) 'Zwischen Ausländerpolitik und Einwanderungspolitik: Migrations-und Ausländerrecht in Deutschland'. In K. J. Bade and R. Münz (eds), *Migrationsreport 2000. Fakten, Analysen, Perspektiven.* Frankfurt, New York: Campus Verlag, pp. 109–40.
Thränhardt, W.-D. (1999) 'Germany's Immigration Policy and Politics'. In G. Brochmann and T. Hammar (eds), *Mechanisms of Immigration Control: a Comparative Analysis of European Regulation Policies.* Oxford, New York: Berg, pp. 29–58.

5
Against Exceptionalism: British Interests for Selectively Europeanizing its Immigration Policy[1]

Andreas Ette and Jürgen Gerdes

Introduction

This chapter provides an analysis of the extent of Europeanization of the policies and politics of immigration in the United Kingdom (UK). In its relationship with the European Union (EU), the UK is often characterized as the odd one out and in comparison to other European member states the British approach towards immigration is considered unique. In contrast to this general assumption of 'Anglo-Saxon exceptionalism' we argue that the British case is in fact only a variant of the general pattern of the Europeanization of immigration policies and does not constitute a fundamentally different case. On the one hand the analysis shows that Britain is exceptional in the extent of its Europeanization, which is at the lowest level compared to other member states of the EU. With respect to the pattern of Europeanization we argue that the European impact on British policies of immigration is highly selective and that the government defends important features of its established politics of immigration. On the other hand, the UK is similar to other leading European member states insofar as it regularly makes use of the European level as a venue to pursue its national interests on immigration policy. Generally, the differences between the UK and other member states concerning the pattern of Europeanization are therefore a result of varying national interests. In particular, three main factors can account for the British case: (1) the mode of Europeanization structuring the British interaction with the EU in this policy area; (2) the increasing difficulties experienced by the UK in regulating migration flows in the national setting; and (3) the particular national preferences of the British government.

The argument on 'British exceptionalism' is regularly evoked in discussions of the relationship between the UK and the EU but also with respect to the British approach towards immigration and the European impact on the policies, politics and polity of the UK. The image of the UK as exceptional is even older than British membership in the EU. The UK refused to participate in the European Coal and Steel Community and the Treaty of Rome – the predecessors of what later came to be the European Communities and the EU. Membership was finally acquired in 1973 after unsuccessful applications in 1961–63 and 1967. From those early days onward, Britain has remained a 'semi-detached' (George 1992) participant in Europe and its 'awkward partner' (George 1998). Helen Wallace (1997) described Britain as fundamentally 'at odds with the theory and practice of integration'. Recent years have seen some improvements in this challenging relationship and the arrival in office of New Labour in 1997 heralded a fresh British approach towards the EU. Nevertheless, for most observers Britain remains 'an uncertain member state; uncertain about the advantages of membership, uncertain about its relationship with the other leading member states, and uncertain about the direction that it would like the European Union to take' (Allen 2005: 120).

Exceptional also are the British experience and approach towards immigration (Freeman 1994, 2004). At least four aspects are attached to Britain's uniqueness: first, the flows of migrants coming to the UK have been different from the experience of most other European countries with respect to the countries of origin, size, timing and composition. Second, the rationales for Britain's immigration policy differ from the European mainstream. Whereas economic reasoning was the major driving force on the continent, foreign policy considerations and in particular the relations with its colonies and New Commonwealth countries have been the central determinants in the UK. A third aspect concerns the problem-solving philosophy of British immigration control. The policy approaches in most European countries focus on internal control schemes as the most effective measures to manage migration. In contrast, Britain's policy rests on the belief of strict external frontier controls but weaker internal controls. Finally, the politics of migration in Britain differ from the European mainstream. Client politics dominated immigration policy-making for a long time on the continent. In the UK, in contrast, immigration was from the late 1950s onward a subject of popular concern. Furthermore, governmental discretion on immigration policies is in most European countries severely limited by interest groups, courts and the nationally incorporated international human rights regime. British politics of immigration, on the other hand, are an outcome of the majoritarian political system with a small number of veto players. They are characterized by a dominating executive and weak legal–constitutional constraints as well as weak interest groups.

The argument about 'British exceptionalism' is also supported by scholarship on the Europeanization of the UK. This applies in the case of the Europeanization of its nation state identity (Marcussen et al. 1999), but also for several policy areas where Britain has been out of line with other member states or complied with Europe only coincidentally (see, for example, Glaeßner 2005; Knill 2001). Similarly, Britain's role in the developing European immigration policy also contributes to this image. The UK did not take part in the drafting of the Schengen Agreement during the 1980s and fundamentally opposed the initiatives during the 1990s to develop a supranational European immigration policy. Furthermore, Britain forged the path of flexibility in the course of the negotiations on the Amsterdam Treaty with its opting out from Title IV on visas, asylum and immigration and the incorporated Schengen *acquis* (Geddes 2000). Recent years, however, have witnessed pronounced British activities concerning the development of a European area of freedom, security and justice in general and of a European immigration policy in particular. Examples of such a shift include the British impact on the EU anti-discrimination directives, the British–Spanish initiative during the June 2002 European Council in Seville on illegal immigration as well as the rather recent British initiatives during its 2005 Presidency of the European Council. Thus, the main task of this chapter is to provide an answer to the following question: does British exceptionalism also characterize the European impact on its politics and policy of immigration? And if so, in what ways is this impact exceptional?

The chapter proceeds in three parts. The first section discusses the extent of Europeanization of Britain's immigration policy. It provides a brief overview of Britain's involvement in European immigration initiatives before the ratification of the Amsterdam Treaty and analyses the legal–institutional structure of the Amsterdam Treaty which regulates British participation in European immigration policy. The main focus, however, is on an analysis of the impact of the developing European immigration policy during the period after 1999 on Britain's immigration policy. The second section provides the analysis of the Europeanization of the politics of immigration. Here, the focus is on the main institutional structures and actors that shape policy-making on immigration in the UK. Finally, the third section discusses three factors that help to understand the British pattern of Europeanization.

Selective Europeanization: the policies of immigration control

Justice and home affairs (JHA) are late entrants to the process of European integration. It was only in 1993 that JHA and immigration policies received proper attention at the European level, and steps towards substantive supranationalization of this policy area have been taken only since the late 1990s. Nevertheless, European cooperation and, in consequence, some form of Europeanization of national policies of immigration had started earlier. Cooperation occurred either in intergovernmental European forums or in bilateral initiatives between European member states. British governments have been active supporters of both forms of cooperation. In intergovernmental European activities, Britain participated in the 1967 Naples Convention which is often seen as the first European initiative dealing with migration of third-country nationals (Geddes 2000). The UK also took part in the Trevi Group from 1975 onward which originally focused on the subject of terrorism but later included issues of trans-border crime and immigration as well. During the 1980s and in particular during the British Council Presidency, the Ad Hoc Group on Immigration was established with the Thatcher government playing a leading role (Layton-Henry 1992: 231–2). Also during the 1990s intergovernmental cooperation between the UK and other European member states continued. Examples include the signing of the Dublin Convention as well as the London Resolution on manifestly unfounded applications for asylum and the drafting of EURODAC, a database for the comparison of fingerprints.

In British bilateral initiatives on immigration, cooperation with France has been paramount. These initiatives include the reciprocal arrangements on juxtaposed controls which permit each state to operate frontier controls on the territory of the other. These provisions were originally introduced in the 1991 Sangatte Protocol, but have received heightened attention during recent years and led to British pre-boarding immigration controls at French ports for travel by sea and at all Eurostar stations for travel by train (Ryan 2004a). These early European or bilateral initiatives have resulted in the harmonization of immigration and particular asylum policies of participating states. Compared to other member states, the extent of these impacts on British immigration policy has been at a low level. However, in comparison to the period after the Amsterdam Treaty, as will be shown below, these early European impacts had more lasting effects on Britain's immigration policy. The associated mode of Europeanization in this early period can be characterized as discursive, with policy learning being the main mechanism by which Europe shaped British immigration policy.

In the development of a European immigration policy, the mode of Europeanization changed with the Amsterdam Treaty. When the Treaty came into effect on 1 May 1999 it included on the one hand substantial provisions concerning the development of a common European immigration policy which was to be implemented over a five-year period. On the other hand it provided for new institutional and procedural regulations. In particular it transferred central immigration matters from the third pillar to Title IV in the first pillar of the Union. Overall, these new provisions had the effect of moving immigration matters away from the dominant intergovernmental decision-making approach and binding major parts of this policy area closer to the traditional Community method, resulting in what Helen Wallace (2005) termed 'intensive transgovernmentalism'. The importance of the Amsterdam Treaty for a European immigration policy is also the main reason for the empirical focus of this chapter on the five years following the ratification of the Amsterdam Treaty – starting in May 1999 and ending in April 2004.

In the British case the mode of Europeanization is more complicated. As already noted, the UK chose the path of flexibility during the Amsterdam negotiations and opted out of Title IV as well as all Schengen provisions. The UK does not need to take part in measures based on this new Title or on the Schengen *acquis*. However, Britain has an 'opt-in' option to measures based on Title IV or Schengen and may inform the Council within three months of receiving a draft of proposed legislation if they wish to take part in it (Hailbronner 1999: 20–1; Peers 2000: 53–60). In this way, the UK decides on a case-by-case basis whether there is any interest in taking part in the European integration of a particular area of immigration policy. These flexibility provisions have important consequences for the interaction between the UK and Europe. Despite the overall shift towards a more prescriptive mode governing EU member state relations on immigration matters, the 'opt-in' option preserves the intergovernmental basis on which the UK interacts with the EU. In consequence, this particular mode of Europeanization provides British governments with much discretion and includes few coercive pressures, except those measures that build on instruments other than Title IV or the Schengen *acquis* and those measures where the UK has already made use of its opt-in clause.

The British 'opt-out' in practice

Despite the assumptions following from Britain's 'exceptionalism' and despite its opt-out of the relevant provisions in the Amsterdam Treaty, British governments have been actively involved in the development of the European area of freedom, security and justice. This is true for Britain's engagement in European policies on immigrant integration (Geddes and Guiraudon 2004), as well as for European policies tackling international organized crime and of anti-terrorism (Glaeßner 2005). It is also true in the case of European immigration and asylum policies. A first indication is provided by the high rate of British participation in all European initiatives in this policy area. In total, the EU has adopted between 1 May 1999, the date of entry into force of the Treaty of Amsterdam, and 30 April 2004, the date when the transitional five-year period ended, a total of 17 regulations, 13 directives and 15 decisions and framework decisions.[2] Compared with the former third pillar under the Maastricht Treaty between 1993 and 1999, this reflects an overall increase in European activity in this policy area. Furthermore, it signifies an impressive shift to the use of legally binding texts (Monar 2004: 127). Of those texts, 7 deal with a common European asylum system, 4 are concerned with legal migration, 7 with irregular migration, 20 with border control and visa issues and 7 with return policy (see Table 5.1).

Overall, the UK has opted into 60 per cent of those 45 legally binding texts. Participation, however, is not equally distributed. On the one hand

Table 5.1   Participation of the UK in regulations, directives and (framework-) decisions taken by the EU between 1 May 1999 and 30 April 2004 in different areas of immigration policy

	Regulations	*Directives*	*(Framework-) decisions*
Asylum policy	2/2*	4/4	1/1
Policies on legal migration	1/1	–/3	–/–
Policies on irregular migration	1/1	3/4	2/2
Border control and visa policy	4/12	–/–	3/8
Return policy	1/1	1/2	4/4

*The first number indicates those initiatives the UK has opted into, whereas the second number shows the total number of initiatives falling into this category.

the UK has opted into all seven texts concerning asylum, into six of seven policy measures tackling irregular migration and also on six of seven return policy measures. On the other hand, the UK opted out of most measures on legal migration and border controls and visas. In other words, Britain has tended to participate in coercive measures that curtail the ability of migrants to enter the EU, whereas less attention has been paid to the more protective measures that to some extent give rights to migrants and third-country nationals (Guild 2004).[3]

The extent of Europeanization

Whereas the preceding section focused on Britain's selective participation in the Europeanization of its immigration policy, the following section focuses on the extent of Europeanization. How deep do these European measures cut into already established British immigration policies? In comparison to other member states analysed in this volume, the extent of Europeanization in British immigration policy remains at a fairly low level. European measures have either been easily absorbed into the British policy approach and its legal system or have required no changes at all because relevant provisions were already available. Nevertheless, the existence of a European immigration policy has altered the UK's traditional system of immigration control by adding new policy measures at the supranational level.

The analysis of the extent of Europeanization follows the typology formulated by Radaelli (2003), who differentiates between four types of changes (see the introductory chapter in this volume): retrenchment, inertia, absorption and transformation. In addition, the following analysis conceives of a fifth type, called 'supplementation'. The first four types are well-known concepts that describe the magnitude of domestic policy change. European cooperation, however, provides a context in which member states jointly develop new policy measures of immigration control. These new policies aim mainly at administrative cooperation and different measures of burden-sharing. Supplementary policies, therefore, characterize new measures that do not alter existing legislation on the national level but add new instruments at the supranational level. The analysis of the 27 European measures the UK has opted into shows that none of them caused transformative changes in Britain's immigration policy. Similarly, none of them caused retrenchment. Nine measures have caused only minimal changes to the British policy approach or legislation (inertia), whereas seven have been absorbed into British policy and caused changes in secondary legislation or some adjustments of primary legislation. Finally, 11 European initiatives establish new policy measures at the supranational level and are therefore characterized as supplementation.

European legislation with only minor impact on Britain's immigration policy consists mostly of European regulations that are directly applicable in the member states and cause only few adjustments to former domestic praxis. Three regulations (333/2002, 334/2002, 1030/2002) serve as an example. They only add 'additional elements and security requirements, including enhanced anti-forgery, counterfeiting and falsification standards' to the original British format of visas and residence permits. European legislation that has been absorbed into British immigration policy consists of all four directives which establish minimum standards in the handling and reception of asylum applications, asylum-seekers and refugees and three European measures on illegal migration. Directive 2001/55, for example, establishes minimum standards for providing temporary protection to refugees in the event of a mass influx. Most elements of the directive do not require implementation because British legislation already accounts for these provisions. Transposition of the directive therefore involved only a number of changes in secondary legislation, for example, a new part 11A in the Immigration Rules. Most importantly, these changes have added the status of 'temporary protection' to British immigration law. Similarly, Directive 2003/9 on reception conditions of asylum-seekers has been transposed by changes in the Statutory Instruments as well. Three legislative changes have been introduced: a new part 11B in the Immigration Rules, the Asylum Support (Amendment) Regulations 2005 and the Asylum Seekers (Reception Conditions) Regulations 2005. These changes incorporated more rights to family unity and the right to be accommodated together for asylum-seekers (Home Office 2005).

Adjustments to primary legislation have been necessary for the transposition of measures on irregular migration and human trafficking. Although UK law already contained offences for intentionally facilitating entry into the UK (section 25 of the Immigration Act 1971), the issue of human trafficking has not so far been regulated by British law. Directive 2002/90 and Council Framework Decision 2002/946 constitute a European framework which has influenced the British system against human trafficking. The core facilitation offences are defined in the directive and are committed either where a person intentionally assists a third-country national to 'enter, or transit across a Member State's territory or where a person for financial gain intentionally assists a third country national to reside in that territory in contravention of the Member State's applicable aliens laws'. The above measures have been implemented by section 143 of the Nationality, Immigration and Asylum Act 2002. The UK has in effect even overimplemented the European requirements. This includes for example the absence of a requirement of gain for the offence of assisting irregular entry, the fact that it is an offence to assist an asylum applicant to enter Britain even where no breach of immigration law has occurred, the confining of the humanitarian exception to cases of organizations which assist asylum applicants and the severity of the maximum sentence (Ryan 2004b: 438).

The UK has for the most part opted into European legislation that supplements existing national immigration control measures with no or only minimal changes to existing legislation or praxis. Policies falling into this type aim mainly at administrative cooperation, financial redistribution, measures of burden-sharing between state actors or a mix of these elements. A first example is Directive 2001/40/EC on the mutual recognition of decisions on the expulsion of third-country nationals and the corresponding Council Decision 2004/191/EC setting out the criteria and practical arrangements for the compensation of the financial imbalances resulting from the application of this directive. The rationale of both initiatives is 'to ensure greater effectiveness in enforcing expulsion decisions and better cooperation between Member States'. Furthermore, they provide that the issuing member state is to reimburse the enforcing state for the cost of expelling a third-country national. Another example is the European Refugee Fund. The fund acts as a financial reserve to be used in the event of a massive influx of refugees but also by supporting projects of refugee integration and the repatriation of persons. It aims to restore balance to the efforts made by member states by introducing a system of financial redistribution in proportion to the burden borne by each state. A final example concerns the Dublin II Regulation. It builds upon the original Dublin Convention and aims at preventing abuse of asylum procedures by applicants submitting asylum applications simultaneously in different member states. The regulation, however, aims predominantly at European cooperation and requires little or no domestic law adjustments (Toner and Hurwitz 2004). All three examples show that many European initiatives aim at new policy measures with only marginal consequences for existing British immigration legislation.

In conclusion, the opt-in of the UK into certain European legislation had only minor impacts on the 'British way of doing things'. In terms of the typology provided by Radaelli, the Europeanization of the policy of immigration in Britain can be characterized as close to the inertia type. Most measures led either to no changes at all or the transposition has been done by changes in secondary legislation and has been easily absorbed. Only a few examples exist which caused new primary legislation. The case of irregular migration and human trafficking is the area where the EU has provided the most thorough impact on existing legislation. Despite the minor legal changes, Europe is taken seriously in Britain's immigration policy. The UK has a generally good record concerning the timely and precise transposition of European directives (see Kassim 2000). This position has also been supported by the analysis of this particular policy sector. Furthermore, the UK has in some cases even exceeded the requirements of European directives when implementing them into national law (for example, new legislation on human trafficking). Finally, supplementary European policies, although with little effect on existing legislation, are now of great importance in British immigration policies because they support the tough immigration control practice in the UK. Here, Europeanization can be regarded as an opportunity structure which helps to resolve British problems of immigration policy that are not to be properly resolved within a national context. Supplementation policies are therefore a way of making strategic use of Europeanization.

Managed Europeanization: the politics of immigration

The previous section focused on the Europeanization of policy, the substantive measures and legal provisions which regulate immigration in the UK. The following section provides an analysis of the European impact on the politics of immigration. These are traditionally characterized by at least three features: (1) they are dominated by a strong executive; (2) the judicial system as well as the constitutional protection for immigrants is weak; and (3) interest groups have only minor impact on immigration policy-making (Geddes 2003; Hansen 2000). This analysis will therefore focus on the European impact on these institutional structures and main actors shaping this policy area. In particular, we focus on the Europeanization of the government and the Home Office, of the legal system and of the incorporation of interest groups. Each part first provides some general characterizations about the European impact and then sketches out its consequences for the policy area of immigration. Overall, the EU membership of the UK has not affected the pattern of immigration politics to a great extent. So far, British governments have successfully played the gatekeeper and managed its participation in a European immigration policy without altering the main tenets of immigration policy-making in Britain. If one compares structures of UK government with the EU a number of potential misfits become obvious. Examples of these incongruences include the necessity of alliance and coalition building in the European Council which contrasts with the majoritarian UK system; the multi-level system of the EU compared with the centralized British system; or the supremacy of EC law and its challenge to the notion of parliamentary sovereignty in the UK (Bulmer and Burch 2004: 7). Research on the Europeanization of the British executive has demonstrated that EU membership has not resulted in any significant departures from the traditional British model of government (Bulmer and Burch 1998). Adjustment to the EU occurred incrementally and differences between both political systems have been overcome by the establishment of highly centralized 'switching mechanisms' in the UK (Bulmer and Burch 2004: 14). In the British governmental system, departments constitute the key policy-making institutions (Smith et al. 1995), and it is the Home Office that acts as the most important player in immigration policy-making. As far as the European impact on the Home Office is concerned, the department is seen as the one with the traditionally weakest European dimension of its work. A study by Marsh et al. (2001: 223) has shown that the Home Office is to a large extent concerned with limiting EU competence, maintaining sovereignty and protecting national interests. The departmental view on Europe is characterized by its interest to 'keep decision-making at an intergovernmental level in order to oppose imposition from the EU'. Recent years, however, have seen important changes in the Home Office. It has significantly enhanced its European engagement and become increasingly involved in European matters concerning immigration, asylum and combating organized crime (Bulmer and Burch 2004: 16). The Home Office has established effective structures to transpose European matters into the British system but also to shape the EU in Britain's interest (Kassim 2000, 2001). Similar to the government system in general, however, the Home Office's adaptation to Europe has been incremental and without deep-seated socialization to new European norms and rules.

The second institutional factor shaping Britain's immigration policy is its weak legal system and its lack of constitutional protections for immigrants. On one hand, the extent of Europeanization of the British legal system appears to proceed at a low level: it experienced little difficulty in adapting to the introduction of Roman-based EU law to operate alongside English common law tradition (Allen 2005: 133).

Furthermore, the overall impact of EU law accounts for under one-sixth of secondary legislation in Britain, the form that is most commonly used to implement EU legislation (Page 1998: 809). On the other hand, EU membership 'has proved by far the most significant constitutional innovation [...] in the twentieth century' (Loveland 2003: 663). The most explicit form of Europeanization of the legal system can be seen in the Human Rights Act 1998 which incorporates the European Convention on Human Rights (ECHR) into British domestic law. In general, the ECHR improves judicial accountability in the UK because it provides people with a broad range of positive rights. Concerning the British government system, the ECHR represents 'an unprecedented transfer of political power from the executive and legislature to the judiciary' (Flinders 2001: 63). This shift, however, occurs in an overall majoritarian system and the government was cautious in drafting the Human Rights Act to respect the sovereignty of the British parliament. It does not empower the courts to strike down legislation. Courts can simply issue a 'declaration of incompatibility' where existing legislation is inconsistent with the ECHR. Therefore, parliament is under no obligation to change the legislation and is in effect still free to judge the constitutionality of its own laws (Flinders 2005: 81–4). In the short term this aspect of Europeanization has not seriously altered the traditional pattern of the politics of immigration in the UK. An early example concerning the impact of the ECHR on Britain's immigration policy was the Anti-Terrorism, Crime and Security Act 2001 and its provisions for keeping potential terrorists of foreign nationality in detention for indefinite periods of time without judicial oversight. The Lords of Appeal issued a 'declaration of incompatibility' and the legislation was subsequently changed although with few improvements for the detained persons. It remains to be seen whether the ECHR and subsequent developments will in the future have more serious impact on the processes and outputs of Britain's immigration policy.

A third group of actors in Britain's politics of immigration consists of interest groups. The British interest group system is characterized by pluralism and the normal policy style in the UK is one of 'bureaucratic accommodation' and the 'logic of negotiation'. 'This is a system in which the prominent actors are groups and government departments and the mode is bargaining rather than imposition' (Jordan and Richardson 1982: 81). This policy style is also obvious in the area of immigration policy. Many policy proposals of the Home Office are preceded by consultation processes with relevant stakeholders. Nevertheless, the relevant studies on Britain's immigration policy have accorded interest groups only minimal impact on the policy of the government (see, for example, Castles and Kosack 1985: 138–45; Freeman 1979: 223; Schönwälder 2001). This result is not surprising because immigration policy is a highly elite-dominated policy area characterized by executive closure. The extent of Europeanization of interest representation would be reflected in the degree to which British interest groups have found in the EU new venues to voice their political positions. Interest groups in other policy areas (such as business and the environment) have done exactly this (Fairbrass 2004). Findings of a recent study on pro-migrant non-governmental organizations (NGOs) in the UK show a similar trend: international NGOs like Amnesty International but also strictly national NGOs like the Refugee Council or the Immigration Law Practitioners' Association 'have become multi-levelled in their activities, which bridge different political levels within the European polity, including those within the nation-state (national, regional and local) as well as trans- and supranational European levels' (Gray and Statham 2005: 16). The EU becomes, in this manner, a new arena for interest groups to push for their national political interests. This strategy of interest groups has been successful in other policy areas as in the case of environmental policies (Jordan 2004) or equal opportunity policies (Sifft 2004) and has changed policy-making in these areas. In the case of immigration policy, however, this strategy seems less likely to have a substantive effect on the established pattern of politics.

In sum, the policy area of immigration is characterized by long-established patterns of policy-making. British participation in European immigration policy has so far had no serious effects on the politics of immigration. Europeanization caused only minor changes aimed mainly at accommodating Europe in Britain and participating effectively at the European level. But the European impact did not restrict the wide scope of discretion of the executive, nor did it strengthen interest representation. Only the Europeanization of the legal system, through incorporation of the ECHR, may in future show some more fundamental consequences. So far, however, British governments have successfully managed to preserve the status quo.

Towards an explanation of the British pattern of Europeanization

We turn now to a discussion of the factors that help to account for the British pattern of Europeanization. Three factors are put forward: first, the mode of Europeanization comprised of the legal–institutional basis of Britain's participation in European immigration policies; second, the increasing Europeanization of immigration flows; and third, the preferences of British governments on immigration. The mode of Europeanization, the first factor, has already been reviewed. It is comprised of the opt-out/opt-in provisions of the Amsterdam Treaty which offer Britain the most obvious opportunity for its selective Europeanization during recent years. Furthermore, they also account for Britain's low level of Europeanization because they allowed the UK – despite the move towards more legally binding European measures – to refuse adoption of the Schengen *acquis* and a range of other directives that would have caused greater Europeanization of Britain's immigration policy. These institutional conditions alone, however, are only necessary but not sufficient conditions for the British pattern.

New patterns of immigration

The second factor concerns the increasing difficulties experienced by the UK in regulating immigration flows in a national framework. Recent changes in the pattern of immigration have reinforced British interest in European cooperation. Traditionally, the UK is seen as Europe's closest approximation to a successful 'zero-immigration country' (Layton-Henry 1994). After a period of laissez-faire policy-making on immigration during the 1950s, the UK developed a firm and effective immigration control system during the 1960s and early 1970s. This restrictive policy affected different categories of migration – labour migration, secondary migration as well as the immigration of asylum-seekers and refugees. But not only have the policies been restrictive; their outcomes have been as well. In the early 1990s, Britain had reduced immigration to a minimum of family reunification and asylum-seekers as well as very low numbers of labour migrants, numbering approximately 50,000 per year (Currle 2004). During the last ten years, however, this picture has changed and each category has seen greatly increasing numbers of migrants. The rising numbers of asylum-seekers and illegal immigrants have been paramount in fostering British interest in European cooperation. At the start of the millennium the UK was – for the first time in its history – the largest recipient of asylum applications in Europe. Gary Freeman (2004: 336) argues that 'Britain is now as vulnerable as its neighbours to asylum influxes', and for Randall Hansen (2004: 341) Britain's former effectiveness in its immigration policy was only a function of other countries' relative liberality. These difficulties in effectively managing migration served as a catalyst for Britain's participation in the development of a European immigration policy. Commenting on the British experience with Europe in general, Helen Wallace (1997: 688) has argued that in the UK 'factors of divergence from the continental pattern have been in constant competition with pressures for convergence'. For asylum and refugee policy as well as for the control of irregular migration, the pressures for convergence now clearly outweigh the factors of divergence – which has increased Britain's preference for cooperation.

British preferences in immigration

The third factor concerns the preferences of British governments with respect to immigration policy. In general, studies on the Europeanization of domestic policies and politics devote scant attention to governments' preferences (see Börzel 2002; Mastenbroek 2005). In contrast, they are important factors in liberal intergovernmentalist as well as social constructivist accounts of European integration (Moravcsik 1993; Risse 2004). This chapter argues that the 'intensive transgovernmentalism' characterizing European cooperation on immigration issues makes national interests an important variable to understand 'how Europe hits home'. The focus of the following analysis is on fundamental British preferences on immigration matters and how they have shaped the decisions to opt out of or into different European measures.[4]

In the British case, three core preferences can be differentiated which have been rather stable during recent decades:

1. First, the UK displays a clear preference for unusually strict immigration policies. This focus on closed borders developed during the 1960s and was supported by liberal race relations. Extensive integration and anti-discrimination policies were therefore predicated on the tight control of immigration. In consequence, British policies of immigration are very restrictive concerning clearly defined rights of entry and settlement but allow wide discretion to the government (see, for example, Hansen 2000).

2. A second preference concerns the particular problem-solving approach of Britain's immigration policy: its focus on external instead of internal controls. The UK has a keen interest in preserving its system of immigration control. At least three arguments are regularly put forward: first, external controls are preferred because of Britain's geographical position as an island. Second, external controls have high symbolic significance and are closely associated with Britain's reputation for having an effective immigration policy. The

third argument points to the high adaptation costs. Dismantling British national border controls would fundamentally alter the British system of immigration control because no system of internal controls of equal standard exists (see, for example, Layton-Henry 2004: 315).

3. Finally, the third argument concerns Britain's open-mindedness and positive attitude towards supranational cooperation. However, this preference needs qualifications: first, it depends on regulations which generally reserve sovereignty and discretion to the nation state. Second, the UK is convinced that its own national immigration policy is more effective than the policies of its European neighbour states. European cooperation is therefore targeted to policy areas where cooperation provides a solution to negative externalities of the policies of other states or where European cooperation allows reinforcing the British approach to immigration control (see Geddes 2004: 5–6).

These general preferences on immigration policy and supranational cooperation also shaped Britain's conduct in developing European immigration policy. An analysis of the justifications by British governments concerning their decisions to opt out of or into different European measures closely mirrored these different preferences. The UK's preference for firm immigration control has led the British government to opt out of most European legislation which extends the rights of migrants. The British government consistently argued for preserving its more restrictive approach, against rights-based policies which were generally seen as an incentive for misuse and fraud. An example is Council Directive 2004/81/EC on residence permits issued to third-country nationals who are victims of trafficking. The UK government decided not to participate in the adoption of this measure because it was not persuaded that the benefits of the proposed arrangements outweighed the disruption to the enforcement of immigration control (House of Commons Select Committee on European Scrutiny 2002c). In particular, the government argued that although they recognize

> the importance of protecting victims of trafficking and ensuring that safeguards are created within which they may feel confident to give evidence against those who trafficked them, but do not believe that this should extend to a guarantee of automatic right to remain in every case. There already exists discretion to grant exceptional leave to remain outside the Immigration Rules in appropriate cases.

We believe that such a system is sufficient, and that a system based on an automatic permit would lead to abuse and exploitation. (House of Commons Select Committee on European Scrutiny 2002a)

Other examples include European initiatives concerning labour migrants and secondary migration. The British government sought to maintain its flexibility in admissions policy and discretion in relation to individuals, arguing that these would be lost by opting into these European measures. A typical example is the Family Reunification Directive. The government's concern was that a decision to opt into this directive would entail a constraint on 'the UK's ability to formulate and adjust policies in relation to family reunification as a matter of domestic law' (House of Commons Select Committee on European Scrutiny 2000b).

As to the second preference, the British government was insistent on preserving its traditional British approach to immigration control. In consequence, the UK opted out of European policies that would entail great adoption costs and overturn established policies and practices in Britain. This is the reverse pattern to the preceding analysis on the extent of Europeanization: whereas measures the UK has opted into caused only minor domestic policy changes, most of the 18 measures the UK opted out of would cause transformative policy changes. The major example concerns the Schengen *acquis*. British participation in Schengen would fundamentally alter the British approach to immigration control. The principle of external frontier control would be jeopardized. Another recent example is Council Regulation 539/2001 including the visa list for third-country nationals. British participation in this regulation would imply a substantive revision of the British visa regime. The government argued that if the UK were to opt into the regulation it 'would require us to impose a visa requirement on some 31 countries not at present subject to a United Kingdom visa regime', of which 26 are Commonwealth countries (House of Commons Select Committee on European Scrutiny 2000a). The national control of its external borders remains a precious cornerstone of British immigration policy.

The third preference was reflected primarily in the context of supplementary policies. These policy measures seem of greatest importance to the British government: they facilitate so-called burden-sharing between the member states of the EU and strengthen the traditional British approach to immigration control. Here, Europeanization offers real opportunities to resolve problems of Britain's immigration policy that are difficult to resolve within the national context. However, the British government consistently maintained the position that these measures should enable the member states to keep their national sovereignty. A prime example concerning the British interest in burden-sharing is Council Directive 2003/9/EC, laying down minimum standards for the reception of asylum-seekers. The British government argued that this directive 'will act as a catalyst to those Member States with less-developed reception arrangements to build upon and improve existing conditions. This would help to ensure that asylum-seekers could expect similar standards of treatment, regardless of the Member State in which the application was being considered' (House of Commons Select Committee on European Scrutiny 2001). In effect, this would introduce more 'level playing fields' and would reduce secondary migration and the disproportionate burden on some member states (House of Commons European Standing Committee B 2002). Another example concerns the Dublin II Regulation. It allows the UK to assert the integrity of its national immigration control policy by shifting the responsibility for certain immigrants to neighbouring states. For the government it is 'important that Member States take responsibility for those on its territory. It should be easy for one Member State to transfer applicants to another when they have been living illegally elsewhere' (House of Commons Select Committee on European Scrutiny 2002b).

To sum up, the mode of Europeanization, the recent experience of immigration and the preferences of the British government seem important predictors for understanding the pattern of Europeanization of the politics and policy of immigration in the UK. Moreover, this analysis shows that in trying to understand patterns of Europeanization in policy areas that are characterized by 'intensive transgovernmentalism' more attention should be paid to incentives for European cooperation, national interests and the type of interaction between member states and the EU.

Conclusion

This chapter had two objectives: first, to provide an analysis of the extent and pattern of Europeanization of the politics and policy of immigration in the UK, and second, to analyse some of the factors that may account for the particular European impact on immigration matters in Britain. Concerning the first point, the analysis has shown that the main characteristic of the Europeanization of Britain's policy of immigration is its selectiveness – with British participation in coercive measures but opting out of protective measures; and its minor extent with only marginal changes to existing legislation but substantive new cooperative European measures. The main characteristic of the Europeanization of the politics of immigration has been its successful management which has not affected the main tenets of immigration policy-making in the UK. The red line concerning the European impact on British immigration policy and politics is therefore clearly defined: British participation in the development of a European immigration policy occurs only as long as this allows reinforcing rather than the overturning of established British policy approaches and does not seriously affect underlying principles and practices of immigration policy-making. Concerning the second point, the chapter highlighted three factors that are of importance in understanding the pattern of Europeanization of Britain's politics and policy of immigration: (1) the mode of Europeanization defined in the Amsterdam Treaty which provides the UK with wide discretion concerning their participation in European policies of immigration; (2) the Europeanization of immigration flows to the UK which increased British interests in European cooperation; and (3) the preferences of British governments concerning immigration.

In contrast to the traditional argument of 'British exceptionalism', this analysis provided evidence to show that the UK is not exceptional with respect to the European impact on its politics and policies of immigration. The Europeanization of its immigration policies is characterized by greater selectivity than in other member states, and the government has taken great care to minimize European impacts on Britain's politics of immigration. The main motivation for European cooperation and consequently the Europeanization of its immigration policies, however, is rather similar to other European member states. The European venue has become a means to enforce or regain national immigration control capacities without constraining effects on already established national policies (Barbou des Places and Oger 2005; Guiraudon 2001). Here, the UK does not differ from European neighbours. Just a few years ago, Christian Joppke (1999: 135) argued that 'the European challenge to British immigration policy is not a restrictive but liberalizing one, bringing into question the very bases of this policy: tight border controls and executive discretion over the fate of immigrants'. This chapter has told a different story: the UK is today the country that profits most from European immigration policies but experiences the least constraining effects on its own discretion.

Notes

1 The authors would like to thank Thomas Faist, Margit Fauser and Andrew Geddes as well as all other participants in the conference 'The Europeanization of National Immigration Policies. Varying Developments across Nations and Policy Areas' (Europäische Akademie Berlin, 1–3 September 2005) for their helpful comments.

2 The analysis is based on the Scoreboard of the European Commission, which includes all regulations, directives and (framework-) decisions that build upon the Tampere Action Plan. However, only those initiatives that were adopted before 30 April 2004 or at least given political agreement prior to that date are included in this analysis. Furthermore, initiatives under the heading 'Fair treatment of third country nationals' are excluded because they concern integration measures.

3 The analysis presented here focuses only on legally binding measures. However, the European immigration policy is also characterized by a growing body of 'soft law'. Even there, the UK is an active supporter of European immigration policy, for example in the case of operational measures to prevent irregular migration (see Cholewinski 2004).

4 The analysis follows the logic of liberal intergovernmentalism: national preferences are negotiated domestically and shape international negotiations afterwards. Recent work by social constructivists has convincingly argued that national preferences are first and foremost shaped by collective norms and understandings in international negotiations. National interests themselves are therefore Europeanized (Risse 2001). For the sake of clarity we apply a naïve understanding of predefined national preferences (Wiener 1999).

References

Allen, D. (2005) 'The United Kingdom: a Europeanized Government in a Non-Europeanized Polity'. In S. Bulmer and C. Lequesne (eds), *The Member States of the European Union.* Oxford: Oxford University Press.

Barbou des Places, S. and H. Oger (2005) 'Making the European Migration Regime: Decoding Member States' Legal Strategies'. *European Journal of Migration and Law*, Vol. 6: 353–79.

Börzel, T. A. (2002) 'Pace-Setting, Foot-Dragging, and Fence-Sitting: Member State Responses to Europeanization'. *Journal of Common Market Studies*, Vol. 40, No. 2: 193–214.

Bulmer, S. and M. Burch (1998) 'Organizing for Europe: the British State and the European Union'. *Public Administration*, Vol. 76, No. 4: 601–28.

Bulmer, S. and M. Burch (2004) 'The Europeanization of UK Government: From Quiet Revolution to Explicit Step-change?' Paper presented at the ESRC/UACES conference on 'Britain in Europe and Europe in Britain: the Europeanisation of British Politics?' Sheffield Town Hall, 16 July.

Castles, S. and G. Kosack (1985) *Immigrant Workers and Class Structure in Western Europe.* New York: Oxford University Press.

Cholewinski, R. (2004) 'EU Measures Preventing Irregular Migration and UK Participation'. *Tolley's Immigration, Asylum and Nationality Law Journal*, Vol. 18, No. 2: 19–31.

Currle, E. (2004) *Migration in Europa – Daten und Hintergründe*. Stuttgart: Lucius & Lucius.

Fairbrass, J. (2004) 'The Europeanisation of Interest Representation: UK Business and Environmental Interests Compared'. Paper presented at the ESRC/UACES conference on 'Britain in Europe and Europe in Britain: the Europeanisation of British Politics?' Sheffield Town Hall, 16 July.

Flinders, M. (2001) 'Mechanisms of Judicial Accountability in British Central Government'. *Parliamentary Affairs*, Vol. 54: 54–71.

Flinders, M. (2005) 'Majoritarian Democracy in Britain: New Labour and the Constitution'. *West European Politics*, Vol. 28, No. 1: 61–93.

Freeman, G. (1979) *Immigrant Labor and Racial Conflict in Industrial Societies: the French and British Experience, 1945–1975*. Princeton: Princeton University Press.

Freeman, G. (1994) 'Commentary'. In W. Cornelius, P. Martin and J. F. Hollifield (eds), *Controlling Immigration: a Global Perspective*. Stanford: Stanford University Press.

Freeman, G. (2004) 'Commentary'. In W. A. Cornelius, T. Tsuda, P. L. Martin and J. F. Hollifield (eds), *Controlling Immigration: a Global Perspective*. Stanford: Stanford University Press.

Geddes, A. (2000) *Immigration and European Integration. Towards Fortress Europe?* Manchester: Manchester University Press.

Geddes, A. (2003) *The Politics of Migration and Immigration in Europe*. London: Sage.

Geddes, A. (2004) *The European Union and British Politics*. Houndmills: Palgrave Macmillan.

Geddes, A. and V. Guiraudon (2004) 'Britain, France, and EU Anti-Discrimination Policy: the Emergence of an EU Policy Paradigm'. *West European Politics*, Vol. 27, No. 2: 334–53.

George, S. (1992) *Britain and the European Community: the Politics of Semi-Detachment*. Oxford: Clarendon Press.

George, S. (1998) *An Awkward Partner. Britain in the European Community*, 3d edn. Oxford: Oxford University Press.

Glaeßner, G.-J. (2005) 'Großbritannien: Ein europäischer Sonderweg in der Politik innerer Sicherheit'. In G.-J. Glaeßner and A. Lorenz (eds), *Europäisierung der inneren Sicherheit. Eine vergleichende Untersuchung am Beispiel von organisierter Kriminalität und Terrorismus*. Wiesbaden: VS Verlag für Sozialwissenschaften.

Gray, E. and P. Statham (2005) 'Becoming European? British Pro-Migrant NGOs and the European Union'. European Political Communication Working Paper Series (9/05).

Guild, E. (2004) 'Transposing the EU *Acquis* on Immigration and Asylum in the UK: an Introduction'. *Tolley's Immigration, Asylum and Nationality Law Journal*, Vol. 18, No. 2: 1–5.

Guiraudon, V. (2001) 'Seeking New Venues: the Europeanization of Migration-Related Policies'. *Swiss Political Science Review*, Vol. 7, No. 3: 99–106.

Hailbronner, K. (1999) 'The Treaty of Amsterdam and Migration Law'. *European Journal of Migration and Law*, Vol. 1, No. 1: 9–27.

Hansen, R. (2000) *Citizenship and Immigration in Post-war Britain. The Institutional Origins of a Multicultural Nation*. Oxford: Oxford University Press.

Hansen, R. (2004) 'Commentary'. In W. A. Cornelius, T. Tsuda, P. L. Martin and J. F. Hollifield (eds), *Controlling Immigration: a Global Perspective*. Stanford: Stanford University Press.

Home Office (2005) 'Explanatory Memorandum to the Asylum Support (Amendment) Regulations 2005, No. 11'. London.

House of Commons European Standing Committee B (2002) *Reception of Asylum Applicants 17 June 2002*. London.

House of Commons Select Committee on European Scrutiny (2000a) *Lists of Third Countries whose Nationals Require Visas and those whose Nationals Are Visa-exempt, Fourteenth Report*. London.

House of Commons Select Committee on European Scrutiny (2000b) *The Right to Family Reunification, Eighteenth Report*. London.

House of Commons Select Committee on European Scrutiny (2001) *Reception of Asylum Applicants in Member States, First Report*. London.

House of Commons Select Committee on European Scrutiny (2002a) *A Common Policy on Illegal Migration, Eighteenth Report*. London.

House of Commons Select Committee on European Scrutiny (2002b) *Determining the Member State Responsible for Examining an Asylum Application, Second Report*. London.

House of Commons Select Committee on European Scrutiny (2002c) *Short-term Residence Permits for Victims of Trafficking Prepared to Cooperate with the Competent Authorities, Thirty-fourth Report*. London.

Joppke, C. (1999) *Immigration and the Nation-State: the United States, Germany and Great Britain*. New York: Oxford University Press.

Jordan, A. (2004) 'The Europeanization of British Environmental Policy'. Paper presented at the ESRC/UACES conference on 'Britain in Europe and Europe in Britain: the Europeanisation of British Politics?' Sheffield Town Hall, 16 July.

Jordan, G. and J. Richardson (1982) 'The British Policy Style or the Logic of Negotiation?' In J. Richardson (ed.), *Policy Styles in Western Europe*. London: George Allen & Unwin.

Kassim, H. (2000) 'The United Kingdom'. In H. Kassim, B. G. Peters and V. Wright (eds), *The National Co-ordination of EU Policy. The Domestic Level*. Oxford: Oxford University Press.

Kassim, H. (2001) 'Representing the United Kingdom in Brussels: the Fine Art of Positive Co-ordination'. In H. Kassim, A. Menon, B. G. Peters and V. Wright (eds), *The National Co-ordination of EU Policy. The Domestic Level*. Oxford: Oxford University Press.

Knill, C. (2001) 'Reforming Transport Policy in Britain: Concurrence with Europe but Separate Development'. In A. Héritier, D. Kerwer, C. Knill, D. Lehmkuhl, M. Teutsch and A.-C. Douillet (eds), *Differential Europe. The European Union Impact on National Policymaking*. Lanham: Rowman & Littlefield.

Layton-Henry, Z. (1992) *The Politics of Immigration. Immigration,'Race' and 'Race' Relations in Post-war Britain*. Oxford: Blackwell.

Layton-Henry, Z. (1994) 'Britain: the Would-be Zero-Immigration Country'. In W. A. Cornelius, P. L. Martin and J. F. Hollifield (eds), *Controlling Immigration: a Global Perspective*. Stanford: Stanford University Press.

Layton-Henry, Z. (2004) 'Britain: From Immigration Control to Migration Management'. In W. A. Cornelius, T. Tsuda, P. L. Martin and J. F. Hollifield (eds), *Controlling Immigration: a Global Perspective*. Stanford, Calif.: Stanford University Press.

Loveland, I. (2003) 'Britain and Europe'. In V. Bogdanor (ed.), *The British Constitution in the Twentieth Century*. Oxford: Oxford University Press.

Marcussen, M., T. Risse, D. Engelmann-Martin, H. J. Knopf and K. Roscher (1999) 'Constructing Europe? The Evolution of French, British and German Nation State Identities'. *Journal of European Public Policy*, Vol. 6, No. 4: 614–33.

Marsh, D., D. Richards and M. Smith (2001) *Changing Patterns of Governance in the UK: Reinventing Whitehall?* Basingstoke: Palgrave.

Mastenbroek, E. (2005) 'EU Compliance: Still a "Black Hole"?' *Journal of European Public Policy*, Vol. 12, No. 6: 1103–20.

Monar, J. (2004) 'Justice and Home Affairs'. *Journal of Common Market Studies*, Vol. 42: 117–33.

Moravcsik, A. (1993) 'Preferences and Power in the European Community: a Liberal Intergovernmentalist Approach'. *Journal of Common Market Studies*, Vol. 31, No. 4: 473–524.

Page, E. (1998) 'The Impact of European Legislation on British Public Policy Making: a Research Note'. *Public Administration*, Vol. 76, No. 4: 803–9.

Peers, S. (2000) *EU Justice and Home Affairs Law*. Harlow: Pearson Education.

Radaelli, C. M. (2003) 'The Europeanization of Public Policy'. In K. Featherstone and C. M. Radaelli (eds), *The Politics of Europeanization*. Oxford: Oxford University Press.

Risse, T. (2001) 'A European Identity? Europeanization and the Evolution of Nation-State Identities'. In M. Green Cowles, J. Caporaso and T. Risse (eds), *Transforming Europe: Europeanization and Domestic Change*. Ithaca, NY: Cornell University Press.

Risse, T. (2004) 'Social Constructivism and European Integration'. In A. Wiener and T. Diez (eds), *European Integration Theory*. Oxford: Oxford University Press.

Ryan, B. (2004a) 'The European Dimension to British Border Control'. *Tolley's Immigration, Asylum and Nationality Law Journal*, Vol. 18, No. 2: 6–16.

Ryan, B. (2004b) 'The United Kingdom'. In K. Hailbronner and I. Higgins (eds), *Migration and Asylum Law and Policy in the European Union*. Cambridge: Cambridge University Press.

Schönwälder, K. (2001) *Einwanderung und ethnische Pluralität: Politische Entscheidungen und öffentliche Debatten in Großbritannien und der Bundesrepublik von den 1950er bis zu den 1970er Jahren*. Essen: Klartext-Verlag.

Sifft, S. (2004) 'The Boomerang Pattern. Pushing for the Europeanization of British Equal Opportunities Policies'. Young Scholars' Conference 'The Impact of Europeanization on Politics and Policy in Europe', 7–9 May, Munk Centre for International Studies, University of Toronto.

Smith, M. J., D. Marsh, D. and D. Richards (1995) 'Central Government Departments and the Policy Process'. In R. A. W. Rhodes and P. Dunleavy (eds), *Prime Minister, Cabinet and Core Executive*. Basingstoke: St. Martin's Press.

Toner, H. and A. Hurwitz (2004) 'The EU Asylum *Acquis* in the UK'. *Tolley's Immigration, Asylum and Nationality Law Journal*, Vol. 18, No. 2: 32–45.

Wallace, H. (1997) 'At Odds with Europe'. *Political Studies*, Vol. 45, No. 4: 677–88.

Wallace, H. (2005) 'An Institutional Anatomy and Five Policy Modes'. In H. Wallace, W. Wallace and M. A. Pollack (eds), *Policy-Making in the European Union*. Oxford: Oxford University Press.

Wiener, A. (1999) 'Forging Flexibility – the British "No" to Schengen'. *European Journal of Migration and Law*, Vol. 1: 441–63.

6

Sweden: Europeanization of Policy, but not of Politics?

Mikael Spång

Introduction

This chapter discusses the impact of EU immigration legislation and policy on Swedish policy and politics.[1] Since domestic impact is perceived from the perspective of supranational legislation and policies, it makes sense to approach it primarily in terms of an adaptation pressure. This pressure is more extensive the larger the misfit between EU and Swedish legislation and policy, and it cuts deeper the more it entails changes to politics, such as policy processes, public discourse and conflicts between political actors (see Börzel and Risse 2003; Radaelli 2003; Risse et al. 2003).

The interrelation between policy misfits and changes to politics provides the focus of this chapter. Policy misfits arise due to, for example, the introduction of new policy elements, consistent changes to already existing elements, and other alterations to core understandings of policy. Such misfits are themselves important when discussing adaptation pressure, but political actors' assessment of these misfits are also of importance in this respect (see Radaelli 2003: 45f.). In this assessment of the adaptation pressure in the Swedish case, I address misfits as they are reflected in domestic legislative and policy changes, as well as the political actors' views about the extent of changes and their desirability. This means that political actors' opinions, standpoints and behaviour in the national implementation process make up the central link between policy and politics. The reason for this approach is partly related to the focus of the study – the implementation of supranational policy – and partly to the central position held by political parties in the Swedish political system. In addition to parties' arguments and behaviour, I will also address some factors such as changes to policy processes and the role of parliament, which are related to EU member-ship more generally. These changes affect immigration politics as well, but are not specific to the policy field at hand.

Following Claudio Radaelli (see Ette and Faist in this volume), I discuss absorption and transformation of policy and politics (Radaelli 2003). Unfortunately, Radaelli does not differentiate between changes to core understandings of policy and changes to politics, a distinction that is of importance when discussing the Swedish case. Swedish immigration legislation and policy have been transformed in several, albeit varying, ways due to the development of EU legislation. That several of the changes have been controversial shows that political actors have perceived the adaptation pressure as high. However, the controversies largely follow the domestic conflict line in immigration politics that emerged prior to EU membership. Furthermore, the political actors' views about the Union play a limited role in their standpoints concerning specific measures. This suggests that in spite of some important transformations of policy, politics has been less Europeanized than might have been expected on the basis of these policy changes.

Europeanization of immigration policies

The domestic policy changes discussed in this section stretch from debates about Schengen membership in the mid-1990s to recently decided but as yet unimplemented EU directives, for example the refugee qualification directive. Some cases, such as the directives on refugee reception and family reunification, entail only minor changes, whereas Schengen membership and some related measures, such as those dealing with carrier sanctions and human trafficking, have transformed Swedish policy. Some other cases, for example temporary residence in situations of mass influx of refugees and temporary residence for victims of trafficking, contain new policy elements or consistent changes of existing elements, but have not transformed Swedish policy.

Border control policies

Among the border control policies considered here are membership in Schengen as well as some changes closely related to the Schengen Agreements, such as the regulation of refusal of entry and extradition, and carrier sanctions. Sweden applied for observer status geared to full membership in Schengen in 1995. An important backdrop to the Swedish application was that Denmark had applied for membership a year previously. This made the future of the Nordic Passport Union a central aspect of the debate about Schengen in the Nordic countries. Sweden signed the Schengen Agreements in 1996 and the process of preparing for membership was launched (Andersson 2000).

The government presented a proposition about membership in December 1997, which did not include any more specific legislative changes but focused on the ratification of the agreements relating to Schengen. The reason for not including any specific legislation, the government argued, was to make it possible for parliament to take a stand on Schengen. Had it been necessary to work out all legislative changes in advance, the discussion in parliament would have been significantly delayed (Regeringens proposition 1996/97: 87: 42). After acceptance of Schengen in parliament, the necessary legislation, policy and organizational changes were prepared in commissions and working groups over the next couple of years, and the government presented the major changes to parliament in February 2000, changes which involved new laws about the Schengen Information System (SIS) and international police cooperation, as well as further agreements between Denmark and Sweden regarding police cooperation. The proposition also contained several changes to the Aliens Act, the Passport Act and the Secrecy Safeguard Act, relating to passport and visa regulations, refusal of entry and extradition (Regeringens proposition 1999/2000: 64).

Sweden became an operative member of Schengen on 25 March 2001. Later, an expert commission was appointed to evaluate Swedish participation in Schengen (SOU 2004: 110). The commission identified several administrative problems that possibly interfere with the efficient combating of cross-border crime, smuggling and trafficking in human beings. These problems may also lead to an increase in the numbers of persons residing in Sweden without valid permits, the commission has argued (SOU 2004: 110: chapters 4, 9–10). The commission has suggested that the regulation of control of persons be taken out of the Aliens Act and made part of a new Border Control Act (SOU 2004: 110: chapter 14). The comments on the proposal are currently being discussed within the government, which may prepare a proposition to parliament.

Schengen membership resulted in changes to Sweden's regulations concerning refusal of entry and extradition. A new paragraph in the Aliens Act, in effect from 2001, stipulates that residence permits may be revoked if a person is registered on the SIS list and there are sufficient other reasons to revoke the permit. In commenting on the question, the government stated that there has to be a very strong national interest on the part of some other Schengen states for Sweden to revoke residence permits (Regeringens proposition 1999/2000: 64: 77).

Later, the directive concerning mutual recognition of decisions on extradition (2001/40/EC) led to the addition that decisions made in accordance with the directive by another member state may be a reason for revoking residence permits. In this case as well, the Aliens Act stipulates that there must be sufficient other grounds for doing so. The working group looking at the domestic implementation of the directive argued that since it does not stipulate that it is obligatory for member states to recognize other states' decisions, the directive should be implemented by adding a new qualification in the Aliens Act (Ds 2001: 76: 25–31). The government followed this recommendation, arguing that it would thereby be possible for Swedish authorities to assess other states' decisions in light of aspects relevant to the case (Regeringens proposition 2001/02: 182: 20–6). The changes to the Aliens Act entered into force on 1 December 2002.

In incorporating Schengen, changes to carrier sanctions figured prominently. Responsibilities on the part of carriers are themselves not a new element in the Aliens Act. These responsibilities, for example covering the costs of return journeys, were extended in the 1989 Aliens Act, but the new law did not include any specific tariffs or similar sanctions against carriers (Wikrén and Sandesjö 2002: 368ff.). During the preparations for Schengen membership, the government considered the existing system to be adequate (Regeringens proposition 1997/98: 42: 72f.). As the more precise preparations were made, however, doubts arose, and other Schengen states, especially France, criticized Sweden in the autumn of 2000 for having an inadequate system of carrier sanctions. The Swedish government affirmed its obligation to follow the Schengen regulations in this respect in the Council in December 2000 (EU-nämndens protokoll 2000/01: 9). Discussions were going on simultaneously about Directive 2001/51/EC, which was adopted by the Council in June 2001. A working group prepared the necessary legislative changes, making it clear that Sweden could not opt for either obligations concerning return travels or sanctions; both had to be made part of Swedish law in order to fulfil the Schengen requirements and the directive concerning carrier sanctions (Ds 2001: 74: 97).

The government presented its proposition in January 2004 (Regeringens proposition 2003/04: 50). The government noted that Sweden was obliged to implement sanctions, arguing that it did not, however, require carriers to implement any sophisticated analysis of travel documents, but only to discover obviously false or forged documents. Neither would it mean any assessment of reasons given by those seeking asylum. The Swedish authorities would continue to perform the assessment of a person's right to enter Sweden. The government concluded that the consequences of increased carrier responsibilities would not differ much from the current situation, although it admitted that sanctions might lead to carriers' implementing more detailed checks than previously (Regeringens proposition 2003/04: 50: chapter 11). The new legislation entered into effect on 1 July 2004.

Later developments in this area include Directive 2003/110/EC, concerning assistance in repatriation through airports, adopted in November 2003, and Directive 2004/82/EC, concerning obligations on the part of carriers to transfer information at the request of national authorities, passed by the Council in April 2004. The implementation of the former directive was prepared in a working group and the government presented a proposition in May 2005, proposing a new law about transit of third-country nationals, which entered into effect in December 2005 (Parliament Records 2005/06: 21; Regeringens proposition 2004/05: 168). Implementing Directive 2004/82/EC has been discussed in a working group, which presented its suggestions concerning changes to the Aliens Act and a new law about a passenger registry in November 2005 (Ds 2005: 48).

Refugee and asylum policies

Several measures adopted by the Union relate to refugee and asylum policy, for example the Dublin Convention and the Dublin Regulation, and directives concerning temporary residence, refugee reception and refugee qualification.

Incorporating the Dublin Convention entailed some changes to the Aliens Act and the Secrecy Safeguard Act (Regeringens proposition 1996/97: 87). Neither the principle of first asylum country, nor the notion that an asylum application shall be processed in the country to which the applicant is connected in terms of family or other significant ties, is new to Swedish legislation, but implementing the Dublin Convention entailed some changes to legislation and practice. The older formulations regarding first asylum country in the Aliens Act was left intact, but supplemented with a stipulation referring to the Convention since it was thought to be unclear whether the older formulation was adequate (Regeringens proposition 1996/97: 87: 10).

The Convention does not prohibit countries from assessing asylum claims, but the government has made it clear that there must be special reasons for the Convention not to be applied (Wikrén and Sandesjö 2002: 191). The way the principle of family ties is regulated in the Convention has meant a change of practice. The nature of those ties, for example that family members in another country shall be recognized as refugees in accordance with the Geneva Convention, was not considered important in earlier Swedish practice (Regeringens proposition 1996/97: 87: 13).

In July 2001 the Council adopted a directive about temporary residence in cases of mass influx of displaced persons (2001/55/EC). Implementing the directive has meant replacing the existing legislation concerning temporary residence. The expert commission looking at the necessary changes had argued that Swedish regulation, which was more extensive than the directive, should be kept intact and supplemented with a new category in the Aliens Act: residence permit on the basis of temporary protection in cases of mass flight (Ds 2001: 77: 43f., 51ff.). The government did not follow this suggestion and instead proposed that the existing regulation be replaced with a new chapter in the Aliens Act. This was also something several authorities and associations had suggested in their comments, arguing among other things that two parallel regulations would make the law unclear. The government also made it clear that the EU directive covered situations in which only one or a few of the EU member states are affected by a mass influx of refugees and that there hence was no need for any special regulation beside that following from the EU directive (Regeringens proposition 2001/02: 185: 27f.).

The new legislation includes the option by government to decide that categories of persons other than those covered by a Council decision can be granted temporary protection. The persons covered by a decision by the Swedish government must have fled for the same reasons and from the same country or region as those covered in the Council decision. The reason for this extension, the government argued, is that persons that have arrived shortly before a Council decision may reasonably be covered by the decision as well (Regeringens proposition 2001/02: 185: 29). Persons that are granted temporary residence can still apply for asylum individually, but it is possible to postpone the assessment of these applications, for example due to workload (Regeringens proposition 2001/02: 185: 55ff.). Temporary residents are given access to social rights in accordance with the Asylum Reception Act (Regeringens proposition 2001/02: 185: 86–91). The change to the Aliens Act entered into effect in early 2003.

The directive concerning refugee reception conditions and standards was adopted in January 2003 (2003/9/EC). The implementation of the directive was made the focus of an expert commission appointed in

January 2003. It presented its report in October the same year and concluded that by and large the asylum reception practices followed the stipulations in the directive, but that several changes had to be undertaken with respect to legal codification of practice (SOU 2003: 89). The proposition has been delayed; in commenting on the delay, the Social Insurance Subcommittee noted in 2005 that current practice conforms to the directive, but that reception conditions need to be regulated in law (Socialförsäkringsutskottets betänkande 2004/05: SfU10).

The directive concerning minimum standards for qualification and status as a refugee was adopted in April 2004 (2004/83/EC). The government appointed an expert commission in September the same year to look at the implementation of the directive. The commission presented its results in January 2006, arguing that most parts of the Swedish legislation conform to the directive (SOU 2006: 6). However, some changes need to be undertaken, most importantly relating to the differences between the directive's category of subsidiary protection and the category 'otherwise in need of protection' in Swedish legislation. Among changes proposed is that protection in case of environmental disasters found in the Aliens Act has to be moved from grounds for subsidiary protection and that the directive's objective risk criteria shall replace the stipulation of well-founded fear in the Aliens Act (SOU 2006: 6: chapter 4). Some changes relating to the directive have already been undertaken, such as strengthening the grounds for asylum to include persecution on the basis of gender and sexuality. Persons persecuted for these reasons will, with the new Aliens Act, which enters into effect on 31 March 2006, be granted refugee status as opposed to status as persons otherwise in need of protection (Parliament Records 2005/06: 41; Regeringens proposition 2005/06: 6).

Secondary migration

The Council adopted the family reunification directive in September 2003 (2003/86/EC). The commission given the task to look at the implementation presented an initial report, covering the mandatory requirements of the directive, in March 2005 (SOU 2005: 15). The final report, relating to the facultative rules of the directive, was presented in November the same year (SOU 2005: 103). The commission has suggested several changes to the Aliens Act and other laws. Whereas the Aliens Act provides that residence permits *may* be granted to persons, the directive stipulates a *right* to reunification. The difference is not significant in practice, however, since the stipulations in the Aliens Act have been interpreted as a right of reunification for spouses, co-habiting couples and minors (SOU 2005: 15: chapters 7 and 8). The commission has suggested that this should be reflected in the law, stipulating that members of the nuclear family as defined above shall be entitled to reunify with persons that have permanent residence in Sweden (SOU 2005: 15: 139f., 152ff.). The commission's final report covers the reunification of adult children, parents and other relatives (SOU 2005: 103). The commission has suggested a liberalization of the stricter rules introduced in the 1997 revision of the Aliens Act. In that revision, so-called 'last link' persons, whose only close relatives live in Sweden, were no longer considered eligible to apply for residence permits (Wikrén and Sandesjö 2002: 67ff.). The changes in 1997 caused much debate and opposition. A commission was appointed to look at a partial liberalization and it presented its report in 2002, suggesting that close relatives could be granted residence permits if special circumstances spoke in favour of it. Being the 'last link' would be such a reason, the commission suggested (SOU 2002: 13: chapter 5).

Since discussions were under way about the EU directive concerning family reunification, the government chose to wait for this directive before going further. The commission investigating the implementation of Directive 2003/86/EC has followed several of the suggestions made by the earlier commission, for example concerning 'last link' persons (SOU 2005: 103: chapters 8 and 9). Another issue discussed in the commission concerns whether it should be required that persons beside the nuclear family be able to support themselves. Some parties advocating a liberalization of family reunification, for example the Liberals, have argued in favour of such a stipulation, but the commission has taken the position that such a requirement would not conform to Swedish welfare policies (SOU 2005: 103: chapter 10).

Irregular migration

The development of policies concerning irregular migration, for example smuggling and trafficking in human beings, has been central to the debate in the EU. The Council adopted a directive concerning unauthorized entry, transit and residence in November 2002 (2002/90/EC). The Council also decided on two framework decisions, one concerning trafficking, adopted in July 2002 (2002/629/JHA), and one concerning unauthorized entry, transit and residence, in November 2002 (2002/946/JHA). Drafts of these framework decisions were accepted by the Swedish parliament during the autumn of 2001 (unauthorized entry) and in spring 2002 (trafficking) (Regeringens proposition 2001/02: 37,

2001/02: 99). The Council adopted a directive concerning time-limited residence permits for victims of trafficking in April 2004 (2004/81/EC).

Parallel with these developments, issues of smuggling and trafficking in human beings were discussed at the national level. When the Swedish government in November 2000 gave a parliamentary commission, originally appointed to consider family reunification, the additional task of addressing smuggling and trafficking, it was done in the context of the French EU Presidency's proposal to develop common legislation and policies regarding smuggling (Regeringens direktiv 2001: 64). Even though the EU directive and the framework decision on smuggling had not been finally adopted when the commission presented its report, which happened in August 2002, it considered the draft proposals in its work (SOU 2002: 69).

The new legislation entails more severe punishment for smuggling, and the 'for profit' proviso previously found in Swedish legislation has been taken away for smuggling through Sweden to another EU country. For other regulations concerning smuggling, however, the proviso is left intact (Regeringens proposition 2003/04: 35). The legal changes entered into force in October 2004. A time-limited residence permit for victims of trafficking was part of these changes; the question whether this fulfils Directive 2004/81/EC was assessed by a working group and it presented its analysis in October 2005, suggesting only minor changes to the Aliens Act (Ds 2005: 24). However, parliament has recently requested that the government prepare legislative changes that will make it possible for victims of trafficking to be granted permanent residence (Parliament Records 2005/06: 41).

Europeanization of politics

As Europeanization of legislation and policies involves more and more changes to domestic policy processes, public debates and political conflicts, the deeper and more far-reaching the consequences become. EU membership has affected the Swedish political system in several ways, ranging from administrative coordination of national positions, which has de facto changed the relationship between government and central authorities (see Beckman and Johansson 2002; Jacobsson 2000), to characteristics of the polity. Constitutional changes, for example those concerning the delegation of decision-making capacity to the Union, have been much discussed, and several elements that play a minor part in the Swedish Constitution, such as the vertical division of power entailed through supranational decision-making as well as a more pronounced role for courts due to the involvement of the EC court, are transforming the constitutional regulation of power in Sweden (see Algotsson 2000). Also, political conflicts have been affected by EU membership. The Swedish electorate is among the most critical of, and sceptical towards, the Union and this is reflected in the sensitivity of the EU issue within several parties.

Policy processes

It has been common in Sweden for policies to be developed through commissions appointed by government to investigate a specific issue and to involve the participation of several actors, including interest organizations and NGOs as well as political parties. These actors can also comment on the commission's proposal before the government presents a proposition to parliament. The policy process also involves commentary on the proposition by the Law Council as part of the judicial preview process. These features of the policy process have often been considered requisite for arriving at reasonable laws and policies that enjoy broad parliamentary and societal support.

The way policies are developed within the Union has changed the context in which the national policy process takes place. It is common to argue that the development of supranational decision-making within the Union strengthens the government and diminishes the possibilities for parliament to play an active role. Sweden is no exception to this pattern, even though the Swedish parliament, like the Austrian, Danish and Finnish parliaments, is often said to have a policy-shaping influence on government (Hegeland 2002; Jungar and Ahlbäck-Öberg 2002: 51f.).

Parliament has two major ways of influencing government regarding Union policies: either through the standing subcommittees or through the Advisory Committee on European Affairs. When a proposal is prepared within the Union, the government is obligated to inform parliament through a memorandum, which is sent to the standing subcommittees and discussed there. This gives parliament the opportunity to enter the policy process at an early stage, but studies have shown that it has been difficult for the standing committees to integrate the debate about EU proposals in their ordinary activities (Blomgren 2005: 84ff.). Discussions between parliament and government also take place in the Advisory Committee. Even though the government has to seek approval of its positions in the committee, giving the committee some leverage, studies have shown that its actual possibilities for influencing the government are limited (see, for example, Hegeland 2002; Jungar and Ahlbäck-Öberg 2002; Lindgren 2000).

Issues relating to immigration have been discussed regularly in the Advisory Committee over the past decade. Even though the government is often urged by the parties to pursue 'liberal' positions in EU negotiations and is often criticized, in particular by the Christian Democrats, the Greens, the Left and the Liberals, for not defending such positions strongly enough, there are no instances in which the government has not enjoyed majority support. In this context it should of course be remembered that the committee does not vote on issues. Instead, the chairperson presents a summary of the discussion. Studies have shown that in no case up to 1999 did the chairperson say that the government did not enjoy the majority's support (Lindgren 2000). In going through the Advisory Committee's debates about immigration policy since 1999, I have also failed to find a single such case.

Looking at the domestic implementation of EU directives, it follows the standard policy process in Sweden, but the implementation of EU legislation and policy deviates from this process in some respects (see Blomgren 2005; Jungar and Ahlbäck-Öberg 2002). Most of the investigations and proposals relating to EU directives have been prepared in expert commissions and working groups in the ministries rather than in parliamentary commissions, which makes it more difficult for the parties to play a role in the implementation process. This situation is not, however, unique to immigration policies, but reflects a general pattern over the past decade. Expert commissions and working groups have become more common. Together with a shortage of time in which to prepare legislation, this affects both the quality of proposals and the support for changes, something that has been much debated over the past decade (Ahlbäck-Öberg and Öberg 2005).

Another and related feature of the implementation process concerns the opportunities for policy development. Even though implementation of directives allows for fewer such opportunities, the parliamentary auditors and others have pointed out that the possibilities that do exist are not adequately taken into account (Konstitutionsutskottets betänkande 1998/99: KU11). One reason for this is the lack of clarity in commissions' mandates, and that commissions are not normally made aware by the government that there is room for interpretation in implementing directives. The reasoning behind suggestions made by commissions and working groups also tends to be vague, which does make the commenting process more difficult (Konstitutionsutskottets betänkande 1998/99: KU11). In most of the cases studied in this chapter, the commissions' and working groups' mandates have been narrow, restricted to an inquiry into necessary changes when implementing EU directives, but not into developing policy. The partial exceptions to this are the commissions appointed to deal with policy on smuggling and trafficking of human beings and the recent evaluation of Schengen.

Political conflicts

Issues relating to migration have become increasingly politicized in Sweden during the last two decades. Several factors, such as the reorganization of asylum reception in the mid-1980s, the government's decision to restrict the grounds for asylum in 1989 (which was later repealed) and the rise of right-wing extremism, have contributed to this politicization. They pushed migration more centrally onto the political agenda, and this is reflected in clearer differences between the political parties. Whereas most decisions prior to the late 1980s were taken with consensus, today disagreements abound in debates and decisions on immigration policies (see, for example, Abiri 2000; Dahlstedt 2000; Demker and Malmström 1999; Hammar 1999).

The Social Democrats and the Conservatives (and to some extent the Centre Party) have collaborated on most of the restrictive changes over the past decade. These changes have been criticized by other parties in parliament, especially the Greens, the Left and the Liberals (and in most cases the Christian Democrats). A more 'restrictive' bloc and a more 'liberal' bloc have thus emerged. These blocs differ both from the traditional left–right divide so important to Swedish politics and from the divide regarding conflicts around the EU in general. The Greens and the Left are critical of the Union and their party programmes include demands for Sweden to leave the Union, while in some other parties – especially the Centre Party, the Christian Democrats and the Social Democrats – there are sizeable groups who are highly critical of the Union (Aylott 2005; Widfeldt 2000).

With some exceptions, however, neither the parties' positions regarding the EU in general nor their views about the desirability of common immigration policies within the Union affect the parties' stances on particular measures. They instead follow the conflict between the 'restrictive' and the 'liberal' blocs. Most measures have been supported by the Social Democrats and the Conservatives whereas the other parties, albeit to varying degrees, have argued against them or suggested significant changes to the government's proposals. The debates about carrier sanctions, smuggling in human beings and to some degree the regulation of temporary residence and the refusal of entry and extradition can be mentioned as examples. Carrier sanctions have been the most controversial issue; the debate dates back to the initial discussions about Schengen in the mid-1990s, and as the issue came up in 2000 and 2001 all parties barring the Conservatives and the Social Democrats argued against changing the regulation of carrier responsibilities. The critics argued that it would affect the possibilities for persons to apply for asylum, could lead to discrimination and involved the exercise of authority over individuals by private companies. Interestingly, even the Conservatives expressed worries and a majority could be formed in the standing subcommittee only after the Conservatives and the Social Democrats had agreed to request that the government perform an overview of practice and inquire into the possibilities of addressing the issue again within the Union (Socialförsäkringsutskottets betänkande 2003/04: SfU11).

The debate about smuggling in human beings was rather similar to that about carrier sanctions. Several parties, among them the Centre Party, the Christian Democrats, the Greens, the Left and the Liberals, voiced concerns about abolishing the 'for profit' proviso, arguing that it must be clear in the law that helping persons on humanitarian grounds is not punishable. The Centre Party, the Greens, the Left and the Liberals argued that the commission and the government had failed to consider that the difficulties of legally entering Sweden and the EU were an important cause of increased smuggling. To many that want to apply for asylum, being smuggled in is the only available option, the parties argued. The critics also thought that punishment for unauthorized entry might be in breach of the Geneva Convention. The majority, Conservatives and Social Democrats, argued that since the 'for profit' proviso is kept when persons enter Sweden to apply for asylum, the exemption on humanitarian grounds has been clarified. The majority acknowledged that the situation is somewhat unclear when a person has first travelled through some other EU or Schengen country, but noted that in normal cases persons will not be punished for helping an individual to enter Sweden when that person applies for asylum. The majority also noted that persons would not be punished for illegal entry when they apply for asylum in Sweden (Socialförsäkringsutskottets betänkande 2003/04: SfU6).

Discussions about temporary residence in cases of mass influx of refugees differs from the two other cases in that an important new element to policy, that decisions in such matters are to be taken by the Council, was not central to the debate. Instead, criticism focused on the possibility of extending temporary residence for as much as three years, the possibility of postponing asylum applications due to workload, and access to social rights. When the possibility of postponement was discussed in the late 1990s, several NGOs, political parties and the Law Council had been against it, arguing that it was in breach of the Geneva Convention. Discussions involving the UNHCR had led, however, to a changed perspective over the last couple of years, the government argued, such that it now considered that mass flight was an exceptional situation in which it might be difficult to make decisions in each individual case (Regeringens proposition 2001/02: 185: 55ff.). The Greens, the Left and the Liberals were hesitant. The Left argued that no postponement option should be included in the law, whereas the Greens and the Liberals thought that there ought to be special reasons for postponing an assessment (Socialförsäkringsutskottets betänkande 2002/03: SfU4).

Another issue discussed by NGOs and political parties was the suggestion of the commission and the government that temporary residents be granted social rights in accordance with the Asylum Seekers Reception Act. NGOs and the Greens, the Left and the Liberals argued that since temporary residence could be granted for such a lengthy period, claimants needed better access to social rights. The Left and the Liberals also opposed allowing the Swedish government the possibility to extend the categories of persons beyond those covered by a Council decision. The Left and the Liberals maintained that such an option would create an insecure situation for persons already in Sweden waiting for their application to be assessed. The majority followed the government's proposition, noting that the possibility of extension was intended as a liberal interpretation of the directive (Socialförsäkringsutskottets betänkande 2002/03: SfU4).

The case in which the pattern of debates and conflicts deviated from the domestic conflict line occurred with the initial debates about Schengen and Dublin, in which positions regarding the Union were visible in the political conflicts. Schengen membership was the subject of much discussion. The Left and the Greens were critical of Schengen membership, arguing, as had some NGOs, that extension of visa requirements was a step in the direction of a more restrictive asylum policy and would lead to the construction of a 'fortress Europe'. Some MPs from other parties voiced similar criticism, but by and large the Centre-Right parties and the Social Democrats favoured membership, arguing that Schengen was an important step in realizing free movement within the EU. The Social Democrats and the Conservatives also argued that Schengen would not affect the right of asylum in any significant way (Parliament Records 1997/98: 91). In the case of Dublin, initially only the Greens and the Left were critical, but interestingly criticism has grown over time, including latterly from, for example, the Christian Democrats, who along with the Greens and the Left argue that Swedish legislation should allow for more scope for asylum claims to be assessed in Sweden (Socialförsäkringsutskottets betänkande 2004/05: SfU10).

In a certain way, this pattern in the conflicts is somewhat surprising because one might expect differences in views about the Union, between Christian Democrats and the Liberals on the one hand and the Greens and the Left on the other, to show up in the respective stances regarding EU legislation. In fact, these differences are more visible in general debates about common migration polices within the Union, for example in the Advisory Committee on European Affairs, since both Christian Democrats and Liberals are in principle in favour of such policies as well as of supranational decision-making. The Greens and the Left are critical of both EU and supranational decisions regarding migration. They often contrast EU and UN cooperation, viewing the latter as preferable in terms of upholding and developing human rights standards and of their intergovernmental character.

Varying Europeanization of policy and politics

EU harmonization has affected Swedish legislation and policies in varied ways. Some of the EU decisions, such as those concerning family reunification and refugee reception, entail some changes to legislation but hardly any to practice, which largely conforms to the directives. Moreover, these changes have not been politically controversial, and in the case of family reunification changes concerning the facultative part of the directive are related to earlier policy debates at the national level. In both cases we hence find a low adaptation pressure.

Some other changes have given rise to a middle-level adaptation pressure since they have entailed the introduction of new policy elements, or consistent changes to already existing elements, without causing major political controversies. Dublin is such a case; it has led to a consistent change of practice concerning first asylum country, which, however, is not a new element. The ratification of the Dublin Convention was at the time not very controversial, but controversy has since grown. Replacing the existing legislation concerning temporary residence in mass flight situations is in itself not a sign of large policy misfits, but the fact that decisions about whether or not such a situation is at hand are to be taken by the Council, rather than the national governments, constitutes a new element. Political controversy related not to this change, but rather to other aspects of the legal changes, such as access to social rights. Temporary residence permits for victims of trafficking are a new policy element, but implementation here has not been very controversial.

The third set of cases has entailed significant changes in practice and/or the introduction of new elements to policy, and has been highly controversial. Schengen is such a case; it has significantly altered migration control, including the understanding of what territory is controlled and what interests are involved in this control. Schengen has brought a wide range of legislative changes and administrative reforms, and has also been the subject of much debate and controversy, at least when related changes are taken into account. Carrier sanctions entail a new policy element and have been the single most controversial issue. The directive concerning smuggling in human beings also belongs to this category of cases that have given rise to a high adaptation pressure. Similar to Schengen more generally, the directive on smuggling in human beings relates to other states' interests, as shown in the changes to the 'for profit' proviso.

The parties' positions have also been focused upon in discussing the implementation of policy and policy misfits because the actors' assessments of policy misfits are of importance to understanding adaptation pressure. The pattern in this respect is interesting since national implementation has involved much debate and contention between parties. This suggests that immigration politics has become increasingly Europeanized due to the development of common policies. Yet these conflicts follow the domestic conflict line between the two 'blocs' in immigration politics established before EU membership and primarily related to domestic developments since the mid-1980s. The Christian Democrats, the Greens, the Left and the Liberals have united in opposing several of the directives in spite of their differences regarding the Union, including their views about the importance of developing a common immigration policy within the Union.

When focusing on the domestic conflict lines it can hence be concluded that the development of EU legislation and policy has had only modest effects on immigration politics. At the same time, several other changes have occurred in politics, in particular relating to policy development, and these have to be taken into account. Even though these changes affect immigration policy processes as well, they are not specific to immigration policy, but rather reflect changes in domestic politics due to EU membership in general. Simply put, these are changes that affect politics to the degree that policies are within the scope of EU policy development. The importance of this point becomes clear when looking at the involvement of parliament in areas that remain outside the scope of Union policy or have only recently become part of it. The Swedish parliament has played an increasingly important role in immigration policy over the past decade, due especially to increasing conflicts between the political parties. In several cases, the parties in parliament have forced the Social Democratic minority government to take policy steps it has either not wanted or at least considered less urgent. Changes to the appeals process for asylum-seekers, debated since the late 1990s, and parliament's decision that a system concerning labour migration from outside the EU must be investigated, supported by the Centre-Right parties and the Greens, illustrate parliament's role.

Both results – the limited effect of differences regarding the EU on the parties' standpoints with respect to specific directives and the fact that parliament in some respects plays a more central role in immigration policies than before – suggest that Europeanization of policies has not transformed the political landscape. As stated at the outset, when discussing this development in terms of Radaelli's categories, one needs to differentiate between changes to politics and core content of policy (Radaelli 2003: 37f.). In several cases, core understandings of policy have been transformed or significantly modified. Adaptation pressure can also be said to be high in some cases. Yet, this has not entailed a significant change in the conflict pattern in Swedish immigration politics.

Conclusions

This chapter has presented evidence to show that Swedish policies and politics have been affected by development of common policies regarding immigration in varying degrees. In some cases, we find a transformation of policy, notably with respect to Schengen and some related changes such as carrier sanctions but also to smuggling in human beings. These cases of high adaptation pressure are distinguished from cases of a middle-level adaptation pressure, such as the Dublin Convention, temporary residence in the event of mass influx of refugees, and temporary residence for victims of trafficking, which have been less controversial than Schengen and related changes. In yet other cases, such as refugee reception and family reunification, adaptation pressure has been low.

The political controversies around some of the EU measures suggest that immigration politics has also been affected, but I have argued that these effects are milder than might be expected. Domestic conflict lines still play a very important role in the parties' different stances regarding specific EU measures. Several changes to domestic politics, especially regarding the development of policy and the role of parliament, have affected immigration politics as well, but these changes are not peculiar to the field of migration. Rather, they are related to shifts within the political and administrative system as a whole due to EU membership.

Note

1 Sweden became a member of the EU in 1995. During the period covered in this chapter, the Centre-Right parties (the Centre Party, the Christian Democrats, the Conservatives and the Liberals) were in government during 1991–94 and the Social Democrats have been in government since 1994.

References

Primary sources

Ds 2001: 74 'Transportöransvaret i utlänningslagen'. Stockholm.
Ds 2001: 76 'Ömsesidigt erkännande av beslut om avvisning och utvisning'. Stockholm.
Ds 2001: 77 'Uppeha[o]llstillstånd med tillfälligt skydd vid massflykt'. Stockholm.
Ds 2005: 24 'Tidsbegränsat uppehållstillstånd för offer för människohandel m.fl'. Stockholm.
Ds 2005: 48 'Överlämnande av passageraruppgifter'.
EU-nämndens protokoll 2000/01: 9.
Konstitutionsutskottets betänkande 1998/99: KU11.
Parliament Records 1997/98: 91.
Parliament Records 2005/06: 21.
Parliament Records 2005/06: 41.
Regeringens direktiv 2001: 64 'Tilläggsdirektiv till Anhörigkommittén'.
Regeringens proposition 1996/97: 87 'Dublinkonventionen'.
Regeringens proposition 1997/98: 42 'Schengensamarbetet'.
Regeringens proposition 1999/2000: 64 'Polissamarbete m. m. med anledning av Sveriges anslutning till Schengen'.
Regeringens proposition 2001/02: 37 'Sveriges antagande av rambeslut om förstärkning av den straffrättsliga ramen för bekämpande av hjälp till olaglig inresa, transitering och vistelse'.
Regeringens proposition 2001/02: 99 'Sveriges antagande av rambeslut om åtgärder för att bekämpa människohandel'.
Regeringens proposition 2001/02: 182 'Ömsesidigt erkännande av beslut om avvisning och utvisning'.

Regeringens proposition 2001/02: 185 'Uppehållstillstånd med tillfälligt skydd vid massflykt'.

Regeringens proposition 2003/04: 35 'Människosmuggling och tidsbegränsat uppehållstillstånd för målsägande och vittnen m m'.

Regeringens proposition 2003/04: 50 'Åtgärder för att klarlägga asylsökandes identitet, m m'.

Regeringens proposition 2004/05: 168 'Återsändande av tredjelandsmedborgare via Sverige'.

Regeringens proposition 2005/06: 6 'Flyktingskap och förföljelse på grund av kön eller sexuell läggning'.

Socialförsäkringsutskottets betänkande 2002/03: SfU4.

Socialförsäkringsutskottets betänkande 2003/04: SfU6.

Socialförsäkringsutskottets betänkande 2003/04: SfU11.

Socialförsäkringsutskottets betänkande 2004/05: SfU10.

SOU 2002: 13 'Vår anhöriginvandring. Delbetänkande av Anhörigkommittén'. Stockholm.

SOU 2002: 69 'Människosmuggling och offer för människohandel'. Stockholm.

SOU 2003: 89 'EG-rätten och mottagandet av asylsökande. Betänkande av utredningen om mottagandevillkor för asylsökande'. Stockholm.

SOU 2004: 110 'Gränskontrollag – effektivare gränskontroll. Betänkande av Gränskontrollutredningen'. Stockholm.

SOU 2005: 15 'Familjeåterförening och fri rörlighet för tredjelandsmedborgare'. Stockholm.

SOU 2005: 103 'Anhörigåterförening'. Stockholm.

SOU 2006: 6 'Skyddsgrundsdirektivet och svensk rätt'. Stockholm.

Secondary sources

Abiri, E. (2000) 'The Changing Praxis of "Generosity": Swedish Refugee Policy during the 1990s'. *Journal of Refugee Studies*, Vol. 13, No. 1: 11–28.

Ahlbäck-Öberg, S. and P.-O. Öberg (2005) 'Glorifiering av handlingskraft tystar det förnuftiga samtalet'. *Axess* (5).

Algotsson, K.-G. (2000) *Sveriges författning efter EU-anslutningen*. Stockholm: SNS Förlag.

Andersson, H. (2000) 'Sweden: a Mainstream Member State and a Part of Norden'. In L. Miles (ed.), *Sweden and the European Union Evaluated*. London: Continuum, pp. 215–30.

Aylott, N. (2005) 'De politiska partierna'. In T. Bergman (ed.), *EU och Sverige – ett sammanlänkat statsskick*. Malmö: Liber, pp. 58–78.

Beckman, B. and K.-M. Johansson (2002) 'EU och statsförvaltningen'. In K.-M. Johansson (ed.), *Sverige i EU*. Stockholm: SNS, pp. 113–28.

Blomgren, M. (2005) 'Riksdagen och EU'. In T. Bergman (ed.), *EU och Sverige – ett sammanlänkat statsskick*. Malmö: Liber, pp. 79–107.

Börzel, T. and T. Risse (2003) 'Conceptualizing the Domestic Impact of Europe'. In K. C. R. Featherstone (ed.), *The Politics of Europeanization*. Oxford: Oxford University Press, pp. 57–80.

Dahlstedt, I. (2000) *Svensk invandrar- och flyktingpolitisk riksdagsdebatt. 1980- och 1990-talsdebatter – översikt och jämförelse*. Umeå: MERGE.

Demker, M. and C. Malmström (1999) *Ingenmansland? Svensk immigrationspolitik i utrikespolitisk belysning*. Lund: Studentlitteratur.

Hammar, T. (1999) 'Closing the Doors to the Swedish Welfare State'. In T. Hammar (ed.), *Mechanisms of Immigration Control: a Comparative Analysis of European Regulation Policies.* Oxford: Berg, pp. 169–201.

Hegeland, H. (2002) 'Den svenska riksdagen och EU'. In K.-M. Johansson (ed.), *Sverige i EU,* Stockholm: SNS, pp. 95–112.

Jacobsson, B. (2000) 'Världen i staten – Europeisering, politik och statens organisering'. Stockholm: Stockholms centrum för forskning om offentlig sektor.

Jungar, A.-C. and S. Ahlbäck-Öberg (2002) 'Parlament i bakvatten?' *Riksdagens roll i EU.* Stockholm: SOU 2002: 81.

Lindgren, K.-O. (2000) 'EU-medlemskapets inverkan på den svenska parlamentarismen'. *Statsvetenskaplig tidskrift,* 103: 193–220.

Radaelli, C. (2003) 'The Europeanization of Public Policy'. In K. C. R. Featherstone (ed.), *The Politics of Europeanization.* Oxford: Oxford University Press, pp. 27–56.

Risse, T., M. G. Cowles and J. Caporaso (2003) 'Europeanization and Domestic Change: Introduction'. In T. Risse (ed.), *Transforming Europe. Europeanization and Domestic Change.* Ithaca: Cornell University Press, pp. 1–20.

Widfeldt, A. (2000) 'The Swedish Party System and the European Integration'. In L. Miles (ed.), *Sweden and the European Union Evaluated.* London: Continuum, pp. 66–78.

Wikrén, G. and H. Sandesjö (2002) *Utlänningslagen med kommentarer,* 7th edn. Stockholm: Norstedts.

7

Selective Europeanization: Europe's Impact on Spanish Migration Control

Margit Fauser

Introduction

Immigration to southern Europe is a new phenomenon. Like Greece, Spain is being confronted with rapidly growing numbers of immigrants only in the last decade or two. In 1985, a year before Spain entered the European Community, the foreign resident population amounted to around 240,000 people – less than 0.6 per cent of the total population. Most of them were affluent retirees from European Community member states, namely the United Kingdom, Germany and Sweden. Since that time, more and more immigrant workers have arrived in Spain every year, primarily from Latin America, North Africa and Asia. At the end of 2005 almost 2.6 million foreigners were living in Spain, or more than 6 per cent of the population – in other words, ten times the number of 20 years ago. Only 22 per cent of those foreigners today are citizens of European member states. The majority are of Latin American (36 per cent) and African (23 per cent) origin, while Asians make up 6.4 per cent of the immigrant population in Spain. The recent regularization of irregular migrants during the year 2005 contributed to the latest increase in the total number of foreigners. Almost 700,000 applications – of an estimated 1.2 million irregulars in Spain – were submitted and most were granted. This should have reduced the number of irregular migrants currently living in Spain to around half a million (Ministerio de Trabajo y Asuntos Sociales 2004; Arango and Jachimowicz 2005; Ministerio de Trabajo y Asuntos Sociales 2005).

Long before these numbers reached significant levels, Spain introduced its first 'Law on the Rights and Freedoms of Foreigners' in 1985. Though the regulation of the rights of non-nationals was required by article 13.1 of the Spanish Constitution of 1978, the timing of the law's approval, which coincided with Spain's entry into the European Community in 1986, led many scholars to see EU admission as the real incentive. Cornelius judged it to be 'almost entirely the result of external pressure associated with Spain's entry into the European Community' (Cornelius 1994: 345; see also Freeman 1995: 895). However, others have questioned the EU's impact in this early phase (Izquierdo Escribano 1993: 300). But generally there is little or no empirical evidence on any of these hypotheses (Baldwin-Edwards 1997: 506).

Since that time, European migration policies have gained a high profile. Therefore the question arises anew as to what extent and in which realms Spanish migration policy has been and is today influenced by European norms.

Not only is Spain a new immigration country, where immigration flows and patterns are evolving rapidly, but its immigration policies are also under a more or less constant state of revision, and with more and more aspects included or regulated. Since its first formulation in the mid-1980s, the Spanish Alien Law saw three major reforms in 1999, 2000 and 2003. The Executive Regulations to the law were revised in 1996, 2001 and 2004. Two asylum laws were formulated in Spain in this short period and many other policy measures were revised and new ones introduced.

To explain the impact of European integration on domestic change, Europeanization scholars have drawn on the concept of goodness of fit (Börzel 2000; Green Cowles et al. 2001) and the concomitant adaptational pressure (see Ette and Faist in this volume). According to this approach the extent of change can be explained by fit or misfit, but the question whether there is Europeanization at all cannot. In cases of great misfit, change caused by European integration is mediated through intervening factors, especially the weakening or strengthening of existing institutions and actors (Börzel and Risse 2000; Green Cowles et al. 2001). In other words, push by European norms and pull by national actors are decisive in order to make Europeanization happen. In environmental policies, to take an example, this meant for Spain that in some cases push by European norms and sometimes the Commission and pull by Spanish NGOs worked against a rather reluctant government to elevate environmental standards (Börzel 2000). But EU norms can also work against human rights advocacy actors – in and outside parliament – that try to inhibit the elevation of restrictions on immigration and asylum. When the EU pushes and the government pulls for a more restrictive policy, oppositional actors might see their position weakened.

This strengthening of governmental actors to the detriment of oppositional actors is what Europeanization obliviously brings about in Spanish migration policy. This is potentially enhanced by the generally strong position of the Spanish executive, especially in times of majority government (Heywood 2002). In this sense, Europeanization seems to reinforce the classical features of the Spanish political system (Molina 2001). For the period in question here, majority governments were in power until 1993 under the Socialists and from 2000 to 2004 under the Conservative Party.

The main argument put forward in this chapter is that Europeanization of Spanish migration policies is rather selective. Selection in turn is based on the interplay between European and domestic factors. Hence, in the Spanish case, Europeanization of domestic policies is promoted by the Europeanization of domestic politics. Put another way, the two dimensions that are the focus of the country comparisons in this book show a special relationship in the Spanish case, with Europeanized politics promoting Europeanized policies.

Empirically, selection means some of the European norms are integrated into Spanish legislation, while others are not. In those realms where European and Spanish norms are most similar, the adoption of European policy-making happens without complications. This is especially true for the newer directives for several reasons. But generally misfit was high, either because Spanish norms differed or because the aspects in question had not been regulated yet due to the emerging character of the whole policy field in Spain. In these cases, just as in environmental issues, the interplay between European and domestic factors is crucial for Europeanization (Börzel 2000); only the actors are different. Whereas in environmental policies adoption took place in Spain due to mobilization of domestic, non-governmental actors, in migration policies the government's efforts account for it. The successive Spanish governments saw their position strengthened by the availability of European policies that fit with their own course on specific matters.

This chapter addresses the following key points. First, Spanish legislation on immigration control will be compared with the European policies in the respective realms, and the politics accompanying the process of Europeanization will be analysed. While the next section concentrates on the rather high level of Europeanization of border and asylum policies, the third section looks at the field of labour migration and regularization of irregular migrants, where Spain shows more reluctance. The fourth section provides an explanation of the differences in the degree and pattern of Europeanization. Finally, the conclusion briefly summarizes the main findings and points to future developments affected by further communitarization and changing positions in the EU and in Spain.

Europeanization of Spanish migration control

This and the following section provide an analysis of the Europeanization of Spanish migration policies. While this section focuses on areas where we can observe Europeanization, the next section looks at realms where European integration has not had significant impact.

In the case of European migration policies different integration dynamics and modes are at work simultaneously, constituting a more or less hybrid constellation (Knill and Lehmkuhl 1999; Lavenex 2001; Vink 2002). There are international agreements, intergovernmental decisions and, more recently, directives that are binding, but there are also numerous recommendations, decisions and summit conclusions that play an important role as well. Thus prescriptive and discursive modes of integration are prevalent in European immigration policy (see Ette and Faist in this volume). In the Europeanization of Spanish migration policy, the predominant operation of the different modes of integration can be related to different points in time. Prescriptive Europeanization can be seen as a consequence of Spain's participation in the Schengen Agreement in the early 1990s. Unlike many other European member countries, Spain together with Portugal joined the Schengen area rather voluntarily at this early stage as the only countries outside the core group that had developed the agreement. All other countries saw themselves subject to the Schengen Agreement after its integration into the Amsterdam Treaty in 1997. Once the agreement was signed, however, at least the more binding implications and subsequent decisions had to be integrated into the domestic framework. In this case prescription might be regarded here as closer to the type of flexible integration that prevails 'when countries have the option of joining EU policy or remaining outside' (Radaelli 2000: 12f.). The softer, discursive dynamics of integration became especially visible in Spain at the end of the 1990s. At that time the European recommendations regarding combating irregular migration became more pronounced, but had not reached the level of common regulations; nevertheless the official policies in Spain were based on those recommendations. Most explicitly, the non-compulsory agreements achieved at the EU Council's Tampere summit came to play an important role. But elements of discursive Europeanization are present throughout all legal reforms by reference to a more general European migration policy framework. And finally, a more strictly prescriptive mode gained importance again with the enactment of Council directives in the realm of immigration and asylum made possible by the Amsterdam Treaty since 2000.

Prescriptive Europeanization: Spanish participation in the Schengen group

As stated earlier, the parallel developments of migration policies in the European Community and in Spain have led to different evaluations. The timing was such that the recommendations made by the European Commission on immigration in 1985 came after the Spanish Law had passed to parliamentary debate. And, contrary to the Spanish Law, the European concerns focused primarily on control of labour migration, access to the EC and crime prevention. The emphasis of the Spanish Alien Law lay on regularization of persons with no legal residence status and on international crime. It did not focus on further immigration or migration control (Gortázar 2002: 5). Thus, even if the law itself was related to Spain's entry to the European Community, its content was not. Since then, however, the linkage to the European context in parliamentary debates and legal proposals has been growing.

In 1991, only five years after entering the European Community, Spain became part of the Schengen Agreement. Although Spain had not participated in the formulation of the agreement, it showed high commitment to it; Spain was among the seven countries that opted for the integration of the arrangement into the Amsterdam Treaty (Baldwin-Edwards 1997: 504). It has been argued, nevertheless, that Spain wanted to integrate into the Schengen group not so much because of a concern for a common immigration policy but because of its desire to participate in the common market (Baldwin-Edwards 1997: 515). But already in the early 1990s the Spanish parliament and the government in various official documents articulated the need to join the Schengen group in order to participate actively in the communitarization of immigration policies (BOE Serie D núm. 165, 22 March 1991).

After the Schengen Agreement, the Dublin Convention was subsequently also signed and ratified. Both documents were integrated into national legislation in the following years and led to some considerable policy changes in Spanish migration control. Various legal instruments were changed on that basis, including other international treaties, laws and executive regulations. For example, though debated for quite some time, entry visa requirements for North African as well as Latin American countries, starting with Colombia, were among the first measures to be introduced in that context at the beginning of the 1990s (Izquierdo Escribano 1993: 300). But the most far-reaching changes were those these treaties called for in the asylum legislation in Spain. The need to reform the existing legislation on asylum and refugee protection was officially agreed upon among the political actors at the beginning of the 1990s. The parliamentary discussion on the reform started in 1992, but had to be reopened in the next legislature due to the early announcement of elections; the reform was finalized in 1994.

One of the main aspects of asylum law reform (LO 9/1994) was the abolition of the distinction between asylum-seekers and refugees established in the previous law. Before the reform, the application of refugee status on the basis of the Geneva Convention was relevant only to a smaller part of those granted protection; the greater part were granted 'asylum' based on Spanish law. The reform based protection exclusively on the Geneva Convention. Also, it introduced a pre-examination to decide on the admission of an asylum claim and it changed the consequences of the refusal of a claim. The possibility of staying in Spain legally for six months in order to apply for residence and a work permit, allowed under the previous law, was abolished.

With this reformed law Spain integrated the Dublin Convention with regard to designating the state responsible for the asylum claim, as well as the related London Resolution. The resolution suggested an accelerated procedure for deciding whether a claim was based on 'manifestly unfounded grounds' and thus not be admitted for further processing.[1] Despite the fact that these recommendations formulated at a meeting of the European Council in London 1992 were not strictly binding, they exercised great influence in many countries.

Other changes were introduced successively, for example the responsibilities of carriers such as airlines or shipping companies originally laid down in the Schengen Agreement. This was part of the Executive Regulation to the Alien Law that was reformed in 1996 (RD 155/1996, art. 41.1). At the same time, Spanish migration policies externalized control to a high degree. Visa requirements, carriers' responsibilities and responsibilities of other European member countries are central instruments of migration control beyond the proper borders of Spanish territory (Ette and Fauser 2005). One of the consequences was that in the years following the reform asylum figures in Spain were cut by half.

With these reforms, Spanish legislation on asylum, entry and border control became on the whole more restrictive in comparison to its earlier liberal character. Thus, at this early stage misfit between the rather liberal Spanish policies and the more restrictive European norms was high. However, the interplay between the dominant domestic actors and those European norms contributed to their implementation. The government's position in this case was strengthened even more as the principal opposition party supported its course. At the same time, the government's loss of its absolute majority during the debate opened the way for oppositional actors to introduce some changes.

In relation to the asylum law reform it is noteworthy that while it was clear to all actors that the existing legislation from 1984 was in need of revision, the existence of a European approach to these issues very much conditioned the proceedings. The two major parties in the Spanish political system, the socialist PSOE (Partido Socialista Obrero Español) and the conservative PP (Partido Popular) followed a favourable and strong course in aligning Spanish legislation with European developments. The leftist IU (Izquierda Unida) and, to a varying degree, the smaller regional parties with representation in the central parliament, showed resistance.

The thrust of the critiques was that the intergovernmental meetings that had led to the treaties were characterized by secrecy, resulting in a poor record on democratic inclusion of national and European parliaments. In addition, in reference to the content of the Dublin Convention, criticism focused on the possible infringement of the right to asylum granted by article 13 of the Spanish Constitution. It was argued that the formula of the 'state responsible for an asylum claim' contained in the Convention did not entail a material harmonization of the right to asylum and would therefore lead to competition among the European countries for the most restrictive measure and that protection of refugees would diminish.

Although the party in government, the PSOE, supported by the major opposition party, the PP, enjoyed a strong position, which allowed many of the restrictive European agreements to be introduced, they had to accept changes to their proposals nonetheless. In this sense, the discussion process benefited from the early elections and the Socialists' loss of their absolute majority in the 1993 election. As a consequence, the parliamentary decision-making process was relatively lengthy because it could not be concluded before the elections. Additionally, this led to the first expert hearing in Spanish parliamentary history, which was installed in the second part of the debate after the elections. These factors made considerable changes possible, for example elevating guarantees for the protection of refugees. In the end, all the parliamentary factions, with one exception, voted in favour of the final version of the asylum law reform. Only the United Left declared its abstention, positing grave concerns regarding the protection of refugees and the accordance of the law with the Geneva Convention.

Discursive Europeanization: the role of the Tampere Conclusions

The implementation of binding European norms in Spain was accompanied more than once by aspects of, and references to, discussions and recommendations that had not reached the level of binding policies, as had happened with the above-described London Resolution. Hence, discursive Europeanization accompanies various legal reforms.

In this sense the integration of the Tampere Conclusions into the Alien Law is a convincing and obvious example. At the special meeting of the European Council on 15 and 16 October 1999 in Tampere the EU member states accorded the development of a comprehensive immigration and asylum policy their top priority (Guiraudon 2003: 264). The summit's conclusions *inter alia* demanded a just treatment of and the granting of rights to third-country nationals, who reside legally in a member country, in equal conditions to EU citizens (European Council 1999; see also Bendel this volume).

In the reform of the Spanish Alien Law in 1999 the rights to assembly, strike, non-compulsory education, unionization and so on were granted to all immigrants, independent of their legal status. A new reform in 2000 limited these rights to legal residents only on the basis of the Tampere Conclusions. In the realm of sanctions and expulsions as well the Spanish legislation was aligned with the policies articulated on the European level. This led to the explicit prescription that illegal residence in Spain was an infraction that could be sanctioned with expulsion.

These newly introduced changes make the Spanish legislation more restrictive, especially in comparison to the previous liberalizing reform, which in turn went far beyond older Spanish policies in assigning important political and social rights to immigrants independent of their residence status. It is difficult to judge, however, whether Spanish norms were in accordance with the European proposals only after their subsequent revision. What is clear is that they signify considerable changes in relation to the previous reform.

These changes were possible only because of the availability of a European framework in parallel with the newly won absolute majority of the PP. The Tampere Conclusions obviously legitimized the new intent of the Conservative Party to reform the law according to their position. It gave them a reason to act for a new bill and thereby to introduce the issue in the election campaign. In this respect, PP officials were successful in combining the European demands with the domestic interest in combating irregular migration and restricting and controlling access to Spanish territory. Oppositional positions were not able to exercise great influence in this situation.

PP parliamentarians introduced the proposal to limit equal treatment of third-country nationals to legal residents shortly before the final discussion of the previous reform in October 1999, and withdrew their support from it. They were ultimately unsuccessful in blocking the legislation. But as they won an absolute majority shortly after, they made a new attempt. The new project was initiated in September 2000 – only nine months after the previous reform had entered into force. After little more than two months, parliamentary discussion was concluded and the bill approved with the government's majority party and supported by two regional parties, Coalición Canaria and the Catalan Convergència i Unió. The reform is intended to 'increase the capacity of the actions of the State concerning the control of illegal immigration, at the same level as other European countries [...] which is an element that is reflected in the conclusions of the European Council in Tampere' (BOE núm. 307 of 23.12.2000 45509).

The change in the government's position at this late stage in the consideration of a bill they had previously supported can be seen in relation to the increasing media coverage of, and public attention to, the arrivals of the *pateras*, small boats bringing irregular migrants from North Africa to the Spanish coasts (Alscher 2005: 9). In this situation the Tampere summit obviously changed the discursive framing of the ruling party and provided an opportunity to introduce the issue in the election campaign.

During the debate government officials and conservative parliamentarians made reference – often in the same sentence – to the responsibilities Spain had to bear, based on Amsterdam, Schengen and Tampere. Most of the other parliamentary fractions did not agree with that position, though. The counter-argument was that the Tampere Conclusions were not binding, nor – and more important in the debate – was the previous reform a violation of the European announcements. 'The agreements of Tampere make reference to the adjustment between the rights of citizens with legal residence status, but they do not mention that the legislations of the member countries couldn't advance further in that direction' (DS Comisiones Núm. 94 of 06.11.2000). Even those parties that generally supported the bill in the final voting, namely Coalición Canaria and Convergencia i Unió, criticized the restriction of rights to regular migrants and maintained their amendments until the end. The parliamentarians argued that the designated rights were fundamental rights that could not be limited to a certain group or made dependent on the status of a person. To do so would be an infringement of such European norms as the European Human Rights Convention, and especially of the Spanish Constitution and the more recent jurisdiction of the Spanish Constitutional Court that defined fundamental rights as rights of personhood, beyond the status of a person, an argument repeated several times by the Basque National Party (PNV). After the approval of the law the socialist delegates brought these articles before the Constitutional Court. There the claim currently remains undecided.

Prescriptive integration: transposition of directives after the Amsterdam Treaty

Since 2000, following from the Amsterdam Treaty Title IV, several Council Directives in the realm of immigration and asylum policies have been approved in the EU. The directives on mutual recognition of decisions on expulsion among the member countries (D 2001/40), on carrier sanctions adding to the Schengen provisions (D 2001/51) and on a common definition on facilitating unauthorized entry, stay and residence (D 2002/90) were transposed within the general reform to the Alien Law in 2003 (LO 14/2003). The directive on carriers' obligation to the communication of passenger data (D 2004/82) has not been transposed as a directive, but is already part of the Spanish legal corpus. This directive originated in Spain and its content was integrated in domestic law parallel with this initiative. Two other directives in relation to minimum standards in Europe, the first on temporary protection in cases of mass influx (D 2000/55) and the second concerning the reception of asylum-seekers (D 2003/9), have been transposed by regulations (*Reales Decretos*), which belong to the competencies of the executive.

Again, at least in relation to the first mentioned directives, Europeanization fosters a change in Spanish migration control towards more restrictive policies. But as this process has already been under way in Spanish migration policy for quite some time, observable changes are minor. The responsibilities of carriers such as airlines or shipping companies originally laid down in the Schengen Agreement, for example, had already been part of Spanish legislation since 1996 through the Executive Regulation to the Alien Law (RD 155/1996, art. 41.1) and had been integrated in the higher norm of a law with LO 8/2000 (art. 53, 2 and 3 and art. 65). Thus, the transposition of the directive supplementing provisions of the Schengen Agreement did not cause major transformations.

Prescriptive Europeanization expressed with the directives leads to adaptation of Spanish migration control policies. Most of the directives were transposed before the final date of implementation. With respect to the government's course in the fight against irregular migration, the directives were in line with their efforts on the domestic as well as on the European level. Most oppositional actors in parliament advocating a different course were marginalized. Nevertheless, as the ruling PP faced growing pressure towards the end of their legislation, they obviously saw a need to find some agreement at least with the major opposition party. This enabled some changes of the reform, but it did not alter the general course.

The integration of the directives on expulsion, carrier sanctions and unauthorized entry in Spanish legislation was embedded in a broader legal reform of the Alien Law that followed the intent to combat irregular migration in general. Hence, the transposition itself was not a major issue in the debates. The Interior Minister as well as parliamentarians from the ruling PP upheld the correspondence of the Alien Law reform with EU migration policy in general. Their spokespersons argued that their approach resonated with the three pillars followed on the European level: facilitating legal immigration, advancing integration policies and combating irregular migration and human trafficking.

Against this line of reasoning, oppositional parties, from the United Left (IU), the Basque nationalists from PNV and the socialist PSOE, criticized the government's version of the directives and the restrictive interpretation of the European model of a common migration policy. Rather than participating in the downgrading of standards, these should be elevated, they argued. Nevertheless, the government could easily, to its advantage, make use of the European norms that strengthened its position. They called into mind the recent summits in Tampere, Seville and Thessaloniki. These in turn were influenced by active Spanish advocacy for the government's approach.

All this happened in an overall climate of harsh critiques of the government over the content of the reform but also over the absence of dialogue among the political and social actors and the timing of the reform – in the midst of municipal and national election campaigns. Most political and social actors had been marginalized by the executive and relevant consultative institutions on matters of immigration, but also the Consejo General de Poder Judicial, which in cases like this has competency to inform the bill, was not heard. Finally the ruling PP achieved an agreement with the Socialists granting them certain changes, which led to a broad approval of the reform.

Inertia instead of Europeanization: Spanish policies on labour migration

Differences in labour market demand between Spain and other European countries have generally been considered an obstacle to the further harmonization of European migration policies (Huntoon 1998). Existing European immigration policies were seen as contradicting Spanish labour market characteristics and needs (Baldwin-Edwards 1997, 1999). For a long time the European Community had focused on free movement and labour migration within the territory of the Community itself and excluded legal immigration from third countries from their agenda. In contrast, Spain launched an active quota policy in 1993 to regulate the foreign workforce. At that time, the European Commission still declared that such an approach would not be an appropriate instrument in a situation of growing unemployment and difficult economic circumstances in Europe (Kreienbrink 2004: 259). Hence it is in the realm of labour migration where Spain shows most inertia.

Originally the Spanish quota worked as a means of regularization for third-country nationals. Though it was not the intention to do so, a high percentage, probably around 90 per cent, of the permits granted in the early years were given to foreigners already resident in Spain. The law reform in the year 2000, article 39, put an end to this practice (Gortázar 2002: 3; Pumares 2003: 55ff.). Furthermore, since 2001 Spain has concluded bilateral agreements on labour migration with third countries in order to channel migratory flows.[2] At the same time, there are rather frequent exceptional regularizations of irregular workers. Regularization processes in Spain can be characterized as 'one-off', meaning campaigns at selected points in time requiring residence within the territory of the state before a given date but not conditioned by a defined duration of that residence (Apap et al. 2001: 280). To date, five extraordinary regularization processes have taken place (1985/86;

1991; 1996; 2000/2001; 2005). These were always protested against among the EU member states as well as the Commission, which feared that these programmes would encourage more irregular migration (Commission of the European Communities 1991; Izquierdo Escribano 1993: 300; Cornelius 1994; Kreienbrink 2004: 259f.).

The Spanish policy on regular and irregular labour migrants throughout the 1980s and 1990s was based on a consensus among political and social actors. Successive governments and oppositional parties agreed on the need for labour migration and the necessity to deal with the situation of irregular migrants. Since the year 2000, however, dispute among the actors has been growing on the domestic course as well as on the definition of what is in accordance with European migration policy. For example, in 2000 the Conservative Party opposed the reopening of an extraordinary regularization campaign demanded by various political and social actors. They worried that this would cause an *efecto llamada*, a snowball effect of attracting irregular migrants, repeating concerns voiced by European governments against the Spanish campaigns in earlier times. Only vigorous protest in the streets as well as in parliament forced them to change their position. They finally reopened the previous regularization process in summer 2001. In 2003 a reform to the Alien Law was carried out without the usual accompaniment of a regularization process even though one had been demanded by many political and social actors. In 2005 the newly elected socialist government conducted a regularization campaign, putting an emphasis on the link to the labour market and the fact that the people concerned were already part of it. In this process of 'normalization', as it has been called, employers had to apply for a permit for their foreign workers based on guaranteed impunity. Supported by political parties, social actors, trade unions, employer organizations, the churches as well as NGOs, this process was heavily criticized by the PP.

Within the EU this recent process found criticism as well as support. Germany and the Netherlands harshly criticized the government in Madrid, arguing that this was a European problem insofar as these regularized migrants could move to other European countries. The German and Dutch Interior Ministers therefore demanded a European solution and suggested a mechanism on mutual information about such activities of individual countries in the future. The Vice President and Commissioner for Justice, Freedom and Security, Franco Frattini, has now taken up the matter formally. At the same time, the Commission's Vice President, Margot Wallström, as well as the Commissioner for

Employment and Social Affairs, Vladímir Spidla, defended the Spanish campaign with the assurance that it was in line with European approaches and directives. It was Franco Frattini who said explicitly that the Commission had not formed its opinion on the subject yet (*El País* 11.02.2005, 12.02.2005, 30.01.2005). This emerging shift in the attitude towards labour migration within the EU is reflected in the Commission's communications during recent years. Today the Commission acknowledges that the economic and demographic challenge in all European countries goes hand in hand with skill and labour shortages that have to be dealt with by economic migration (Commission of the European Communities 2003).

It is still unclear how far common European efforts in the realm of labour migration will develop. At the moment, the EU provides national actors with different frames they can rely on when defending their own positions. The Spanish Minister for Labour and Social Affairs could contend that Spain was 'the envy of Europe' because of its treatment of irregular migrants and Commissioner Spidla demanded this course be followed in other countries. At the same time, a conservative parliamentarian could criticize this position by referring to the serious opposition being heard from important European governments (DS Congreso Pleno Núm. 91 of 18.05.2005: 4565f.).

Explaining varying Europeanization in Spain

The changes in Spanish immigration control considered in this chapter can most appropriately be characterized as ranging between absorption and transformation (see Ette and Faist in this volume). At the beginning the changes taking place were more transformative in nature, when the rather liberal or unregulated realms were revised in the direction of the more restrictive European policies. In cases of the transposition of the recent directives there is only a limited extent of change, or, in other words, a process of absorption. This is not to say that essential structures are not really modified or that change is happening only superficially. But the extent of change is shrinking, primarily because the degree of fit between Spanish and European norms is improving. Several factors can explain the alteration in the degree of fit over time. When Spain entered the Schengen Agreement in 1991 the country had not had any influence on the treaty's content. In the following years, Spain's role in the formulation of a common European migration policy was not especially pronounced either. But through early participation and adaptation, misfit in the following years was minimized.

Since the year 2000 the conservative government acted in favour of a common line against irregular migration at the European level which might lead to greater fit in the future as well.

At the same time, fit is not improving in all policy fields related to migration control. Europe's impact on Spanish migration policies is still selective. In the realm of labour and irregular migration the nature of Europeanization can best be described as inertia or even retrenchment. Domestic interest here is still in contradiction to the European course. Whether these remain dissimilar or become more distanced from Europe depends on the course European policy will take in this realm. Considering the extensive criticism of Spanish policies in that realm from European institutions and governments of some member countries, growing Europeanization seems unlikely here unless the EU itself changes its course.

We consider now, first, the different factors explaining the growing degree of fit between Spanish and European norms that contribute to unproblematic Europeanization in some realms. Second, we attempt to explain selectivity based on the role of governmental actors empowered in the process of Europeanization.

Participation without representation

Europeanization literature has suggested that potential misfit is minimized by a country's active participation in the formulation of European policies because it can introduce a model to the European level that is closer to the domestic one (Geddes and Guiraudon 2002).

As stated earlier, Spain was not represented in the formulation of the Schengen Agreement. However, the country participated in the agreement very early on. As a result it transformed its legislation on asylum and immigration to align with the obligations and subsequent decisions taken as a consequence of the agreement. As the Schengen area was an idea dominated primarily by the northern European major receiving countries at that time, southern European countries showed considerable differences with these policy lines (Baldwin-Edwards 1997). This is the reason that change in this early phase of adaptation is significant in Spain.

Anticipated compliance

Once domestic asylum and border control policies were brought in line with European decisions, misfit was minimized. 'Anticipated compliance' is the cause of the reduced extent of change since 2000. Adaptation to the first European policies took place throughout the

1990s. Due to more flexible integration because of the originally voluntary participation in the Schengen Agreement, but also due to framing
integration as a mechanism of adaptation, Spanish policies were
already closer to the European course on asylum and migration
control. The country by that time had adapted to many EU rules, such
as the carrier sanctions in 1996. Therefore the integration of the
respective directive did not cause greater changes. Moreover, when the
Schengen Agreement was integrated in the Amsterdam Treaty, those
countries that were already members of the agreement naturally
showed the least extent of misfit.

Making Europe more Spanish

Another factor that contributed to the shrinking of differences between
European and Spanish policies on migration is Spain's growing
influence on the EU level. From the end of the 1990s onward, the
Spanish government more actively supported a common European
migration policy. They advocated in favour of common policies within
the EU's third pillar on Justice and Home Affairs (JHA) and favoured a
special summit on these issues. Consequently the Spanish president
and state officials claim an important contribution to the Tampere
summit (Closa and Heywood 2004: 234ff.; Niehus and Freisinger 2004:
102).[3]

'More Europe' was the slogan of the Spanish EU Presidency in 2002.
But it has been asked whether this was rather not 'more Spain' in
Europe in many respects, including migration policies (Powell 2003).
Recent activities of the Spanish government brought items from the
national agenda successfully onto the European level (Cuervós 2005).
The Seville summit conclusions in this sense further developed many
aspects taken up in the Tampere Conclusions in the field of combating
irregular migration (European Council 2002).[4] This course for further
development of restriction and control on migration in Europe is
reflected in the Spanish initiative for a directive on the communication
of passenger data by carriers. The initiative is almost literally identical
with the reform of the Alien Law that was introduced at the same time
in the national parliament. The proposal was designated as a directive
at the end of April 2004 (D 2004/82).

At the same time these activities had retroactive effects on the
national level. This becomes especially visible when noting the importance Spanish state officials attributed to their influence on the
Tampere summit, whereas at the same time government based its legal
reform on these very same approaches as has been analysed earlier in

this chapter. Hence, there is strong evidence to consider the interaction of top-down influences by the EU and bottom-up processes stemming from the national level as decisive to the explanation of the process of Europeanization.

Explaining selectivity

The extent of change Europeanization brings about is becoming smaller and smaller in Spain. Nevertheless, what has become clear in the discussion on Spanish's labour migration policy is that there are also realms where Spain follows its own course.

When considering the impact of Europeanization on the dimension of politics, we observe a general strengthening of the executive and governmental actors. Unlike the experiences of many other European countries, the mode of Europeanization in itself does not account for the differential impact of European norms and decisions on Spanish migration policies (see Ette and Faist in this volume). Rather the empowerment of governmental actors in this process and the selections undertaken by them provide an explanation. Hence, the Europeanization of politics allows for Europeanization of policies.

Conclusion

Following from the analysis presented in this chapter, Europeanization in Spain can be characterized as selective. On the whole, the level of Europeanization is high in Spanish migration policy, contrasting with Spain´s classically low level of incorporation of EU norms (Colomer 1996: 204). But Europeanization is high only in certain policy fields. When comparing different subpolicy fields, we can observe that Europe's impact on Spanish migration policies is selective.

Selection for its part can neither be explained by the existence of fit or misfit between Spanish and European norms, nor can it be related to the specific modes of Europeanization. What does explain selectivity is the role of actors and politics in the process of Europeanization. We can thus draw the following conclusions.

First, Spanish migration policy resembles European norms in many realms as fit between the two improves. At the beginning of the 1990s misfit was high because of the emerging character of the policy field in general in Spain. In the course of time, misfit is shrinking in some policy areas, though, because of three factors. Spain participated early on in the Schengen Agreement but was not represented in the process of decision-making. It therefore had no influence on the formulation of the agreement, whose provisions differed sharply from Spanish procedures at that time. Over the following years, previous adaptation to, and anticipated compliance with, European norms reduced the distance for policy adjustment. In recent years Spain's influence in European fora is growing. This might lead to diminishing misfit in the future as the European course might be more closely aligned with the Spanish model.

Second, in the Spanish case differences in the impact of European norms do not depend on the mode of Europeanization. Different modes lead to the same consequences. Discursive and prescriptive Europeanization both lead to considerable changes in border and asylum policies. Simultaneously, the same mode can also lead to different consequences. In the field of labour migration Spain shows least adaptation to European demands. At least potentially, discursive Europeanization is also possible in this realm; but discursive reference to the European policy framing contributed to transforming Europeanization in the case of asylum policies, while inertia or reluctance prevail in the field of labour migration and the treatment of irregular migration.

Third, what can explain Europeanization even in cases of great misfit is the reinforcing effect the European norms have for certain actors. In a scenario of a strong executive, the political actors in power obviously derive strength from the environment of Europeanization. It is on their account that the restrictive policies on immigration control and asylum issued by the European Community through the 1990s were integrated into the Spanish legislation. On labour migration and regularization of irregular workers none of the actors showed an interest in approaching the European course. This is where selectivity enters the picture.

Today, labour migration and especially the treatment of irregular workers have become a highly contested issue in Spain. During the PP majority rule the party distanced itself more and more from previous practice. In 2001 only very strong pressure in parliament and in the streets forced the government to accept a regularization campaign; in 2003 they resisted claims for a new campaign. With the change in government in 2004, the Socialists again took up regularization as a measure, a move that was heavily criticized by the Conservatives. But also – and perhaps more surprisingly – disagreement is growing on the European level: various commissioners and member states' representatives showed support, while others criticized the campaign. Future development in that sense partly depends on the course the currently ruling Socialist Party will follow in the European fora. Taking a cue from their domestic course, they might even intervene for the purpose of an active European policy on labour migration, possibly bringing European proposals more in line with Spanish policies. Thereby, selectivity might be reduced in the future when European policies show greater fit with Spanish domestic policies – at least until other actors come into power and follow other positions.

Notes

1   In cases where either a country was not responsible for accepting a claim or when the person had passed through another safe third country or came from a safe country of origin, his or her claim can be categorized as unfounded.

2   At the moment, there are agreements with Colombia, Ecuador and Morocco (2001), Dominican Republic, Romania and Poland (2002) and with Bulgaria (2004) (Database of the Parliament, International Conventions).

3   On different occasions President Aznar and the Minister for Foreign Affairs Matutes repeatedly mentioned their efforts and success in the planning of the Tampere summit in the press and during parliamentary debates; see for example *El País* 16.10.1999; *El Mundo* 28.10.1999; DS, Congreso, Pleno, Núm. 24 of 19.05.2004, p. 13.

4   It should be noted that these issues only came on the agenda immediately before the Council meeting in Seville; in response to the electoral victories of extremist right-wing parties in France (Le Pen) and the Netherlands (Pym Fortuyn), Aznar travelled to all 15 member states to ensure that bilateral accords include asylum and immigration in the agenda. The main argument was that reluctance in those fields had led to populist and xenophobic consequences and therefore needed to be addressed with urgency (Powell 2003).

References

Primary sources

BOE núm. 307 of 23.12.2000.

BOE Serie D núm. 165, 22 March 1991.

Commission of the European Communities (1991) *Commission Communication to the Council and the European Parliament*, SEC (91) 1855 final. Brussels: Commission of the European Communities.

Commission of the European Communities (2003) *Communication from the Commission to the Council, the European Parliament, the European Economic and Social Committee and the Committee of the Regions on Immigration, Integration and Employment*, COM (2003) 336 final. Brussels: Commission of the European Communities.

DS Comisiones Núm. 94 of 06.11.2000.

DS Congreso Pleno Núm. 91 of 18.05.2005.

El País 11.02.2005.

El País 12.02.2005.
El País 30.01.2005.
European Council (1999) *Presidency Conclusions*, Tampere, 16.10.1999.
European Council (2002) *Presidency Conclusions*, Seville, 22.06.2002.
Ministerio de Trabajo y Asuntos Sociales (2005) *Informe Estadístico. Extranjerios con trajeta o autorización de residencia en vigor a 30 de septiember 2005.* Madrid, Ministerio de Asuntos Sociales y Trabajo, Secretaría de Estada de Inmigración y Emigración, Observatorio Permanente de la Inmigración.
Ministerio de Trabajo y Asuntos Sociales (2004) *Anuario Estadístico de Extranjería 2003.* Madrid, Ministerio de Trabajo y Asuntos Sociales, Secretaría de Estado de Inmigración y Emigración, Observatoria Permanente de Inmigración.

Secondary sources

Alscher, S. (2005) 'Knocking at the Door of "Fortress Europe": Migration and Border Control in Southern Europe and Eastern Poland'. CCSI Working Paper.

Apap, J. P. et al. (2001) 'Regularisation of Illegal Aliens in the European Union. Summary Report of a Comparative Perspective Study'. *European Journal of Migration and Law*, Vol. 2: 263–308.

Arango, J. and M. Jachimowicz (2005) 'Regularizing Immigrants in Spain: a New Approach'. *Migration Information Source.* http://www.migrationinformation.org/Feature/display.cfm?ID=331 (last accessed on 26 June 2006).

Baldwin-Edwards, M. (1997). 'The Emerging European Immigration Regime: Some Reflections on Implications for Southern Europe'. *Journal of Common Market Studies*, Vol. 35, No. 4: 497–519.

Baldwin-Edwards, M. (1999) 'Where Free Markets Reign: Aliens in the Twilight Zone'. In J. Arango and M. Baldwin-Edwards (eds), *Immigrants and the Informal Economy in Southern Europe.* London: Frank Cass Publishers, pp. 1–15.

Börzel, T. A. (2000) 'Why There Is no "Southern Problem": On Environmental Leaders and Laggards in the European Union'. *Journal of European Public Policy*, Vol. 7, No. 1: 141–62.

Börzel, T. A. and T. Risse (2000) 'When Europe Hits Home: Europeanization and Domestic Change'. *European Integration online Papers* (EIoP) 4(15).

Closa, C. and P. M. Heywood (2004) *Spain and the European Union.* Basingstoke: Palgrave.

Colomer, J. M. (1996). 'Spain and Portugal. Rule by Party Leadership'. In J. M. Colomer, *Political Institutions in Europe.* London, New York: Routledge, pp. 170–210.

Cornelius, W. A. (1994) 'Spain: the Uneasy Transition from Labor Exporter to Labor Importer'. In W. A. M. Cornelius, L. Philip and James F. Hollifield (eds), *Controlling Immigration: a Global Perspective.* Stanford, Calif.: Stanford University Press, pp. 331–69.

Cuervós, C. (2005) 'El papel de España en la política de inmigración de la Unión Europea'. España en la construcción de una política de inmigración. I Seminario inmigración y Europa, Barcelona, Fundació CIDOB.

Ette, A. and M. Fauser (2005) 'Externalisierung der Migrationspolitik. Der britische und spanische Fall'. In S. Haug and F. Swiaczny (eds), *Migration in Europa.* Materialien für Bevölkerungswissenschaft, No. 115, Bundesinstitut für Bevölkerungsforschung, Wiesbaden.

Freeman, G. P. (1995) 'Modes of Immigration Politics in Liberal Democratic States'. *International Migration Review*, Vol. 29, No. 4: 881–902.

Geddes, A. and V. Guiraudon (2002) 'The Anti-Discrimination Policy Paradigm in France and the UK: Europeanization and Alternative Explanations to Policy Change'. *Theorising the Communitarisation of Migration*, the University Association for Contemporary European Studies Study Group on the Evolving European Migration Law and Policy, the Foresight Centre, University of Liverpool.

Gortázar, C. (2002) 'Two Immigration Acts at the End of the Millenium'. *European Journal of Migration and Law*, Vol. 4: 1–21.

Green Cowles, M. et al. (2001) 'Europeanization and Domestic Change: Introduction'. In M. Green Cowles, J. Caporaso and T. Risse (eds), *Transforming Europe: Europeanization and Domestic Change*. Ithaca, NY: Cornell University Press, pp. 1–20.

Guiraudon, V. (2003) 'The Constitution of a European Immigration Policy Domain: a Political Sociological Approach'. *Journal of European Public Policy*, Vol. 10, No. 2: 263–71.

Heywood, P. (2002) *The Government and Politics of Spain*. Basingstoke: Palgrave Macmillan.

Huntoon, L. (1998) 'Immigration to Spain: Implications for a Unified European Union Immigration Policy'. *International Migration Review*, Vol. 32, No. 2: 423–50.

Izquierdo Escribano, A. (1993) 'The EC and Spanish Immigration Policy'. In A. Almarcha Barbado (ed.), *Spain and EC Membership Evaluated*. London: Pinter Publishers, pp. 293–301.

Knill, C. and D. Lehmkuhl (1999) 'How Europe Matters. Different Mechanisms of Europeanization'. *European Integration online Papers* (EIoP) 3(7).

Kreienbrink, A. (2004) *Einwanderungsland Spanien. Migrationspolitik zwischen Europäisierung und nationalen Interessen*. Frankfurt am Main: IKO-Verlag für Interkulturelle Kommunikation.

Lavenex, S. (2001) 'The Europeanization of Refugee Policies: Normative Challenges and Institutional Legacies'. *Journal of Common Market Studies*, Vol. 39, No. 5: 851–74.

Molina, I. d. C. (2001) 'La Adaptación a la Unión Europea del Poder Ejecutivo Español'. In C. Closa (ed.), *La europeización del sistema político español*. Madrid: Istmo, pp. 160–96.

Niehus, G. F. and H. Freisinger (2004) 'Die Außenpolitik des demokratischen Spaniens'. In W. L. Bernecker and K. Dirschler (eds), *Spanien heute Politik Wissenschaft Kultur*. Frankfurt am Main: Vervuert Verlag, pp. 79–119.

Powell, C. (2003). 'Política exterior y de seguridad de España'. *Anuario Internacional CIDOB 2002*. Barcelona: CIDOB.

Pumares, P. (2003) 'L'immigration subsaharienne et la politique migratoire de l'Espagne'. *Cahier de Migrations Internationales* (54F): 52–94.

Radaelli, C. M. (2000) 'Whither Europeanization? Concept Stretching and Substantive Change'. *European Integration online Papers* (EIoP) 4(8).

Vink, M. P. (2002) 'Negative and Positive Integration in European Immigration Policies'. *European Integration online Papers* (EIoP) 6(13): 1–19.

8
Ulysses Turning European: the Different Faces of 'Europeanization' of Greek Immigration Policy

Georgia Mavrodi

Introduction[1]

A striking feature of the 'Greek case' is the magnitude of its unexpected, undesired and rapid transformation from a country of emigration to one of immigration, directly connected to the collapse of the former communist regimes in the Balkans and in the former Soviet Union. Whereas in the mid-1980s the number of foreign residents was estimated at 65,000, the total number of immigrants (both legally and illegally resident) rose to approximately 1 million in the year 2000 (Cavounidis 2002: 48) and remains at 960,000 at present (*Agelioforos* 26 June 2005). If these estimations are correct, foreign residents currently account for almost 9 per cent of the Greek population, one of the highest immigrant population rates among the European Union (EU) member states. Compared to other member states, Greece's immigrant population displays three distinct characteristics: it overwhelmingly originates in directly neighbouring countries; it is dominated by a single ethnic group, namely Albanian citizens; and it has been involved in clandestine entry and/or residence.

Amidst a prevailing sense of crisis caused by the political and economic turbulence in the Balkans at the beginning of the 1990s and having traditionally been a country of emigration, Greece responded to extensive immigration flows by adopting a 'zero immigration' policy, a choice that remained dominant until the end of the decade. Legislation introduced in 1991[2] – granting full responsibility for managing the status and rights of aliens to the Ministry of Public Order[3] – was principally aimed at immigration control (Triandafyllidou and Veikou 2002: 202). Legal provisions, characterized as 'draconian' (Sitaropoulos 2000: 107), were directed towards controlling external borders; restricting immigration of third-country nationals of non-Greek ethnic origin;[4] safeguarding internal security; and fighting illegal immigration. Since the mid-1990s, Greek immigration policy has been slowly but steadily liberalizing, but the extent of liberalization varies across policy areas.

Due to the size of Greece's immigrant population, the country's recent experience with immigration flows and its fairly long EU membership, Greek immigration policy constitutes an interesting case for studying possible Europeanization effects, both in terms of policy output and policy-making procedures. In addition to the standard focus of most studies, namely the impact of adopted binding legislation at the EU level on national policy change, it is also possible, and indeed fascinating, to detect Europeanization effects arising from non-binding decisions or even policies in the development stage at the European level. In this chapter I carry out this task by focusing on two policy areas: admission of third-country nationals for reasons of family reunification, and asylum policy. Although falling within the realm of secondary migration, family reunification nevertheless constitutes a big part of current immigration flows to both Greece and the EU; at the same time, it also constitutes a Europeanized policy area. Asylum, on the other hand, forms a somewhat distinctive policy area, not least because of the existence of an important international refugee protection regime. Nevertheless, asylum policy has been at the forefront of the Europeanization process, making it an especially interesting policy case to explore. Finally, both policies have followed a similar pattern as to the timing of significant changes, the end of the 1990s being an important point of reference.

In my analysis, the main focus is on the EU impact on Greek immigration and asylum legislation since the beginning of the 1990s. This implies at least two conscious choices: one in favour of legislative, as opposed to administrative, policy change; and the other in favour of policy adoption instead of implementation. Regrettably, these choices entail limitations on explanatory rigour and might even obscure policy change defined in a wider way.[5] Nevertheless, legislative change provides the legitimate and authoritative foundations – even within more or less flexible limits, depending on the distinct national institutional settings – for administrative practice and implementation. Policy adoption, although it might not fully account for 'real' eventual policy change, nevertheless sets fundamental policy standards (rationale, principles, rights, obligations) on which policy implementation is expected to rely.

Family reunification

Family reunification provisions were first introduced into Greek legislation by the 1991 Basic Immigration Act,[6] although in a somewhat restrictive spirit. Third-country nationals were granted this right only after a minimum of five years of continuous legal residence. Family members of third-country nationals legally resident in Greece were provided with full access to the social security system and children were granted free access to public primary and secondary education, but working rights for spouses were restricted. Additionally, these provisions affected only a limited number of foreign workers and their families, those who could immigrate legally and continuously maintain their legal status for the period required.

Two years after entry into force of the Amsterdam Treaty (2001) and in parallel with the process of drafting legislation at the EU level, the second basic Greek law on aliens was debated and voted upon by the Greek parliament.[7] While not abandoning – and partly even strengthening – immigration control policy measures,[8] the new law passed on the responsibility for dealing with immigration issues to the Ministry of Internal Affairs and established more favourable provisions for the activation of certain important rights for third-country nationals, such as the right to family reunification. The minimum period of continuous legal residence required for the activation of this right was reduced from five to two years,[9] although a requirement to fulfil certain income and housing requirements was introduced.[10] Third-country nationals admitted on grounds of family reunification were also granted the right to work without time restrictions.[11] Legal residence was recognized to be accompanied by the entitlement to certain rights, such as the right to social security and education as well as freedom of movement and settlement within the country, the latter right granted with some restrictions on the basis of national security concerns.

The 2005 immigration law[12] went further in establishing more favourable provisions: after five years of legal residence, those admitted on the grounds of family reunification are now granted an autonomous right to residence. A special status has been introduced for third-country nationals who are family members of Greek citizens or nationals of other EU member states, which grants them a residence permit of an initial duration of five years and the right to permanent residence after five years of legal residence in Greece. Residence permits issued on grounds of family reunification also entitle their holders to the right to work.

Asylum

In timing similar to that for immigration issues, the first Greek legislative Act to regulate refugee matters was Law 1975/1991.[13] Before that law came into force, the procedure for refugee recognition was based on ministerial decisions, which nevertheless had no legal validity (Skordas 1999: 679). As a rule, refugees remained in the country until their resettlement to a third host country was possible (Skordas 2002: 211). Shortly thereafter, Greece ratified the Dublin Convention on the determination of the state responsible for the examination of asylum applications submitted in one of the EC states.[14] The provisions of Law 1975/1991 referred to the Geneva Convention and did not introduce any new substantive elements for refugee recognition (Skordas 1999: 679). Apart from providing for administrative Acts[15] and residence on humanitarian grounds,[16] the rest of the provisions[17] dealt with non-admissibility criteria, manifestly unfounded asylum claims, withdrawal of refugee status and the temporary character of residence of asylum-seekers in Greece. Admissibility criteria included the direct arrival from the country where persecution had occurred and the immediate submission of an asylum application after entering Greek territory. Manifestly unfounded asylum claims were to be rejected and their applicants subject to expulsion without a right to appeal. In exceptional circumstances and for humanitarian reasons, the Minister of Public Order could allow a rejected asylum-seeker to remain 'on tolerance' in the Greek territory, but only temporarily and until departure was made possible. This special 'humanitarian' status fell short, however, of providing protection for third-country nationals entering Greece en masse due to armed conflicts (Skordas 1999: 681). Thus, the extremely restrictive spirit of the law was made evident.

Five years later, Law 1975/1991 was amended by the framework law on refugees,[18] entailing a complete revision of procedural conditions for granting asylum (Skordas 1999: 683) but maintaining the predominantly administrative character of the Greek asylum system introduced in 1991. Along with the regular examination procedure, an accelerated procedure for examining applications submitted in ports and airports, or on manifestly unfounded grounds or from asylum-seekers entering Greece from a 'safe third reception country' was introduced.[19] Thus, the concept of 'safe third country' was for the first time incorporated into Greek legislation, although no procedure for the determination of these countries was established (Skordas 1999: 684, 690). Other innovations included the abolition of non-admissibility conditions, the introduction of provisions concerning family reunification of refugees and a special regime for temporary protection of aliens taking refuge in Greek territory in cases of *force majeure*, such as international or non-international armed conflicts (Skordas 1999: 695).

The most significant changes in Greek refugee policy regarding recognition of refugee status were introduced in 1999 by Presidential Decree 61/1999. The decree particularized the relevant provisions of the 1996 framework law on refugees (Skordas 1999: 683), by extending time limits on the procedural stages for the examination of asylum claims and the exercise of appeals against negative administrative decisions. It also included adult physically or mentally disabled children of the applicant in the definition of 'family members' covered by an asylum application.[20] Family reunification for recognized refugees was also regulated, within certain restrictive income requirements and other conditions;[21] and the duration of renewable residence permits for recognized refugees, including their family members, was increased from one to five years. The creation and appointment of a six-member administrative appeals board for review of cases of rejected asylum-seekers were characterized as a 'major leap ahead' in restoring confidence in the Greek asylum procedure (Stavropoulou 2000: 96).

A series of presidential decrees, issued on the basis of the 1996 framework law on refugees,[22] significantly enhanced the rights of third-country nationals in need of protection. Employment rights now included not only recognized refugees, but also asylum-seekers and individuals with temporary residence permits for humanitarian reasons;[23] refugee reception centres became the responsibility of the Ministry of Health and Welfare (as opposed to the previously responsible Ministry of Public Order); and the right to free medical care and hospital treatment was awarded to refugees, asylum-seekers and residents on humanitarian grounds alike.[24]

Despite legislative changes that have taken place since 1991, however, the Greek asylum system still lags behind when it comes to the status of temporary protection, reception standards of asylum-seekers and the procedure of appeal against rejections of asylum applications. Refugee social welfare in Greece has been described as rudimentary (Sitaropoulos 2000: 113), while refugee reception remains a highly problematic issue. The scope of the designated temporary protection status has not been adequately specified, and serious drawbacks exist with the provision of accommodation and subsistence means to asylum-seekers and refugees. Both non-governmental organizations and the UNHCR have stressed the lack of adequate reception standards for aliens in need of protection, allegedly due to Greek fears that improved reception and living conditions of asylum-seekers could cause an increase in the number of asylum applications (Skordas and Sitaropoulos 2004: 38, 45).

Europeanizing policy

In ways that parallel the developments in other EU member states that have recently become countries of immigration, such as Spain (Fauser, this volume), Greek immigration and asylum legislation has been developing in tandem with the development of a European immigration and asylum policy. The first Greek basic immigration Act on immigration and asylum (1991) was passed five years after the adoption of the Schengen Agreement (1986), and almost simultaneously with the adoption of the Dublin Convention (1991) and the transfer of national competence on these issues to the EU (1992).

Conditionality

The dominant argument concerning the development of immigration and asylum policy in southern European countries since the beginning of the 1990s posits that EU-level immigration policy has had a restrictive impact on national immigration policies (Freeman 1995; Baldwin-Edwards 1997, 1999; Watts 2002). Most authors cite the example of obligations derived from the Schengen arrangements as evidence for the importance of adopting policies previously formulated at the European level in order to be able to achieve the desired participation in European institutional arrangements. Becoming a party to the Schengen system meant that candidate countries had to put into force specific legal provisions concerning border controls, visa policy and the fight against clandestine immigration. In other words, Europeanization of national policies is argued to have been a precondition for joining common European institutions.

Following this argument, the Europeanization of Greek immigration policy might be seen as an issue of conditionality. The importance of EU developments in formulating Greece's first basic immigration Act was made evident during parliamentary debates prior to its adoption. The pressure to adopt and implement those policy provisions that would guarantee the 'European' character of Greek immigration legislation as well as secure Greek participation in Schengen was obvious during the 1991 parliamentary debate: most of the references made to international law and its developments at that time concerned

European treaties, and the vast majority of the latter were focused on the provisions and policy framework of the Schengen Treaty. The importance of adopting a strict border control policy and measures against illegal immigration was stressed by the Minister of Public Order, who characterized Schengen as a 'relatively hard Treaty' and predicted its adoption by more EEC member states in the future. He insisted that, despite harsh criticism from the opposition parties, Greece become a signatory in order to be able to voice its positions and play a role in any possible future modifications of the Schengen system (Greek Parliament Plenary Sessions 15/10/1991: 205). Furthermore, the Deputy Foreign Minister acknowledged that certain articles of the law to be voted upon were designed to be Schengen-adaptive, among them article 14 on family reunification of legally resident third-country nationals. She also stressed that Greece had only recently applied for observer status to the Schengen Treaty and a decision by the Schengen parties would be forthcoming on 25 October 1991, just two weeks after the anticipated adoption of the basic immigration Act in parliament (Greek Parliament Plenary Sessions 15/10/1991: 210).

The predominance of references to the Schengen provisions during the 1991 parliamentary debate supports the claims already made in the literature concerning the impact of the Schengen Treaty on the formulation and adoption of national immigration policy in Greece at the beginning of the 1990s. So also does the fact that the desire to join that treaty was used as a basis for government reasoning for adopting certain provisions of the 1991 immigration law. However, the scope of the Schengen impact on national immigration policy was restricted to the legal provisions for third-country nationals concerning entry to, and temporary residence in, Schengenland. It is, moreover, noteworthy that although Greece hoped to become a party to Schengen from the early 1990s, it managed to meet the standards required by the other Schengen parties only in 1998. Furthermore, it is worthwhile considering whether the Greeks' eagerness to adopt policy provisions agreed upon at the EEC/EU level was sustained after Greece had fully joined the process establishing a common European immigration policy.

Formal obligation

Once membership in common European institutional arrangements on immigration and asylum issues is established, a major source of EU impact on national legislation is naturally to be sought in binding legislation adopted at the EU level and incorporated into the national legal order. Such impact has gained importance especially after the

Amsterdam Treaty came into force (1999). However, the adoption of a series of EU directives on the reception of asylum-seekers, asylum procedures and exclusive competence and burden-sharing among EU member states[25] has not yet led to any legislative change in Greek asylum policy. There are three probable reasons for this state of affairs. First, as in the case of Council Directive 2004/83/EC, EU policy provisions constitute the 'lowest common denominator' of legislation among EU member states, causing a minimal 'misfit' between national and European asylum policy. Second, even where considerable 'misfit' exists, the Greek government seems to have been waiting for the 'finalization of the first major phase of European immigration and asylum legislation' (Papagianni and Naskou-Perraki 2004: 146) and the lapse of the stipulated deadlines before proceeding with legislation reform. Third, the slow-moving character of Greek bureaucracy may also explain the delay in transposing EU legislation into national law within the deadlines provided by the EU.

Serious 'misfits' can be observed in certain policy areas, specifically the status of temporary protection, standards of reception of asylum-seekers as well as judicial appeal procedures. The elaboration of a presidential decree fully transposing Council Directive 2001/55/EC on temporary protection and burden-sharing into Greek legislation has been documented (Papagianni and Naskou-Perraki 2004: 148),[26] but adaptation of Greek legislation is still pending. In the meantime, Greek legislation on temporary protection remains problematic because the necessary ministerial decision specifying the scope of the provided temporary protection status has not been issued (Skordas and Sitaropoulos 2004: 38). Concerning the reception of asylum-seekers, serious drawbacks have been documented in Greece with respect to the provision of basic social welfare, accommodation and subsistence to asylum-seekers and refugees (Skordas and Sitaropoulos 2004: 45). Since Regulation (EC) 343/2003 amending the 1990 Dublin Convention was adopted (known as 'Dublin II'),[27] these have intensified due to the increase in asylum claims triggered by implementing the regulations. Moreover, Greek legislation prohibits asylum-seekers from leaving the country before a final decision on their application has been reached[28] and allows for the interruption of the examination of their asylum applications and their detention and expulsion upon return. These provisions have been causing serious problems in cases of asylum-seekers readmitted to Greece under the 'Dublin II' provisions (UNHCR 2004).

Additionally, Greek legislation does not allow for judicial appeal against the rejection of an asylum application, save at the very last stage. This sharply contrasts with article 38 of the draft Council Directive on minimum standards for granting and withdrawing refugee status.[29] Upon its adoption, the directive is therefore expected to cause a 'profound change in the legislative framework' in Greece (Papagianni and Naskou-Perraki 2004: 150) by decreasing the extensive role and powers of the executive in favour of the judiciary.[30] Generally speaking, because of the formal obligation to adapt to EU asylum legislation, it is therefore to be expected that Europeanization of Greek asylum legislation will be intensified.

On the matter of family reunification, the relevant EU directive that could have raised the obligation to adapt Greek legislation was adopted only in 2003.[31] Bearing in mind that the Greek initial policy framework of 1991 had already been changed by the second basic immigration Act in 2001, the provisions of the latter could not be attributed to the direct impact of binding EU legislation. By contrast, a series of provisions of the 2005 immigration Act, including those on family reunification,[32] have resulted from the Greek obligation to transpose EU directives into national law and harmonize the latter with the EU legal framework. This fact has been clearly stated by the government in its introductory report on the 2005 immigration Act (Greek Ministry of Interior 2005: 2).[33]

Voluntary incorporation and framing

Even in the absence of formal obligation, however, the incorporation of EU non-binding legislation has in some cases been documented. Such was the case of PD 61/1999 on the procedure for the recognition of refugee status. Perhaps the most interesting characteristic of that decree was the explicit incorporation of EC 'soft law' on asylum policy. Article 4 introduced a new, accelerated procedure for certain categories of asylum applications,[34] establishing that the Resolutions of the Ministers of the EC responsible for immigration of 30 November–1 December 1992 should be used as guidelines concerning 'manifestly unfounded' asylum claims and 'safe third country' issues.[35]

An examination of changes made in 2001 to family reunification provisions also suggests that the hypothesis of voluntary incorporation of European policy developments deserves to be investigated. Greek immigration policy promulgated in 2001 was defended as 'fully echoing current [policy] understandings and tendencies that have been formed in the European Union' (Greek Ministry of Interior 2001: 2). During parliamentary debates, the government claimed that its legislative initiative was keeping a balance between specific, Greek domestic interests and the country's international, mostly EU, obligations. Extensive references to the gradual development of an immigration policy at the EU level, to the conclusions of the European summit at Tampere and to the formulation of EU directives were made by the Deputy Minister of Interior, in his attempt to convince the opposition parties of the necessity to take into account Greek membership in the EU while formulating the principles and provisions of Greek legislation (Greek Parliament Plenary Sessions 6/3/2001 – afternoon; 13/3/2001).

Nevertheless, despite proposals of the Scientific Committee of the Parliament (2001: 5) and of the National Committee on Human Rights (2001: 3–4), as well as the pressure exercised by the left-wing parties during parliamentary debate, the government refused to include more favourable provisions on the issue of family reunification based on the Commission proposals under discussion at the EU level at that time. Instead, the Minister of Interior argued that the government considered it more appropriate to deal with national Greek concerns, such as the legalization and registration of illegal residents. Furthermore, it was considered inappropriate for Greece to incorporate those EU-level provisions before becoming obliged to so. Responding to requests to reduce the minimum period of legal residence required to enjoy the right to family unification from two years to one, the Minister of Internal Affairs acknowledged that one year would most probably be stipulated in the relevant Council Directive to be adopted, but insisted that Greece wait for the European developments to take place first and then adjust its policy accordingly (Greek Parliament Plenary Sessions 20/3/2001: 6134; 27/3/2001: 6348).

The significant changes to the provisions on family reunification in 2001 cannot, therefore, be considered to be the result of obligations flowing from EU membership; nor, contrary to the efforts of the opposition parties, were they the result of voluntary incorporation of non-binding, EU policy provisions in progress. However, government rationales as well as opposition argumentation did rely partly on the policy developments taking place in the EU parallel to the process of Greek legislative change, thus using EU immigration policy as a frame of understanding for domestic immigration policy. In general, the importance of EU membership in shaping domestic debates on immigration is also confirmed by the fact that references to political, social and economic developments in the EEC/EU and its member states were dominant in the discussions of the international dimension of immigration in the first two major legislative initiatives (1991 and 2001).

The 'framing' dimension of Europeanization may in fact have considerable importance in the case of Greece, where European political and social developments have often been considered as synonymous with modernization. As Skordas (2002: 219) notes, the incorporation of policy objectives within the Greek 'legal order due to 'external' pressures emerging from the broader legal, societal and political environment of the EU [...] [s]eems to be a more general feature of the Greek modernization process after the restoration of democracy in 1974'. In this framework, 'fundamental changes are not always initiated within the country as strong societal demands, rather the necessity to introduce them is often "imported" from abroad'.

Investigating the counterfactual

At this point a question can be raised as to whether changes in Greek legislation, which have generally introduced more liberal provisions both in asylum and family reunification issues, can in fact be attributed to EU immigration policy. After all, we should avoid 'ascribing political and institutional changes to the impact of the EU without first being sure that it was actually the EU that drove these changes rather than domestic or other international factors. The congruence of EU developments does not make the EU a cause of all change in the member states' (Geddes 2003: 27).

A possible domestic explanatory factor, relevant for both the issue of family reunification and asylum policy, would be the shift in Greek public opinion toward third-country nationals since the beginning of the 1990s. A more positive stance towards immigration, greater public support for the enhancement of immigrant rights and the mere acceptance of long-term settlement of third-country nationals and their families in Greece could suggest that public opinion has played a role in liberalizing Greek policy. Public opinion surveys seem to run counter to this type of explanation, however. According to the Eurobarometer,[36] during the 1990s Greeks became more sceptical concerning the immigration phenomenon and displayed an increasingly negative stance towards immigrants (Table 8.1). In fact, they occupy one of the most 'immigration-sceptical' positions among the European publics. Moreover, the results of the 2003 European Social Survey reflect a profile of Greek public opinion that is the most xenophobic and least tolerant towards immigrants and foreigners in western Europe (*Eleftherotypia* 6/11/2003). A recent survey of the European Migration Observatory also confirms these findings (*Kathimerini* 18/12/2005). Rising xenophobia in Greece was one of

Table 8.1   Greek public opinion towards immigrants during the 1990s (%)

	Spring 1993	Autumn 1994	Autumn 1997
'There are too many foreigners in the country'	57	64	71
'I feel disturbed by the presence of other nationalities in the country'	28		34
'I feel disturbed by the presence of people of different race in the country'	25		31
'There should be no acceptance of economic immigrants from the southern Mediterranean'	32		29
'There should be no acceptance of economic immigrants from Eastern Europe'	31		30
'There should be no acceptance of asylum seekers'	24		24

Source: Eurobarometer Standard Reports, Nos 39, 42, 48 (Commission of the European Communities 1993, 1994, 1997).

the main concerns during parliamentary debates on immigration legislation in 2001 and it was admitted that the Greek public appeared to be the most xenophobic among the 15 EU member states (Plenary Parliamentary Debates 6/3/2001 – afternoon: 5637, 5641, 5643–4).

Given a rather hostile public opinion, the role of civil society and domestic pro-immigrant actors may have been a factor influencing the legislative process. As far as the 2001 policy changes on family reunification were concerned, the government side claimed that there was a significant impact of trade unions and non-governmental organizations promoting the rights of immigrants (interview with Th. Tsiokas,[37] 5/1/2005). Nevertheless, civil society does not seem to have played a significant role since non-governmental organizations were not yet very active in immigration issues (interview with T. Papadopoulou, 21/1/ 2005[38]). The trade unions were mostly concerned with the legalization of illegal residents and the integration of immigrant workers into the social security system (interview with P. Linardos-Rylmond,[39] 19/1/2005). Enhancing the right to family reunification was not among their top priorities. During parliamentary debates on immigration legislation in 1991 there were no hearings in which civil society organizations participated. In 2001, hearings were limited to the representatives of two organizations for the promotion of human rights, who argued for more favourable provisions concerning the rights of third-country nationals admitted on the grounds of family reunification. Their suggestion concerning the right of family members to work was indeed incorporated into the 2001 basic immigration Act. However, their claim for the reduction of the residence requirement for family reunification to one year was rejected.

The transfer of competence on immigration issues from the Ministry of Public Order to the Ministry of Internal Affairs in 2000 was a significant development for public administration. This transfer of competence, first and foremost a political choice, also meant a dominant role for the Ministry of Internal Affairs in drafting legislation. It seems plausible to argue that this development entailed a general change in approach to immigration issues and can explain, at least partially, the departure from the 'policing spirit' and the very strict provisions of the 1991 law to more favourable provisions for third-country nationals introduced in 2001.

Moreover, when new immigration legislation was being drafted in 2000 and 2001, it had already been a decade since Greece had become a country of immigration. There was a growing realization – evident during the debates in parliament among the governing party and parties of the Left – of the problems that extensive clandestine immigration, social exclusion of immigrants and the lack of appropriate legislation had caused: rising xenophobia among the local population, rising criminality rates, social alienation of immigrants and increasing corruption in public administration. Indeed, it was repeatedly argued in parliament that it was far better to have third-country nationals joined by their families for reasons of social integration and prevention of immigrant criminality. Third-country nationals admitted on grounds of family reunification were also granted the right to work without time restrictions in order to avoid their absorption into the informal employment sector (Plenary Parliamentary Debates 20/3/2001: 6/33).

It was hoped, moreover, that the legalization and greater social integration of immigrants into Greek economic and social institutions would help the survival of the ailing social security and pensions system. In contrast to the early 1990s, experience now showed that immigrants had come to Greece to stay: that was evident in the growing number of immigrant families and the number of pupils of foreign nationality in primary and secondary education. The turn to more liberal legislative provisions on family reunification adopted in 2001 can thus be explained by lessons derived from domestic experience with the immigration phenomenon throughout the 1990s, as well as by attention paid to the domestic social welfare agenda.

Unlike immigration issues, asylum issues were not subject to extensive discussion during the 1991 parliamentary debate; nor was there a detailed debate on the 1996 framework law on refugees. This significantly lower level of political interest in asylum issues has in fact been characteristic of Greek policy-making, attributable to the difference in numbers between third-country nationals seeking asylum and those entering Greece for economic reasons, and the subsequent lack of interest on the part of the Greek public and politicians in refugee matters (Sitaropoulos 2000: 107, 110; Skordas and Sitaropoulos 2004: 49). Indeed, the number of asylum applications as well as the refugee recognition rate in Greece are among the lowest of the EU member states (Sitaropoulos 2000: 106),[40] whereas the size of the (economic) immigrant population is one of the highest. Without public interest in and parliamentary debates on asylum issues, the investigation of alternative explanations of legislative changes is difficult. However, the role of domestic institutional actors, especially that of the Greek Ombudsman, seems to have been to exercise significant and growing pressure towards enhancing refugee rights. His role has been documented both in the specification of rights provided by the existing legal framework[41] and in the drafting process of legislative initiatives.[42]

Europeanizing politics

In other countries, the transfer of national competence to the European level in immigration issues is considered to have weakened the legislature's agenda-setting and policy-making powers in favour of the executive. This assumption needs further investigation in the Greek case. This concern is of special importance in the case of asylum policy: the extent to which the EU has impacted on the politics dimension is still unclear, because the process of adopting EU legislation has not yet been completed.

In the Greek political system the executive has traditionally been strong, and EU policy-making is therefore not expected to have a major impact on the domestic balance of power between government and the parliament. In the two policy areas of family reunification and asylum, the role of the executive has been strong since the first basic immigration and asylum Act in 1991. Indeed, all major legislative changes have called for the issuing of a series of presidential decrees and ministerial decisions to regulate specific issues. That has provided the executive with considerable flexibility to initiate policy changes, without having to subject them to legislative scrutiny and open parliamentary debates. This privilege notwithstanding, it might be noted that incorporating European directives in a series of important immigration and asylum policy issues through the adoption of new legislation at the national level actually opens a window of opportunity for the legislature, as long as it calls for the adoption (and open parliamentary discussion) of new legal Acts.

Still, a stronger role for the executive can be observed in the area of asylum in comparison to immigration policy. The main body of legal provisions on refugee protection has been incorporated in presidential decrees, according to both Law 1975/1991 and its amendment, Law 2452/1996. Both Acts contained only two articles on asylum, allowing for regulation of a variety of important issues – such as the procedure for refugee status recognition, refugee reception and the social rights of refugees – by a series of presidential decrees and ministerial decisions. This way, 'the Greek executive avoided providing direct statutory solutions that would be subjected to parliamentary debate and scrutiny' (Sitaropoloulos 2000: 110).

Furthermore, asylum applications and the refugee recognition procedures have remained under the sole authority of the Ministry of Public Order. This fact may indeed provide an explanation for the dominant role of the executive in formulating asylum policy, given the emphasis placed by the Ministry of Public Order on (national) security issues, which are traditionally shielded from information disclosure and extensive public debate. On the other hand, competence on immigration issues was transferred from the Ministry of Public Order to the Ministry of Internal Affairs in 2000. This transfer of competence, a significant development for immigration policy, meant a dominant role was to be played by the Ministry of Internal Affairs in drafting immigration legislation, while cooperating 'horizontally' with other ministries on a variety of issues.[43] Most of these institutions lack the 'policing spirit' of the Ministry of Public Order and instead are more prone to information disclosure, public debate and parliamentary scrutiny of their areas of interest. Even in the area of asylum policy, a significant weakening of executive powers – in this case in favour of the judiciary – is expected to take place upon adoption of the EU Directive on minimum standards for granting and withdrawing refugee status. In general, however, a more in-depth analysis of the procedural dimension of Greek immigration and asylum policy awaits the full incorporation of the recent EU directives into the Greek legal order.

The different faces of Europeanization: concluding remarks

In following the development of Greek immigration and asylum legislation since 1991, my analysis has revealed the role of Greek membership in the EU along with domestic political and institutional factors in bringing significant policy changes during the last decade. Naturally, the limited scope of this case study does not allow for generalizations. However, the analysis has shown that Europeanization may vary in its intensity, forms and effects across policy areas.

Europeanization may have different 'faces' or 'mechanisms', depending on both the timing of policy formulation and change, and the institutional characteristics of different policy areas at the domestic and at the European level. The present analysis has revealed four of these 'faces': conditionality, formal obligation, voluntary incorporation and framing. Conditionality was the predominant mechanism in the early 1990s in relation to the Schengen system and the Greek intention to join in the development of a common European immigration policy still outside the Community framework at that time. Formal obligation, entailing among other things the incorporation of EU binding legislation into the national legal order, was a significant driver of the EU impact on domestic policy once Greek membership in common European policy arrangements became reality.

Europeanization has also entailed the voluntary incorporation of EU non-binding legislation into domestic policy. Furthermore, policy developments at the European level have provided a frame for the understanding of domestic policy initiatives: this was evident in the 2001 legislation change where, despite the lack of formal obligations, open parliamentary debate nevertheless brought EU policy to the fore and used it as a framework for the argumentation on Greek immigration policy change.

Taking into account the entire period since 1991, both policy areas – family reunification and asylum – have 'absorbed' EU policy developments (Radaelli 2000: 11), albeit through different mechanisms. The European impact on family reunification policy has come about predominantly through formal obligation to adapt national legal provisions to binding EU legislation, whereas Greek asylum policy has voluntarily incorporated non-binding decisions made at the European level. Since 1999, however, Greek asylum legislation has been characterized by 'inertia' in the form of delays in transposing EU directives (Radaelli 2000: 11). It appears that different policy areas, subject to distinct domestic institutional factors, 'react' differently to European pressures for adaptation. Passing immigration policy on to the Ministry of the Interior has allowed the legislature to play a more significant role in legislative change. By contrast, resting responsibility for asylum policy with the Ministry of Public Order has maintained a restrictive policy system, prone to resisting change and maintaining the dominant powers of the executive. There, Europeanization has been up to now at the discretion of the latter. Nevertheless, adaptational pressures are high and likely to cause profound changes in Greek asylum policy. Therefore, the impact of the imminent transposition of a number of EU directives into the Greek legal order – and therefore, the extent of Europeanization especially in the case of asylum – remains to be seen.

Notes

1 I am indebted to Katerina Panourgia, head of the first section of Parliamentary Committees at the Greek parliament, for her valuable help with my research at the Parliamentary Archives in Athens. My warmest thanks go to Tatiana Papadopoulou, Theoharis Tsiokas and P. Linardos-Rylmond for their generosity in participating in interviews. Those interviewed expressed their personal opinions and their responses cannot be interpreted as official statements of any kind. I also wish to thank the editors of this volume for their helpful comments on earlier drafts, Virginie Guiraudon for her encouragement and understanding, and Georgia Papagianni for her kind help and assistance in organizing my research. The author has been conducting her PhD research at the European University Institute, Florence, as a bursar of the Greek Scholarship Authority (IKY).

2 Law 1975/1991.

3 Contrary to the situation in other EU member states, the Greek Ministry of Public Order (responsible for policing and security issues) is independent of the Ministry of Internal Affairs.

4 A part of the immigrant population consists of persons of Greek ancestry from the former Soviet republics (mainly Georgia, Armenia and Russia) and Albania. An estimated 100,000 ethnic Greeks from Albania settled in Greece in the 1990s, whereas 58,000 arrived from the former Soviet republics from 1990 to 1995 (Fakiolas 1999: 194). Their status has been regulated by a separate legal framework on their admission and residence.

5 Instead of changing national immigration legislation, immigration policy change can take the form of changing the administrative interpretation of policy principles and means provided by the existing legal framework, as was the case in Sweden during the 1970s (Hammar 1985: 279–87).

6 Law 1975/1991, article 14.

7 Law 2910/2001.

8 Law 2910/2001 was heavily criticized in parliament because of its provisions for strengthening internal immigration controls by obliging both public administration personnel and individuals in various professional

capacities to report to the police on clandestine immigrants and illegal residents.

9   Provided that the applicant possesses the adequate means for the maintenance and health insurance of the persons involved (article 28 of Law 2910/2001).

10 Law 2910/2001, article 29.

11 Law 2910/2001, article 31.

12 Law 3386/2005.

13 In fact, Law 1975/1991 was meant to amend an immigration Act dating back to 1929. For the purposes of this chapter, I therefore consider Law 1975/1991 to be the first Greek law regulating immigration issues in modern years.

14 Law 1996/1991.

15 Law 1975/1991, articles 24 and 25.

16 Law 1975/1991, article 25.

17 Law 1975/1991, article 25.

18 Law 2452/1996.

19 Law 2452/1996, article 2.

20 Upon asylum application, the term 'family of the applicant' now included the spouse, their minor children, the parents of both the applicant and his/her spouse, as well as their adult children who are unable to submit an asylum application independently, due to mental or physical inability.

21 Conditions include, *inter alia*, that the recognized refugee must show a certain, specified income and family members should be in possession of regular travel documents and visas to enter Greece (Skordas 1999: 693).

22 PD 189/1998; PD 61/1999; PD 266/1999 and PD 366/2002. The first two among them replaced presidential decrees which had been issued on the basis of the previously applicable law 1975/1991, namely PD 83/1993 on the procedure of examination of asylum applications; and PD 209/1994 on employment rights of recognized refugees.

23 PD 189/1998, replacing PD 209/1994. However, self-employment of residents under humanitarian status is not allowed (Skordas and Sitaropoulos 2004: 38).

24 PD 266/1999; PD 366/2002.

25 Council Directive 2001/55/EC 'on minimum standards for giving temporary protection in the event of a mass influx of displaced persons and on measures promoting a balance of efforts between Member States in receiving such persons and bearing the consequences thereof', *OJ 7.8.2001*; Council Directive 2003/9/EC 'laying down minimum standards for the reception of asylum seekers', *OJ 6.2.2003*; Council Directive 2004/83/EC 'on minimum standards for the qualification and status of third-country nationals or stateless persons as refugees or as persons who otherwise need international protection and the content of the protection granted', *OJ 30.9.2004*.

26 It is reported that the 'draft [Presidential Decree] incorporates the directive word for word' (Papagianni and Perraki 2004: 148).

27 Council Regulation (EC) 343/2003 'establishing the criteria and mechanisms for determining the Member State responsible for examining an asylum application lodged in one of the Member States by a third-country national', *OJ 25.2.2003*.

28 PD 61/1999, article 2.
29 Amended proposal for a Council Directive on minimum standards on procedures in Member States for granting and withdrawing refugee status, COM(2002) 326 final/2, Brussels, 03.07.2002, p. 17.
30 In 2002, the adoption of a draft presidential decree amending PD 61/1999 was called off by the Council of State on the grounds, *inter alia*, of Council Resolution of 20 June 1995, concerning minimum guarantees for the procedures of examining asylum applications (Greek Ombudsman 2003).
31 Council Directive 2003/86/EC of 22 September 2003 on the right to family reunification, *OJ L 251 03.10.2003*.
32 See articles 53–60, Law 2005.
33 In total, 32 out of 98 articles of the law served the full or partial incorporation into the Greek legal order of various Council Directives, as well as EU secondary law.
34 For applications submitted in ports and airports; for 'manifestly unfounded' asylum claims; and for applications submitted by a third-country national entering Greece from a 'safe third country'. PD 61/1999, article 4.
35 Interestingly enough, these Resolutions were not even a part of 'soft law' adopted in the framework of the third pillar provided for by the Maastricht Treaty, as the treaty entered into force in 1993.
36 Eurobarometer Reports and questionnaires are not based on the same questions over the entire period under consideration. Therefore, comparability of data becomes problematic (except from those reports that contain exactly the same questions regarding a specific issue). However, a general trend in public opinion towards foreigners in the country can be deduced. Positive statements or affirmative stance concerning the potential positive effects of the presence of non-EC/EU foreign citizens in Greece can be interpreted as a positive stance of the Greek public opinion vis-à-vis immigrants; negative statements concerning third-country nationals and the presence of residents 'different' in terms of race and nationality can be regarded as a negative stance towards immigration.
37 Mr Tsiokas is an MP elected with PASOK, which was the governing party in 2001. He was a member of the Permanent Parliamentary Committee on Internal Affairs, Public Order and Justice, and sponsor of the government's legislative initiative in parliament.
38 Mrs Papadopoulou is a Legal Adviser to the Greek Ministry of Foreign Affairs.
39 Mr Linardos-Rylmond is an analyst in the Institute of Working Issues (INE) of the General Confederation of Workers in Greece (GSEE).
40 In 2002, the refugee recognition rate reached the bottom line of 0.3 per cent (UNHCR 2003).
41 For example, such has been the case of refugee entitlement to disability benefits (Skordas 2002: 214).
42 Concerning the draft presidential decree amending PD 61/1999 on the procedures of refugee recognition, formulated in 2002, most of the suggestions made by the Greek Ombudsman (Greek Ombudsman 2002: 3–7) were incorporated into the text (Greek Ombudsman 2003).
43 Most significantly the Ministries of Foreign Affairs; Employment; Economics; Health; and Public Order.

References

Primary sources

Agelioforos [Newspaper in Greek]
Eleftherotypia [Newspaper in Greek]
Kathimerini [Newspaper in Greek]
Plenary Sessions of the Greek Parliament (in Greek): 10/10/1991, 15/10/1991, 16/10/1991, 17/10/1991, 22/10/1991, 6/3/2001, 13/3/2001, 20/3/2001, 27/3/2001.
Commission of the European Communities (1993) *Eurobarometer. Public Opinion in the European Community*. No. 39, Spring 1993. Brussels.
Commission of the European Communities (1994) *Eurobarometer. Public Opinion in the European Community*. No. 42, Autumn 1994. Brussels.
Commission of the European Communities (1997) *Eurobarometer. Public Opinion in the European Community*. No. 48, Autumsn 1997. Brussels.
Greek Ministry of Interior, Public Administration and Decentralization (2001) *Introductory Report to Draft Law on Entry and Residence of Aliens in the Greek Territory. Acquisition of Greek Citizenship through Naturalisation and Other Provisions* (in Greek), Athens. http://www.parliament.gr/ergasies/nomosxedia/EisigisiEpitropon/E-allod.pdf (last accessed on 1 June 2006).
Greek Ministry of Interior, Public Administration and Decentralization (2005) *Explanatory Report to Draft Law on 'Entry, Residence and Social Integration of Third Country Nationals in the Greek Territory'* (in Greek). Athens. http://www.parliament.gr/ergasies/nomosxedia/EisigisiEpitropon/E-IPIKOI-eis.pdf (last accessed on 1 June 2006).
Greek Ombudsman (2002) *Comments on the Draft Presidential Decree for the Modification of Provisions of Presidential Decree 61/1999 Concerning the Procedure for the Recognition of Refugee Status* (in Greek). Athens. http://www.synigoros.gr/reports/pd_16_1999.doc (last accessed on 1 June 2006).
Greek Ombudsman (2003) *Commenting on the Draft Presidential Decree for the Modification of Presidential Decree 61/99 Concerning the Procedure for the Recognition of Refugee Status* (in Greek). http://www.synigoros.gr/reports/pd_16_1999_eisagogi.doc (last accessed on 1 June 2006).
National Committee on Human Rights (2001) *Additional Comments on the Draft Law 'Entry and Residence of Aliens in the Greek Territory. Acquisition of Greek Citizenship through Naturalisation'* (in Greek), 8 January. Athens.
Scientific Committee of the Greek Parliament (2001) *Report on the Draft Law 'Entry and Residence of Aliens in the Greek Territory. Acquisition of Greek Citizenship through Naturalisation'* (in Greek). 29 January. Athens.
UNHCR (2003) *Positions of the UNHCR on Important Matters of Refugee Protection in Greece* (in Greek). Athens. http://www.unhcr.gr/download/strategy2003.htm (last accessed on 1 June 2006).
UNHCR (2004) *Note on the Access to the Asylum Procedure of the Asylum Seekers who are being Readmitted to Greece, inter alia, according to Regulations on the Determination of the Member State that is Responsible for the Examination of an Asylum Application or of the Concept of Safe Third Country*. Athens. http://www.unhcr.gr/protect/DUBLIN_ per cent20NORWAY.zip (last accessed on 1 June 2006).

Secondary sources

Baldwin-Edwards, M. (1997) 'The Emerging European Union Immigration Regime: Some Reflections on Its Implications for Southern Europe'. *Journal of Common Market Studies*, Vol. 35, No. 4: 497–519.

Baldwin-Edwards, M. (1999) 'Where Free Markets Reign. Aliens in the Twilight Zone'. *South European Society and Politics*, Vol. 3, No. 1: 1–15.

Cavounidis, J. (2002) 'Migration in Southern Europe and the Case of Greece'. *International Migration Review*, Vol. 40, No. 1: 45–70.

Fakiolas, R. (1999) 'Greece'. In S. Angenendt (ed.), *Asylum and Immigration Policies in the European Union*. Berlin: Europa Union Verlag, pp. 193–216.

Freeman G. P. (1995) 'Modes of Immigration Politics in Liberal Democratic States'. *International Migration Review*, Vol. 29, No. 4: 881–902.

Geddes, A. (2003) *The Politics of Migration and Immigration in Europe*. London: Sage.

Hammar, T. (ed.) (1985) *European Immigration Policies: a Comparative Study*. Cambridge, UK: Cambridge University Press.

Papagianni, G. and P. Naskou-Perraki (2004) 'Greece'. In I. Higgins (ed.), *Migration and Asylum Law and Policy in the European Union. FIDE 2004 National Reports*. Cambridge, UK: Cambridge University Press, pp. 135–60.

Radaelli, C. M. (2000) 'Whither Europeanization? Concept Stretching and Substantive Change'. *European Integration Online Papers*, Vol. 4, No. 8.

Sitaropoulos, N. (2000) 'Modern Greek Asylum Policy and Practice in the Context of the Relevant European Developments'. *Journal of Refugee Studies*, Vol. 13, No. 1: 105–17.

Skordas, A. (1999) 'The New Refugee Legislation in Greece'. *International Journal of Refugee Law*, Vol. 11, No. 4: 678–701.

Skordas, A. (2002) 'The Case of Recognized Refugee Families in Greece: the "Undesirable" Integration'. *WAR-Bulletin*, Vol. 4: 210–21.

Skordas, A. and N. Sitaropoulos (2004) 'Why Greece is not a Safe Host Country for Refugees'. *International Journal of Refugee Law*, Vol. 16, No. 1: 25–52.

Stavropoulou, M. (2000) 'The Practice of the Greek Appeals Board: a Major Leap Ahead'. *International Journal of Refugee Law*, Vol. 12, No. 1: 90–6.

Triandafyllidou, A. and M. Veikou (2002) 'The Hierarchy of Greekness: Ethnic and National Identity Considerations in Greek Immigration Policy'. *Ethnicities*, Vol. 2, No. 2: 189–208.

Watts, J. R. (2002) *Immigration Policy and the Challenge of Globalization: Unions and Employers in Unlikely Alliance*. Ithaca and London: Cornell University Press.

Part III

The European Impact on National Policies and Politics of Immigration – the Case of New Member States and Peripheral States

9
Advanced yet Uneven: the Europeanization of Polish Immigration Policy

Anna Kicinger, Agnieszka Weinar and Agata Górny

Introduction

The political transition of the late 1980s in Central and Eastern Europe resulted in a new geopolitical and economic European order. Along with changes in its economy and politics, a radical shift occurred in Poland's migration situation. Having once been artificially excluded from population movements during the communist era, Poland joined the European migration flows after the final liberalization of its passport law in 1990. Although still an emigration country, Poland has started to receive growing numbers of migrants, mainly from the ex-USSR, as well as transit migrants heading for the West (Koryś 2004; Okólski 1996).

Polish immigration policy, virtually non-existent in the late 1980s, has slowly moved up the legislative agenda since 1989. As immigration policy developed and took shape in the early 1990s, the process of its Europeanization started. We argue that it was its diffusion through distinctive channels, including diverse international agreements, treaties and activities, that facilitated policy transfer and policy learning (Geddes 2003; Dolowitz and Marsh 2000). Subsequently, the 1998 opening of official negotiations on Poland's accession to the European Union, and, in particular, the start of negotiations on the Justice and Home Affairs (JHA) chapter during May 2000, spurred and intensified the development of Polish immigration policy. Meanwhile, since 1998, the channels of Europeanization have fallen under the umbrella of the European Commission's actions and the EU conditionality mechanism, which now plays a decisive role in the process of policy Europeanization.

This chapter aims to demonstrate the extent to which immigration policy and politics have been Europeanized in Poland. The strong influence of Europe was felt on Polish immigration policy without question during the EU accession process. But within the various aspects of immigration policy the extent of Europeanization has varied. In our opinion, the beliefs and norms shared by Polish policy-makers and the discourse regarding Polish immigration policy are relatively well Europeanized. In contrast, the institutional side of immigration policy-making and execution, especially concerning generally accepted 'ways of doing things', seems rather resistant to European influences. The lack of lobbies and parties interested in immigration matters has allowed the policy-making process to take place behind closed doors and to remain substantively unchanged since the early 1990s.

In this chapter we begin with an analysis of the channels by which Polish immigration policy and politics were subject to Europeanization before and after 1998. In our view, the Europeanization of Polish immigration politics cannot be understood apart from these channels. We then examine Polish legislation on immigration to illustrate the scope of European influence specifically on this field. Finally, we explore the extent of the political Europeanization of immigration through an analysis of its institutional setting, Polish policy-makers' attitudes and parliamentary discourse on immigration law. The latter is also important for determining the extent of Europeanization on the level of beliefs, since parliament is the primary institution for policy-making in the Polish political system. In order to compare the degree of Europeanization in different policy subsectors, we focus on asylum policy and the introduction of a visa requirement for Ukrainian, Belarusian and Russian citizens to enter Poland. These two aspects constitute examples of, respectively, highly Europeanized and more nationally oriented areas of immigration policy.

Channels of Europeanization

The Europeanization of policy and politics is a multidimensional process. For politics to be Europeanized, a diffusion of 'soft' elements such as European (EU) norms, shared beliefs and 'ways of doing things' is necessary (see, for example, Radaelli 2003: 30). To be successful, diffusion of these elements requires fora for interaction and cooperation between European actors and agents of the Europeanizing party (see, for example, Checkel 2001). We call such occasions for interaction 'channels of Europeanization'. We argue that these channels were crucial for the Europeanization of Polish immigration politics, even though their unique importance may have diminished in 1998, when the EU conditionality mechanism took effect and implied a specific, EU-driven pattern of policy learning.

Before 1998, channels of Europeanization comprised various fora of cooperation between East and West. The first such fora were the intergovernmental meetings on security and migration within the Budapest process, initiated by the 1991 Berlin conference, on combating illegal migrations in Europe, and meetings within the Vienna process, initiated by the 1991 Vienna Conference, on population movements in Europe. These intergovernmental meetings permitted Western, Central and Eastern European countries to debate and develop solutions to their common problems of illegal migration, smuggling and trafficking, as well as to deal with such phenomena as illegal trade in arms and drugs, and international criminal networks. At the same time, cooperation on asylum was initiated in several fora, the most prominent of these being CAHAR,[1] within the Council of Europe framework, and CIREA,[2] a consultative forum of the EU. Cooperation with the UNHCR and the Helsinki Foundation was also launched in that period.

In the period after 1997, interaction between Polish and EU representatives occurred at several venues, of which the most important were the meetings during the accession preparatory phase (law screening), negotiations and twinning projects. All three were focal points of Europeanization, when Polish policy-makers were exposed to policy learning and norm diffusion mechanisms (see, for example, Finnemore 1996). The negotiations started in 1998, with preliminary law screening in the JHA chapter conducted separately.

Negotiations took place in written form, but also included meetings, albeit irregular ones, between the EU delegations and national experts. According to the Polish participants – mainly civil servants – the meetings deepened their understanding of the issues at stake on the European level. The twinning projects created opportunities for 'hands-on' policy learning. Polish policy-makers, who have participated in a number of such initiatives since 1997, generally perceived twinning projects as a tool serving two main objectives: learning by doing, and networking. The experience was highly personalized, and helped to promote policy transfer on many levels.

Interactions within virtually all the demonstrated channels of Europeanization focused on the security dimension in immigration policy. In the context of the early 1990s, the security dimension focused on a feared mass influx of persons from the East fleeing instability in the post-Soviet republics. The fear was justified, to a certain extent, by Poland's long and underprotected border with the ex-Soviet republics and its visa-free regime with those states (Anioł 1996: 18–19).

Even after 1997, although negotiations touched on a broad spectrum of immigration policies, border security was of utmost importance to the EU partners. All aspects of border security were addressed on a regular basis: inspections, controls, illegal crossings, organized crime and trafficking. Twinning projects mainly concerned border security, in keeping with the security priorities of negotiations.

Immigration policy

Turning to the West in search of solutions (1990–97)

The increase in Polish nationals' international mobility, as well as that of foreigners coming through and to Poland after 1989, placed the country in a new migration situation. As in many other policy fields, Poland turned westward for solutions on how to cope with and regulate migration. The evolving channels of cooperation during the 1990s with Western countries unquestionably impacted on the nascent Polish immigration policy; their effect has been especially visible in later changes to Polish law. It can thus be claimed that the process of Europeanization of Polish immigration policy started as early as the beginning of the 1990s through a process of learning from the West (Bulmer and Radaelli 2004) or 'policy emulation' (Cornelius and Tsuda 2004: 17–20).

The first policy changes related to asylum. Polish authorities, amazed at the influx of protection-seekers (most of whom were headed for the West and used Poland only as a transit country), were unprepared for this new phenomenon and so looked towards more experienced Western countries (Szonert 2000). Accession to the Geneva Convention on refugees in 1991, the opening of the UNHCR Liaison Office in Warsaw in 1992 and finally accession to the Convention for the Protection of Human Rights and Fundamental Freedoms (ECHR) in 1993 laid the foundations for the system of refugee protection in Poland. It is worth noting that, despite the relatively small influx of asylum-seekers, the refugee protection system was developed not only through participation in the pre-existing worldwide refugee protection system but also by joining in its European specifics as per the provisions of the ECHR.

Cooperation between Poland and its Western neighbours in the field of migration was fostered by signing the readmission agreement in March 1991 between Poland and the Schengen group of countries, and was then broadened with the special bilateral agreement between Poland and Germany signed in Bonn in May 1993. According to the agreements, the Schengen countries dropped the visa requirements for Polish nationals; however, Poland became obliged to take back its nationals as well as third-country nationals who had illegally entered Schengen territory via Poland. By signing readmission agreements, Poland became charged with cordoning off Western countries while having to transform itself quickly from a refugee-sending or transit country to a refugee-accepting one (Lavenex 1998: 282). On the other hand, through enhanced cooperation with Germany and significant German investment in the Polish border infrastructure, Poland prepared itself to become a gatekeeper of the eastern EU border (Anioł 1996: 41–2).

The post-1989 intensification of immigration flows forced changes in the Polish law on migration. The 'old' Act on Aliens of 1963,[3] created during the communist era when foreigners were rather an exotic phenomenon, did not correspond to the reality of the 1990s. The 1963 law had many loopholes and was created more to keep track of foreigners than manage migration flows (Łodziński 1998). The first changes after 1990,[4] primarily the incorporation of the institution of refugee status into Polish legislation and improving the non-functioning deportation system, proved to be only the beginning of the changes that would have to be made given the new migration reality. Work on a new law started in 1995, one year after the Polish Minister of Foreign Affairs lodged an application for the country's membership in the EU, and culminated with a new Act on Aliens, which passed into law in June 1997.[5] The law represented a mixture of EU-inspired solutions and emerging Polish interests in the field of migration, which were focused on security issues at that time. As aptly summarized by Łodziński (1998), the new law enabled the state authorities to improve their control of the flow of foreigners and limit the influx of undesired foreigners to Poland.[6] The changes that were obviously influenced by Western regulations included the temporary residence permit, popular in Western countries but previously non-existent in Polish law, and provisions regarding the responsibility of sea and air carriers for the passengers they transport.

Issues of asylum were the ones most inspired by European influences in their legislative treatment. New additions to Polish law included the 'safe third country' and 'safe country of origin' concepts as well as those of 'manifestly unfounded application' and 'accelerated procedure'.[7] It is worth noting that although the influx of asylum-seekers into Poland appears almost negligible compared to the skyrocketing numbers of asylum applications in Western countries, the new law introduced concepts and institutions that had previously been applied with success by EU countries in their battle against the so-called asylum crisis (Loescher 1989) and which appeared on the agenda of emerging EU cooperation in the field.

It should be noted that, concurrently with the parliament's work on the new Act on Aliens, work on a new national constitution was under way, which was to result in the Constitution of 2 April 1997.[8] The Constitution encompassed some provisions relating to migration issues – such as the right to leave the country (art. 52.2), the right to asylum and refugee status with reference to the Polish law and international agreements (art. 56), the basic rules regarding acquisition of Polish citizenship (art. 34), the right to settle in Poland for persons of Polish origin (art. 52.5) – and affirmed the close ties with the Polish diaspora abroad (art. 6). The constitutional provisions as outlined could serve as a basis for further elaboration of a migration doctrine in Poland (see also IPSS 2004).

In summary, in 1999 when the Treaty of Amsterdam came into force, Poland already had a new law and some basic principles regarding migration, as specified in the 1997 Constitution. Poland had also benefited from valuable experience in cooperating with Western countries in various EU and non-EU fora in the field of migration and asylum. However, apart from evident European influences, some items representing strictly Polish interests (for example, the repatriation of ethnic Poles living in post-Soviet republics) also found their place on the developing Polish immigration policy agenda.

Following the moving target of the EU acquis (1998–2004)

The framework guiding the development of Polish immigration policy was definitely narrower after 1997, when negotiations between Poland and the EU officially started. The 'accession conditionality levers of the Union' (Grabbe 2002) had the strongest influence on the shaping of Polish immigration policy in this period. The negotiations on the JHA chapter, which started in 2000, prompted the concurrent drafting of an amendment to the Polish Act on Aliens, which took place in 2000–1. The driving force for change in the work on the amendment came from the requirements for European integration, and from the repeated appeals in every European Commission report to enhance the protection of the eastern border and toughen entry rules (see Iglicka et al. 2003: 18). It is worth noting that the JHA chapter, relating directly to security issues, was not subject to any transition periods or any substantive negotiations because Poland's future role as an EU gatekeeper made the issue of borders and immigration not only a matter of technical standards, but also unavoidably an issue of politics and perception (Piórko and Sie Dhian Ho 2003: 180).

The 2001 amendment of the Act on Aliens[9] brought many important changes to Polish migration law. Some new, Western- and EU-inspired, institutions were introduced; these included the 'marriage of convenience' concept, along with regulations aiming to combat this practice, and the institution of temporary protection, previously non-existent in Polish law. The latter institution had its origins in Poland's experiences, and those of other European countries, with the influx of people fleeing the wars of former Yugoslavia (Koser and Black 1999).[10] Similarly, the regulations on family reunification introduced by the amendment were consistent with Western standards and EU discussions on its family reunification directive.[11]

Other important changes brought about by the 2001 amendment included the change in the definitions of 'safe third country' and 'safe country of origin', which took into consideration not only the formal participation of a given country in international instruments for human rights protection but also the actual state of affairs. Furthermore, conditions for a residency permit were changed; new ways to ascertain and control the legality of foreigners' presence on Polish soil were introduced, and a new administrative tool – the obligation to leave the territory of Poland – was introduced to supplement expulsion orders.

All in all, in contrast to the law of 1997, the 2001 amendment was created under much more of a European influence, and this influence was strikingly evident. However, it has been aptly observed by, for example, Ewa Kępińska and Dariusz Stola, that 'adopting the EU *acquis* turned out to be similar to following the moving target' (2004: 164). The constant evolution of EU law meant having to amend Polish legislation frequently and to adopt new EU measures in various fields, including migration and asylum. The successful conclusion to the negotiations in December 2002 and the signing of the Treaty on Accession (April 2003) did not bring to a close the harmonization process of Polish law with binding (and sometimes non-binding) EU measures.

The following year, 2003, brought two new Acts: a new Act on Aliens[12] and the Act on Granting Protection to Aliens within the Territory of the Republic of Poland,[13] both of which were passed in

June 2003. The distinction between all forms of humanitarian migration and general provisions on aliens was new to Polish law, but brought it into line with practices in many European countries. The newly introduced Act on Aliens was detailed and highly elaborate, especially on such matters as the rules on border crossing, on the issuance of visas, residence permits and Polish travel or identity documents to foreigners, on keeping foreigners in guarded detention centres or under arrest, on registering and tracking foreigners and so on. Generally, there were no radical innovations to Polish legislation this time with regard to the immigration policy; instead, the Act polished and refined the already established institutions and procedures and further adjusted them to the EU *acquis* for the forthcoming EU accession, with its special focus on the Schengen *acquis* (visa issuance and a uniform format for visas and residence permits).

The Act on Granting Protection to Aliens within the Territory of the Republic of Poland combined the four forms of protection that could be granted to foreigners in Poland, that is, refugee status based on Geneva Convention provisions, asylum, temporary protection and legal residence permits. The latter form was an innovation in Polish legislation, introduced to offer basic protection to asylum-seekers not meeting the Geneva Convention criteria, whose expulsion to their country of origin would be impossible for humanitarian reasons. Special treatment within the asylum procedure was provided for unaccompanied minors, for aliens whose psychophysical state suggests that they have been victims of violence and for aliens with disabilities, in line with the European directive on minimum standards for asylum-seekers.[14] The provisions on temporary protection were also developed further in order to be consistent with the EU directive on minimum standards when granting temporary protection.[15]

These changes to immigration policy, supported by EU legislation and influenced by the accession incentive, were introduced relatively smoothly. In contrast, the requirement to introduce visas to Poland for citizens of Ukraine, Belarus and Russia brought some resistance from Polish stakeholders. In this matter, Polish and EU interests obviously diverged. The visa-free regime with these countries, as a vestige of the former 'ties of socialist brotherhood', had been left in force in the new, post-1989 era. This proved to be one of the most important immigration policy decisions for Poland in terms of its effects on migration flows.[16] Such a step was in accordance with Polish foreign policy interests, which included supporting democratic and market economy changes for Poland's eastern neighbours in order to achieve a stable and predictable geopolitical order in the region. Facilitating contacts between Polish citizens and citizens of countries in the east was seen, from the beginning, as a way to achieve such goals. The maintenance of the visa-free regime for citizens of Ukraine, Belarus and Russia proved to be the most visible sign of Poland's commitment to the 'close contacts' principle in its foreign policy towards post-Soviet East European countries.

The common EU visa regime, with Russia, Belarus and Ukraine on the visa-countries list[17] (meaning these countries' citizens required visas), was thus at odds with the principles, goals and broad interests of Poland's foreign policy. The introduction of the visa requirement for citizens of these countries was therefore put off as long as possible. Even after the introduction of the visa requirement, movement across the Polish eastern border has not noticeably lessened because visas are issued fast and efficiently. The liberal issuing of regular visas and no-fee tourist visas for Ukrainian nationals illustrates one example of securing Polish interests on the one hand while fulfilling Poland's obligations as an EU member on the other. Furthermore, in preparation for entrance into the Schengen area and the specific Schengen visa regime, Poland, along with other new member states, supported the Commission's initiative to establish a separate regime governing local border traffic at the external borders of the member states (European Commission 2003), a proposal that is still under consideration in the EU.

In the lead-up to EU accession on 1 May 2004, the Polish migration law had undergone frequent alterations in order to keep pace with the EU *acquis* in the field. The extent of European influences on changes to Polish immigration policy has been considerable since the early 1990s, and especially powerful after 1997, when negotiations on EU accession were launched, negotiations which also served as the primary channel for Europeanizing Polish immigration policy. Poland's accession to the EU did not bring those legislative processes to a halt. Yet another amendment to the Act on Aliens took place in April 2005,[18] so we can observe that the Europeanization of Polish migration law is continuing. Preparations for participation in the Schengen area are now the main driving forces of change, now that Poland belongs to the EU.

Europeanization of Polish politics of immigration

Institutional setting and stakeholders

The institutional framework of immigration policy-making in Poland has not changed in substance for more than 15 years. Since the beginning of the 1990s, the core of the policy-making team has remained the same. This relatively small group of policy actors, based in the Ministry of the Interior, was involved in the construction of Polish immigration policy and in interaction with EU institutions in the whole pre-accession period, before 1998 and after.

Since the early 1990s, immigration policy has been crafted according to a distinctive procedure. The process starts with a first draft written by civil servants involved in the policy area, who must accommodate external constraints and address Polish reality. Before 1998, these policy-makers relied on legislative examples from other European countries. Since 1997, the *acquis* has been the major point of reference in the policy-making process, involving a rigorous adoption of EU regulations or their adaptation to the Polish situation. After the drafting stage, interinstitutional discussion over the proposed measures takes place among the Border Guard service, the police forces, the respective ministries and, as of 1995, the UNHCR and the Helsinki Foundation. The latter two organizations became active in the field of asylum policies in Poland in the early 1990s. Their presence had a strong impact on the implementation of the first provisions, especially when the representatives of the UNHCR or the Helsinki Foundation lodged appeals against the relevant measures at the National Administrative Court. Thus, since 1995 the two organizations have been regularly invited to participate in the actual drafting of immigration-related laws.

The majority of sensitive issues are thus usually discussed and agreed upon prior to the parliamentary stage, and therefore beyond democratic scrutiny. Policy proposals reach the two houses of parliament only in the last stage of development, and there is thus no opportunity for a decisive impact on their creation. The whole procedure stands in clear contrast to the European-level ways of doing things, where decisions concerning immigration laws involve a broad spectrum of lobbyists, social groups and interested politicians.

Since 2001, the Office for Repatriation and Aliens (ORA) has been the main affiliation of the immigration policy-making team. The ORA was created at the suggestion of EU experts, and drew its staff from the Ministry of the Interior's migration and asylum department. It is now the central governmental organ responsible for all matters related to migration policy in Poland, and indeed the only institutional development in this field. It should be noted, however, that the mere existence of ORA has not brought any substantial changes in the make-up of the team of civil servants dealing with legislation on migration, nor has it decisively influenced how immigration policy is made. The same staff continues work in the same building on the same matters, following the same pre-ORA institutional rules. All in all, in Poland, the institutional setting, the generally accepted 'ways of doing things' and the policy-making process all remain largely unchanged since before 1998. Europeanization in this area can therefore be considered rather limited.

Policy-makers' attitudes towards immigration policy formation[19]

In the pre-accession period, Poland was under a time constraint to shape its policy. Moreover, Poland was in a relatively weak position vis-à-vis its EU partners to shape policy according to domestic needs. What was rather an ad hoc response at the beginning evolved into a more steady realization of an objective within the broader perspective of EU accession. The transfer of legal and procedural regulations has been successful; we can also discern the Europeanization of norms concerning the politics of migration, that is the beliefs and ideas about immigration policy implicit in political behaviour, culture and discourse. Interviews with the key immigration policy-making stakeholders in Poland demonstrate that Polish policy-makers grew increasingly aware, through their various interactions in the channels of Europeanization, of the complexities of immigration policy. They also understood that, although their attention was drawn mainly to border security, they need to consider immigration policy in a broader context of economic and demographic planning (I.13).[20]

Having observed Western policy models and tracking problems and their solutions for more than a decade, the Polish elites became aware of the dilemma underlying the immigration issue: 'If Poland were a country where there are tens of thousands [of immigrants] accepted every year, if there were some racial crimes, as in London, or entire sections of cities taken, as it is in Paris... well, in Poland it is a marginal issue' (I.2). The interviewees realize that long-term immigration can become a social and political problem, so they opt for rather restrictive policy choices, relying on Europe-wide shared beliefs. That such a restrictive attitude prevails puzzles many: 'I can understand that German policy makers are xenophobic, with 90,000 asylum-seekers per year, but I cannot understand why Polish policy makers should be xenophobic with merely 5000' (I.7). The above statement, uttered by one UNHCR employee, reflects how people from outside the administrative process are baffled that immigration is perceived as a policy problem in a country with insignificant immigration flows. The fears of the policy-makers obviously echo the EU-level securitization of immigration policy (Huysmans 2000).

This European influence notwithstanding, there have been two important beliefs defining Polish politics of immigration, which suggest there is a limit to the Europeanization of migration politics. First, there is a clear discursive division of 'us vs them', which reflects the idea that immigration policy is a problem of EU-rope but not of Poland (yet); second, Polish migration policy is conceptualized as a problem of the future. The first belief above, an 'us vs them' dichotomy, derives from Poland's idiosyncratic policy-making reality, in which immigration is completely depoliticized, in sharp contrast to the EU-15. To slow down the negative consequences of immigration, such as exclusion, marginalization, racism and xenophobia, Polish elites try to maintain the status quo, to prevent the crises unfolding elsewhere from taking place in Poland. There is a well-grounded fear that, as the influx increases, the attitudes of society and politicians may radicalize (I.13, I.10, I.16). 'We have it all in miniature. And we have to answer the question of what we should allow in the future. Because the phenomena in miniature are manageable. Any greater process is unlikely to be managed' (I.13). The key to keeping the issue non-political is keeping the numbers low. Almost all interviewees ascribed immigration policy's apolitical nature to the limited influx: 'It [immigration policy] is not used politically because we are still a country where this problem is rather small, numerically, compared with the Western Europe ...' (I.5). This objective – avoiding the stirring up of social unrest – influences the way policy is created. This style of immigration policy-making is no longer plausible in the EU-15, as immigration there has long since become a political issue.

The second belief, namely the idea that immigration is more a problem of the future than of the present, is expressed through immigration policy planning. Europeanization is clearly visible in the interviewees' assessments of the impact of European integration on Polish immigration policy. In their view, EU membership fosters the adoption of attitudes towards immigration policy similar to those that are present in other member states. Moreover, for them EU membership means growing volumes of flows, and increasing difficulties of control (I.13, I.16). Immigration is viewed as an irreversible consequence of democratization, capitalism and European integration, and thus part of Poland's inevitable future. Polish policy-makers are aware of this: 'When we are in the EU, we should know what our expectations are, what our share will be, what Poland wants to have here, what is our immigration policy' (I.13).

While it may seem that Europeanization of the beliefs and attitudes of Polish policy-makers has been significant, immigration is still not perceived as a political issue or as a present-day social problem. Therefore, the change of attitudes has not yet been translated into action.

Parliamentary debates on immigration laws, 1997–2003[21]

Since immigration has not yet become politicized in Poland, parliamentarians have a very limited interest in the issue:

> Apart from this very limited circle of people who have to get familiar with this field, because they give speeches on behalf of the parliamentary caucuses, there is no one who can spare his or her time to think about it. Of course, the MPs are worried about the borders, about jobs, they are a little bit scared of terrorists, but the general attitude is rather superstitious – better not to talk about it so that it will not come to us. (I.4)

During the period in question, the discussants did not argue much over immigration laws, and the only debatable issues were usually those related to the legal provisions for asylum and the visa regime. These two instances constitute special cases in the parliamentary debates on immigration policy in Poland, the first one for its deep Europeanization, the second – for the resistance to it.

The legitimizing use of 'Europe'

In the Polish debate on national immigration policy, the concept of 'Europe' was widely used. The terms 'Europe' and 'European' were used both by the author-bureaucrats of the Act on Aliens, and by the MPs presenting the standpoints of the parliamentary caucuses. The main term popping up in the debate was 'Europeanness', used in the parliamentary proceedings on the Aliens Acts and their amendments. It appeared in the discourse in many forms, quite often used interchangeably for the EU or Council of Europe, especially in the years preceding negotiations.

EU membership became a categorical imperative, which forestalled any discussion from the start. Disputants would justify new laws by referring to European standards. Consistency with EU norms, or with norms prevailing in the member states, was thus a crucial indicator of the value of each of the Acts. This dimension was often highly symbolic; the disputants would recall the years of communist seclusion and the difficult path of returning to normality, symbolized by the

European Community. Here, Europeanization meant precisely the modernization of the state system. Arguments were Eurocentric; for example, particular policy choices were legitimized by the authority of EU experts, even when they contradicted the opinions of domestic experts. The most controversial issues presented by the independent experts were also justified by the *acquis communautaire* requirements.

Another approach was the revisualization of Europe according to the geography of the Schengen area. In this revisualization, Poland would take on the role of the gatekeeper of the EU. It seems that this role was particularly well verbalized by the authors of the regulations. Consequently, the debate focused on the duty of Poland, as a candidate country and a future member state, towards the Western European countries. The historical role of Poland as gatekeeper of Christendom was often even evoked to justify the new, restrictive measures.

Two dimensions of Europeanization

The question of asylum has represented one example of the extensive use of 'Europe' as a norm in all the above-mentioned dimensions. Since asylum-seekers were a relatively small group in Poland, the legitimization of the adopted provisions reflected the Europeanization of the politics on the issue, mainly because there was no discourse originating in the domestic arena with which to compete. Moreover, its development over the years reflected shifts in 'European' attitudes among the stakeholders. In the mid-1990s, Poland's policy towards asylum-seekers was rather restrictive and so its critics often evoked 'Europe' as the symbol of modernization of the Polish laws (especially in terms of human rights). In the later stages of negotiations and after accession, as the EC started promoting more exclusive asylum laws, the restrictionists would use 'Europe' to justify policy choices. Discussion on migration policy ran parallel to the shift on how and where the Polish government saw itself at the EU level (I.15). The debates resulted in a redefinition of the Polish reason of state, most fully expressed in the opinion that Poland should care about the common interest of the enlarged Union. This reflected the new geopolitical situation of Poland and its role as EU gatekeeper.

The enactment of a visa regime was discussed in a different framework. The matter was highly politicized in Poland, as the introduction of the regime would hurt cross-border commerce and family relations. Apart from the political, social and economic reasons, visas were poorly regarded for very emotional reasons – for many MPs, they were reminiscent of the situation of Polish nationals attempting to enter the

USA or Canada. Visas were believed by some to be a sign of disrespect for their bearers. In such circumstances, it was impossible for Polish policy-makers or any other domestic force, if there had been any, to focus attention on the security benefits, which were the dominant issue concerning visas in the EU-15. It seemed that the visa regime, unlike the asylum laws, economically and emotionally touched a nerve and the EU request ran contrary to Polish national preferences. Thus the introduction of visas was mainly presented as a necessary evil: Poland had to accept the visa regime for the sake of accession, but it should soften its consequences. Visas were legitimized by the mention of the EU conditionality.

Conclusions: explaining the extent of Europeanization

According to Geddes, 'policy in the Central and Eastern European Countries has arisen almost entirely as a result of the requirements of EU accession and [...] EU policy models and ideas about borders, security and insecurity have been exported to CEE countries' (Geddes 2003: 173). It certainly cannot be denied that, especially since 1998, the crucial (although not the sole) factor influencing Polish immigration law was the process of integration with the EU. Consequently, the extent of the Europeanization of Polish immigration policy and law is substantial – witness the full adoption of EU measures, policies and standards in the field of migration and asylum. In our opinion, there were two factors that favoured Europeanization of immigration policy in Poland and can explain the degree to which it has embedded itself.

First, since 1990, Polish immigration policy has been constantly under construction within a changing environment where immigration is concerned. The European influences happened to match, to a greater or lesser extent, the institutions, regulations and practices that were being created. Generally speaking, the extent of Europeanization in immigration policy was large, as the entire policy was developed almost from scratch, first by looking to the West and later by adjusting to the EU *acquis*. The second important factor was the nature of the negotiations on accession, in which Poland as a candidate country was in an obviously weaker position. The process of enlargement and negotiations on the accession 'represented a colossal exercise in policy transfer' (Bulmer and Radaelli 2004: 2), in which the EU conditionality mechanism was decisive. The fact that EU accession was the strategic goal for Poland and other aspiring countries limited the scope of possible resistance against the EU *acquis*, especially since candidate countries had little if no opportunity to influence the JHA requirements before accession.

Europeanization of the politics of immigration has been clearly observed in policy-makers' attitudes and discourse on immigration. It seems that the perception of uncontrolled immigration as a threat and the 'fortress Europe' approach have been effectively transferred to Poland despite its small numbers of immigrants. Furthermore, 'Europe' was frequently cited in discussions on Polish immigration policy in the 2000s and became an inherent element of the debates, occasionally used forcefully to justify some unpopular legal solutions. However, the extent of Europeanization, at least in public and political discourse, varies depending on the subcategory of immigration policy. Polish asylum policy, which echoes EU provisions and concern for human rights, is relatively highly Europeanized. Visa policy, on the other hand, although adopted from the EU, was shaped to accommodate Polish interests pertaining to the countries lying east of its border. There are no signs that Polish policy-makers share their Western counterparts' attitude towards the visa regime – in Poland it is clearly construed as 'not our policy'. The institutional dimension of the politics of immigration matters have proved to be rather resistant to Europeanization, in our view. The formation of the ORA – perceived as an important EU-driven institutional change – did not result, in fact, in any substantive changes in practices relating to developing immigration policy. Moreover, in contrast to the EU-15 countries, there are very few lobbies and parties interested in immigration in Poland.

Overall, immigration policy is highly Europeanized in Poland and in this respect we can talk about the breadth of its transformation (see, for example, Radaelli 2003), whereas in the politics of immigration we can observe diversity in the extent of Europeanization. The sphere of beliefs, norms and attitudes and as well as the discourse itself seem to be under strong European influence. It can be argued, however, that the extent of Europeanization of these aspects of politics has not been tested in practice. Immigration to Poland is still relatively low and policy-makers perceive the problem of immigration as a future issue, in contrast to the EU-15 where immigration has been topical for some time. There is only minor interest in immigration matters in Poland among social and political actors and no crucial changes in the nature of a policy-making process have been observed in the field.

Appendix I

List of interviews by the interviewee's affiliation

I.1 Ministry of Internal Affairs and Administration
I.2 Parliamentary Commission on Internal Affairs and Administration
I.3 Parliamentary Commission on Internal Affairs and Administration
I.4 Parliamentary Commission on Internal Affairs and Administration
I.5 Helsinki Foundation
I.6 Office of the Committee for European Integration, negotiating team
I.7 UNHCR
I.8 Border Guard Service
1.9 Border Guard Service
I.10 Refugee Council
I.11 Office of the Committee for European Integration, negotiating team
I.12 Office of the Committee for European Integration, negotiating team
I.13 Office for Repatriation and Aliens
I.14 UNHCR
I.15 Helsinki Foundation
I.16 Office for Repatriation and Aliens
I.17 Office for Repatriation and Aliens

Notes

1 Ad Hoc Committee of Experts on the Legal Aspects of Territorial Asylum, Refugees and Stateless Persons.
2 Centre for Information, Reflection and Exchange on Asylum Matters.
3 *Dziennik Ustaw (Dz.U.)* [Journal of Laws] 1963, No. 15, item 77. Changed in 1974, 1977 and 1983.
4 *Dz.U.* 1991, No. 119, item 513.
5 *Dz.U.* 1997, No. 114, item 739.
6 The Act specified and toughened the conditions of entry of foreigners to Poland (the obligation to possess sufficient means to cover the cost of stay in Poland was a new one). Additionally, the Act added new criteria related to state security as grounds for refusal or invalidation of a visa or temporary residence permit or an expulsion order (danger to state security, public health, well-founded suspicion of terrorism, suspicion of taking part in smuggling or human trafficking, etc.).
7 It is worth noting that all these issues were the subject of 'soft' EU regulations at that time. See the Resolution of 30 November 1992 on manifestly unfounded applications for asylum; Resolution of 30 November 1992 on a harmonized approach to questions concerning host third countries;

Resolution of 30 November 1992 on countries where there is no general risk of prosecution; and Council Resolution of 20 June 1995 on minimum guarantees for asylum procedures, *OJ C 274 19.09.1996*.

8   *Dz.U.* 1997, No. 78, item 483.

9   *Dz.U.* 2001, No. 42, item 475.

10   The regulations were inspired by these events and experiences; however, the EU directive on the matter was agreed upon later that year. See the Council Directive 2001/55/EC of 20 July 2001, *OJ L 212 7.08.2001*.

11   The first proposal for the Council Directive on family reunification for third-country nationals was presented as early as December 1999 by the Commission. The divergence of states' positions on this matter resulted in prolonged negotiations and the directive was not agreed upon until September 2003.

12   *Dz.U.* 2003, No. 128, item 1175.

13   *Dz.U.* 2003, No. 128, item 1176.

14   Council Directive 2003/9/EC of 27 January 2003; *OJ L 31 6.02.2003*.

15   Council Directive 2001/55/EC of 21 July 2001; *OJ L 212 7.08.2001*.

16   Citizens of these countries, especially of Ukraine, who were staying in Poland numbered between 100,000 and 500,000, according to various sources. The vast majority find illegal seasonal employment in Poland in agriculture, domestic services, child care and construction, filling significant gaps in the Polish labour market. Moreover, the borderlands shared by Poland and its eastern neighbours used to be very closely tied economically by various petty trade links.

17   Council Regulation (EC) No. 539/2001 of 15 March 2001, *OJ L 81 21.03.2001*.

18   *Dz.U.* 2005, No. 94, item 788.

19   The analysis of attitudes of immigration policy-making stakeholders is based on 17 semi-structured expert interviews conducted in 2002–3 with key actors involved in developing immigration policy in Poland during the period discussed. In this chapter, we present only fragments of the analysis of this material. For more, see Weinar (forthcoming).

20   The bracketed number following citation of an interview refers to the interviewee's affiliation. The various affiliations are listed in Appendix I at the end of the chapter.

21   The process of legitimization of the proposed legal solutions. As concerns the field of migration, based on parliamentary proceedings of the Act on Aliens 1997 (*Dz.U.* 1997, No. 114, item 739), the amended Act on Aliens of 2001 (*Dz.U.* 2001, No. 42, item 475), the Act on Aliens of 2003 (*Dz.U.* 2003, No. 128, item 1175) and the Act on Granting Protection to Aliens within the Territory of the Republic of Poland of 2003 (*Dz.U.* 2003, No. 128, item 1176).

References

Anioł, W. (1996) *Poland's Migration and Ethnic Policies: European and German Influences*. Warsaw: Friedrich Ebert Stiftung.

Bulmer S. J. and C. M. Radaelli (2004) 'The Europeanisation of National Policy?' *Queen's Papers on Europeanisation*, Vol. 1.

Checkel, J. T. (2001) 'The Europeanization of Citizenship?'. In M. Caporaso, T. Cowles and T. Risse (eds), *Transforming Europe: Europeanization and Domestic Change*. Ithaca, NY: Cornell University Press, pp. 180–97.

Cornelius W. A. and T. Tsuda (2004). 'Controlling Immigration: Limits of Government Intervention'. In W. A. Cornelius, T. Tsuda, P. L. Martin and J. Hollifield (eds), *Controlling Immigration: a Global Perspective*. Stanford, Calif.: Stanford University Press, pp. 3–48.

Dolowitz, D. and D. Marsh (2000) 'Learning from Abroad: the Role of Policy Transfer in Contemporary Policy-Making'. *Governance: an International Journal of Policy and Administration*, Vol. 13, No. 1: 5–24.

European Commission (2003) *Proposal for a Council Regulation on the Establishment of a Regime of Local Border Traffic at the External Land Borders of the Member States*, COM 502 final.

Finnemore, M. (1996) 'Norms, Culture and World Politics: Insights from Sociology's Institutionalism'. *International Organization*, Vol. 50, No. 2: 309–33.

Geddes, A. (2003) *The Politics of Migration and Immigration in Europe*. London, Thousand Oaks, New Delhi: Sage Publications.

Grabbe, H. (2002) 'European Union Conditionality and the *Acquis* Communautaire'. *International Political Science Review*, Vol. 23, No. 3: 249–68.

Huysmans, J. (2000) 'The European Union and the Securitization of Migration'. *Journal of Common Market Studies*, Vol. 38, No. 5: 751–77.

Iglicka, K., P. Kaźmierkiewicz and M. Mazur-Rafał. (2003) *Managing Immigration. The Case and Experience of Poland in the Context of Relevant Directives of the European Commission*. Report for the Migration Policy Group in Brussels.

IPSS (2004) *Raport w sprawie polityki migracyjnej państwa* [Report on the state's migration policy]. Warsaw: IPSS.

Kępińska E. and D. Stola (2004) 'Migration Policy and Politics in Poland'. In A. Górny and P. Ruspini, *Migration in the New Europe: East–West Revisited*. Houndmills, Basingstoke, Hampshire: Palgrave Macmillan, pp. 159–76.

Koryś I. (2004) *Migration Trends in Selected EU Applicant Countries*. Vol. III: *Poland. Dilemmas of a Sending and Receiving Country*. Vienna: International Organization for Migration.

Koser K. and R. Black (1999) 'Limits to Harmonization: the "Temporary Protection" of Refugees in the European Union'. *International Migration*, Vol. 37, No. 3: 521–43.

Lavenex S. (1998) 'Asylum, Immigration, and Central-Eastern Europe: Challenges to EU Enlargement'. *European Foreign Affairs Review*, Vol. 3: 275–94.

Łodziński, S. (1998) *Problemy polityki migracyjnej Polski w latach 1989–1998 (czerwiec) a nowa ustawa o cudzoziemcach* [Problems of the Polish Migration Policy 1989–1998 and the New Law on Aliens]. Report No. 47. Warsaw: Biuro Studiów i Ekspertyz Sejmu RP.

Loescher G. (1989) 'The European Community and Refugees'. *International Affairs*, Vol. 4: 617–36.

Okólski M. (1996) 'Recent Trends in International Migration. Poland 1996'. ISS Working Papers, Migration Series, Vol. 16. Warsaw: Institute for Social Studies, Warsaw University.

Piórko I. and M. Sie Dhian Ho (2003) 'Integrating Poland in the Area of Freedom, Security and Justice'. *European Journal of Migration and Law*, Vol. 5: 175–99.

Radaelli, C. M. (2003) 'The Europeanization of Public Policy'. In K. Featherstone and C. M. Radaelli (eds), *The Politics of Europeanization*. Oxford: Oxford University Press, pp. 27–56.

Szonert M. (2000) 'Rok 1990 – początki opieki nad uchodźcami' ['The year 1990 – the beginning of refugee protection']. In J. E. Zamoyski, *Migracje polityczne XX wieku* [Politically Motivated Migration of the 20th Century]. Warsaw: Wydział Geografii i Studiów Regionalnych UW, pp. 35–64.

Weinar, A. (forthcoming) *Europeizacja polskiej polityki wobec cudzoziemców* [The Europeanization of Polish Policy on Foreigners]. Warsaw: Scholar.

10
EU-ization matters: Changes in Immigration and Asylum Practices in Turkey

Ahmet İçduygu

Introduction

Turkey's transformation over the course of the last two decades into a land of immigration is one of the most significant features of its recent history and very much an issue of debate in the European Union (EU). As Turkey has been increasingly confronted with large-scale immigration and asylum flows, this relatively new migration phenomenon has had a number of social, economic and political implications, not only for the country, but also in the wider context of Europe (İçduygu 2004: 93; 2003: 7; Kirişçi 2002: 7–10). In particular, the EU's Helsinki decisions of December 1999, which declared the candidacy of Turkey to the EU membership, brought forward new questions and concerns in the area of immigration policies and practices in Turkey. One of the most widely debated issues in this context is the 'management of migration and asylum flows' arriving in the country, and in particular the question of how Turkey's state institutions and legal frameworks would handle the phenomena of immigration and asylum. These debates have made clear that the health and stability of Turkey's integration into the EU depend not only on the economic, social and political transformations in the country, but also on specific policy matters. This chapter addresses the transformation of national immigration policies and practices in Turkey with regard to the role played by the EU's promotion of the notion of 'migration management' in the process of European integration. The issue of 'migration management' is seen here to be a component of the country's Europeanization or the EU-ization process.[1] In other words, European integration has an enormous impact on the transformation of the qualities and conditions of 'migration and asylum management' in the country. Nevertheless, this is an area that demands more empirical analysis before broader academic discussion can take place. Terms like 'immigration and asylum' and 'Europeanization', particularly in a dynamic context such as Turkey's European integration, are subject to contestable interpretations. Moreover, as the 'Europeanization' of national immigration and asylum policies and practices is not only a matter of policy but also a matter of politics, the efforts to elaborate this process appear to be uneven and vigorously debated (İçduygu 2004: 93; Kirişçi 2005a: 355–7).

Research on the changing qualities and conditions of immigration and asylum in Turkey in connection with the country's Europeanization should start from how Featherstone and Radaelli (2003) describe 'the politics of Europeanization' namely, the question of 'what is the power of Europe in national contexts?' (see Ette and Faist in this volume). As Europeanization is defined as 'processes of construction, diffusion, and institutionalization of formal and informal rules, procedures, policy paradigms, styles, "ways of doing things" and shared beliefs and norms to a European model of governance, caused by forms of cooperation and integration in Europe' (Bulmer and Radaelli 2004: 4), the notion of 'migration management' remains very central to the Europeanization process. In few places is this more obvious than in Turkey, where different kinds of national immigration and asylum policies and practices are infused with historical legacies, social validity, cultural notions and political importance which in turn are intensely contested by the European influence.

It is obvious that immigration and asylum policies and practices differ from one national setting to another, and various factors are employed to define their meanings and contents based on varied intentions. At different levels, in the process of Europeanization, national immigration and asylum policies and practices in Turkey are challenged by various social, cultural, economic and political values because the creation, definition and manipulation of these interactions are an ongoing process. For instance, the new draft Law of Settlement,[2] which has been prepared to replace the old Law of Settlement (Law No. 2510, dated 14 June 1934),[3] and can be seen as part of Turkey's EU harmonization efforts, is a significant indicator of the possibility of change in legislation that assertively favours the inflows of persons of 'Turkish descent and culture'[4] and limits the rights of foreign nationals to settle in Turkey. In fact, the Law on Settlement of 1934 is the major piece of legislation that sustains the conservative philosophy of various immigration- and asylum-related policies and practices in Turkey; and consequently it seems to be subject to renewal within the EU integration process. Despite this attempt to create a new liberal legal framework, frequent disputes over immigration and asylum issues are still common, and have continuously imbued the notion of immigration as having concrete and metaphorical importance for national homogeneity and security. As will be discussed in some detail in this study, for instance, the issue of lifting the geographical reservation of the 1951 Geneva Convention, which is very central to the asylum regimes in Turkey, is also often regarded as an element of change which may subsequently harm the notion of homogeneous national identity. There is no doubt that these examples reflect the highly political character of immigration and asylum issues, which become even more political through the Europeanization process.

That the EU process of introducing the new perception and new law on the management of immigration and asylum flow in Turkey plays a role is indisputable. In fact, it is no longer challenged that the EU exerts influence on the qualities and conditions of immigration and asylum for candidate members as well as member states. But, as we shall see, the Europeanization of immigration- and asylum-related policies and practices is not a smooth process, and often involves ups and downs and occasional refusals to comply. It shall be shown, further, that the EU process may easily affect some aspects of immigration and asylum issues such as new legal arrangements, but it may also face serious difficulties in influencing other aspects such as implementation of the law.

The aim of this chapter is to elaborate the impact of Europeanization on various dimensions of immigration and asylum policies and practices in Turkey. In drawing on immigration and asylum developments in the country and policy responses to these changes, this chapter seeks to explore the degree, direction and dimensions of transformations in the conventional understanding of immigration and asylum issues in Turkey. This has been done by applying a multifaceted analysis which offers a differentiated assessment of the changes that have occurred in the course of Turkey's EU membership process. In other words, we take Europeanization, or EU-ization, as one of the basic sites at which the transformation of immigration and asylum issues in Turkey can be elaborated more analytically and critically. The analytical approach we apply here allows us to capture the unique influence of the EU process on each separate dimension of immigration and asylum in the country. To what extent has change actually occurred in the domestic implementation of immigration and asylum policies? In order to answer this question, Radaelli's (2003: 35–8) categorization of four possible outcomes of Europeanization – retrenchment, inertia, absorption and transformation – will be used as a guide. In our conclusions, we will argue that the impact of the EU was much more obvious on some dimensions than on others. We will also argue that this transformation of policies and practices of immigration and asylum in Turkey, which occurs as a product of Europeanization, particularly since 2001, is a process that would lead to a new type of 'migration and asylum management' which is neither fully identical to the modern European model nor totally the same as the conventional understanding of migration and asylum issues in Turkey.

Immigration and asylum flows to Turkey: a snapshot

Turkey has long held the reputation of being a country of emigration,[5] and, in contrast to the unknown reality, has not reflected any direct image of being a country of immigration. In fact, this is a false picture. Since its establishment in the early 1920s, modern Turkey has experienced the paradox of being a country of both immigration and emigration (İçduygu 2004, 2005b; Kirişçi 2003). Until the 1980s, however, immigration has remained limited to inflow of the ethnic Turks living in other parts of the world, particularly from neighbouring areas, who were rejoining the motherland; in fact, this was a part of the nation-building process in the country. In the last two decades, however, large numbers of foreigners began immigrating to Turkey (İçduygu and Keyman 2000; İçduygu 2000, 2004). This is a fairly new phenomenon and presents itself in many different forms. In addition to the immigration of ethnic Turks, which also sometimes includes asylum-seekers, there are four main types of inflows of foreign nationals to Turkey (İçduygu 2003: 12): (1) irregular labour migrants, (2) transit migrants, (3) asylum-seekers and refugees and (4) regular migrants. It seems that the first three types often overlap and fluctuate as migrants may drift from one status into another, depending on circumstances and opportunities. It also seems that the main European concern is with these three forms of movement of people associated with Turkey. Accordingly, in order to meet European expectations, Turkey needs to apply all relevant instruments in combating irregular migratory flows, preventing transit migration and liberalizing its asylum system.

In fact, in recent years irregular migration has been one of the chief characteristics of the immigration flows to Turkey. These irregular flows consist of three main trends (İçduygu 2003: 17). The first involves mainly migrants from the Commonwealth of Independent States (CIS) and East European countries, such as the Russian Federation, Ukraine, Romania and Moldova, who come to Turkey in search of work. These migrants sell their labour in various sectors such as sex and entertainment, construction, textile industry, domestic work and agriculture. Many enter Turkey legally and subsequently overstay or fail to renew their visas. The second form of irregular migration to Turkey consists of transit migrants who come to Turkey mainly from the Middle East (predominantly Iranians and Iraqis) and from various Asian (for example Bangladesh, Pakistan and Sri Lanka) and African (such as Congo, Nigeria and Somalia) countries. They often target Turkey as a transit zone in their attempt to reach and enter various European countries. Most of them fall within the illegal entry and departure category, while others drift into illegality as they overstay their tourist visas. The third group of irregular migrants includes rejected asylum-seekers who are reluctant to return home and are in search of illegal jobs and/or opportunities to migrate illegally to another country.

As a country that has been confronted with various types of immigration and asylum flows mentioned above, Turkey seems to attach great importance to the newly emerging migration and asylum questions and their 'management' (İçduygu 2004: 88). This focus has been precipitated by Turkey's desire to enter the EU and by the conditionality imposed by the EU which has fuelled the need for the creation and implementation of a variety of migration- and asylum-related policies. In other words, strategic bargaining and sociopolitical learning seem to be jointly reinforcing processes in the Europeanization of national immigration and asylum policies in the country.

Current national immigration and asylum policies and practices in Turkey: an overview

Though widely challenged by global trends of immigration and asylum flows of recent years, conventionally all states try to convey the impression that they uphold the integrity of the state through the control of (1) their own borders, (2) the residential status of foreign citizens in their territories and (3) the access of these foreign citizens to the labour markets within their borders. Turkey is no exception: in line with the country's various nation-state-based and security-focused concerns, it has established and reinforced its systems of border control, and of regulation and control on immigration through its visa policy and systems of residence and work permits. These policies and practices have also dictated the rules and regulations governing the asylum system in the country.

Immigration-related policies and practices

As noted earlier, since the early years of the republic, Turkey has been a country of immigration, but until the early 1980s this has been mainly limited to the arrivals of ethnic Turks. The immigration of ethnic Turks particularly in the early years of the republic was part of the nation-building process that gave preferential treatment to immigrants of Turkish descent and culture. It was within this context that the *Law of Settlement* was adopted in 1934 (Law No. 2510, dated 14 June 1934). Today this law continues to determine the main rules of immigration and asylum into Turkey. It contains provisions on who can immigrate, settle and acquire refugee status in the country, and it clearly favours individuals of Turkish descent and culture who apply as immigrants and refugees. This law has had very direct impact on regular immigration flow to the country: nearly 2 million immigrants who are considered ethnic Turks arrived and settled in Turkey between 1923 and 2005. It also has an indirect effect on irregular migration: some irregular immigrants of Turkish origin, including asylum-seekers or rejected cases of asylum-seekers, have been allowed to stay in the country on an unofficial basis, or have been allowed to benefit from those provisions that allow people of Turkish descent to settle, work and eventually obtain Turkish citizenship.[6]

Although Turkey imposes severe restrictions on the permanent settlement of foreigners in the country, it has had quite a liberal visa regime for some time. The conditions for foreigners to obtain entry visas for Turkey are outlined in the Turkish Passport Law (Law No. 1764, dated 24 July 1950). According to this law, foreigners who want to reside in Turkey must enter the country legally, and some foreign citizens must possess an entry visa. Until recently, there were more than 40 countries whose citizens were not required to obtain a visa. For instance, despite their ongoing involvement in irregular migration, citizens of Iran, Morocco and Tunisia still have three-month visa exemptions. In addition, nationals of more than 30 countries may obtain sticker-type visas at the Turkish border. For instance, citizens of Belarus, Russia or Ukraine may obtain sticker visas for two months, those of Azerbaijan, Jordan or Moldova for one month, and those of Georgia for 15 days.[7] Stricter measures are applied for nationals from 'high risk emigration countries'.[8] Meanwhile, as mentioned above, serious steps have been taken only recently to adopt the EU negative visa list[9] – those third countries whose nationals must be in possession of a visa when crossing external borders, and those whose nationals are exempt from that requirement (Apap et al. 2004; Kirişçi 2005b).

The principal legal instrument that determines the residence and working status of migrants in Turkey is the Turkish Law on Foreigners (Law No. 5683, dated 15 July 1950).[10] According to this law, foreigners must apply for a residence permit that is issued by the local police department after a thorough examination.[11] If the applicant has a valid work permit or sufficient financial sources and demonstrates no intention of disturbing public order in the country, a residence permit may be issued initially for one year,[12] renewable for a period of three years, and then again for a period of five years. It is often the case that a work permit is a prerequisite for a residence permit. Foreign spouses of Turkish citizens may obtain a three-year residence permit on their first application, which is then renewable after five years. Upon termination of marriage or death of the Turkish spouse, they do not have any legal right to renew their residence permit.

Until recently, work permits for foreigners were issued independently of residence permits. Even if a foreigner did not have a residence permit in Turkey, (s)he could still have free access to the labour market. These work permits were not issued to the foreigners themselves but to the institutions or the companies that employed them. There were several authorities responsible for the issuing of work permits.[13] Foreign citizens were restricted by the Law on Activities and Professions in Turkey Reserved for Turkish Citizens (Law No. 2007, dated 16 June 1932) from practising certain professions.[14] The new Law on Work Permits for Foreigners (Law No. 4817, dated 15 March 2003) allows work permits to be issued to individual foreigners and institutionalizes the process by making the Ministry of Labour and Social Security the sole authority responsible. In nullifying the Law on Activities and Professions in Turkey Reserved for Turkish Citizens, the new law makes it possible for foreign workers to practise any profession. The new law reflects the attitude that work permits for foreigners should be administered on the basis of labour market demands.

Asylum-related policies and practices

For immigration-related legislation, policies and practices, there are three main legal documents that also directly affect the inflows of asylum-seekers and refugees, and indirectly influence irregular migration flows. These are: (1) the *Law of Settlement* adopted in 1934, (2) the 1951 *Geneva Convention on the Status of Refugees* and (3) the 1994

Regulation on Asylum. The implications of these legal arrangements for asylum flows and irregular migration have been subject to debate in recent years.[15]

The implications of the Law of Settlement of 1934 for immigration and asylum practices in Turkey have already been discussed. As noted earlier, although Turkey was one of the signatories of the 1951 Geneva Convention on the Status of Refugees, she was among those who accepted the introduction of a geographical and time limitation to the Convention: accordingly, legal obligations would be applied only to persons who were fleeing persecution in Europe as a result of events prior to 1951. In 1967, when Turkey acceded to the Additional Protocol on the Status of Refugees, it dropped the time limitation but maintained the geographical limitation. This limitation has been a key feature of the country's asylum policies and practices (Kirişçi 2001: 13–14). In order to tackle the unprecedented influx of asylum-seekers from the Middle East and to assume responsibility for determination of refugee status, a new regulation on asylum was adopted in November 1994.[16] This regulation is entitled the Regulation on the Procedures and Principles Related to Mass Influx and Foreigners Arriving in Turkey or Requesting Residence Permits with the Intention of Seeking Asylum from a Third Country. With this regulation, the Turkish authorities have taken the responsibility of granting refugee status – previously the responsibility of the UNHCR – into their own hands.[17]

Based on its ongoing geographical limitation in the 1951 Geneva Convention Turkey still does not accept non-European refugees on *de jure* basis, but it is a de facto situation that the country receives numerous asylum-seekers from neighbouring non-European countries. The fact that Turkey does not accept non-Europeans as asylum-seekers and refugees has several implications for irregular migration (İçduygu 2003; Kirişçi 2002). Most asylum-seekers and illegal transit migrants, mainly from Iran and Iraq, make illegal border crossings to Turkey with the help of smugglers and traffickers. Some irregular migrants apply for asylum although they have no grounds to do so. By limiting the application of the 1951 Geneva Convention to certain geographical areas, Turkey hopes to be immune to the flows of politically or economically deprived people coming from poor and unstable countries in Asia and Africa. In reality, however, the opposite seems to be the case: the country has been faced with increasing flows of people from these regions, including the Middle East. Turkish authorities have long feared that the abolition of the geographical limitation would bring even greater numbers of asylum-seekers to Turkey, or increase the numbers of foreigners settling in the country, which would have repercussions for Turkey's definition of national identity and even national security (Kirişçi 2005a: 355–7).

With no regulations pertaining to the status of non-European asylum-seekers, Turkey has applied its domestic laws to foreigners entering the country, meaning that incoming foreigners are expected to possess valid documents and can remain only within the permitted period of stay. At the same time, on the basis of various de facto refugee cases, the Turkish authorities for reasons of pragmatism have granted non-European asylum-seekers some form of protection (Kirişçi 1995). These non-European asylum-seekers are considered to be under temporary protection and are expected to leave the country. If their asylum applications to the Turkish authorities and the UNHCR are processed and accepted, they can resettle in a third country; if their cases are rejected, they must return to their homeland. According to the new Law on Work Permits for Foreigners, only those asylum-seekers and refugees who have residence permits of at least six months may have access to legal employment opportunities under certain specific conditions.

Towards harmonization with EU legislation and implementation

Before discussing the details of the harmonization efforts taking place in Turkey regarding immigration and asylum policies and practices, it is helpful to point out the crucial turning points in recent developments in these areas. In this context, three periods of changes can be identified: the pre-1994 period which was a time of ignorance; the transition to international norms from 1994 to 2001; and finally the post-2001 period which is characterized by EU-ization types of changes (İçduygu 2004: 90–1). As noted earlier, the 1994 Regulation marked a turning point at which certain immigration- and asylum-related policies and practices changed and some new sets of rules became institutionalized. With the mass influx of asylum-seekers from Iraq in early 1991, the Turkish authorities had become more conscious about the immigration and asylum flows to the country, and initiated this new legal arrangement. Although this was a positive attempt to regularize some rules and measures regarding asylum (and in part immigration as well), it did not reflect any liberalization of policy: rather, this move helped consolidate the authoritarian role of the state in immigration and asylum issues and increased its power over these areas. However, partly because of growing international criticism of the implementation of the 1994 Regulation, which had caused the violations of the principle of non-refoulement,[18] and partly because of the growing importance of immigration and asylum issues in Turkey, which attracted both national and international concerns, the post-1994 period saw some slow but tangible steps towards the harmonization of immigration and asylum policies and practices in the country to international norms and standards. The crucial turning point in this field came with the EU-related changes occurring after 2001 (TMI and UNHCR Ankara 2005: vi). These changes include the related legislation and the implementation projects complementing the administrative structure and the institutional infrastructure for Turkey's immigration and asylum system that must be harmonized with the EU *acquis* and system throughout EU accession negotiations.

The issue of 'migration management' in Turkey has only in the last couple of years moved to the forefront of official concern. As already noted, this is partly because the country's experience with immigration is of relatively recent origin and partly because Turkey lacks established immigration policies and practices – except in the case of the influx of ethnic Turks during the early years of modern Turkey. Today most official initiatives to manage immigration occur in response to external pressures, such as that from the EU, rather than local policy concerns. Thus, in this period of the pre-EU accession process, the issues of immigration, border controls, asylum and the introduction of appropriate legislation are of considerable importance for Turkey, as reflected in the EU 'Accession Partnership' (AP) document adopted on 8 March 2001 and subsequently revised on 26 March 2003. According to this document, Turkey must harmonize its immigration and asylum legislation to meet the following four objectives in particular:

1. Pursue alignment of visa legislation and practice with the *acquis*;
2. Adopt and implement the *acquis* and best practices on migration (admission, readmission, expulsion) with a view to preventing illegal immigration;
3. Continue alignment with the *acquis* and best practices concerning border management so as to prepare for full implementation of the Schengen *acquis*; and
4. Start an alignment of the *acquis* in the field of asylum including lifting the geographical reservation to the 1951 Geneva Convention; strengthening the system for hearing and determining applications for asylum; and developing accommodation facilities and social support for asylum-seekers and refugees.

Following the pre-accession requirements of the EU, in the National Programme for the Adoption of the Acquis (NPAA) in 2003 Turkey declared its own intentions to introduce some major changes to its immigration and asylum policies and practices (Apap et al. 2004: 11; Kirişçi 2005b: 347; Tokuzlu 2005: 339). These intentions included primarily the drafting of two new laws in 2005: the Law on Aliens and the Law on Asylum. It appeared, however, that the political will was not strong enough to realize these targets to establish a new comprehensive legislative framework on immigration and asylum issues. On 25 March 2005 when the Turkish government adopted an Action Plan for Asylum and Migration (TMI and UNHCR Ankara 2005), it became clear that the comprehensive codification, through the Law on Aliens and the Law on Asylum, has been postponed to 2012. The Action Plan is a fully detailed document which contains the description of existing policies and practices as well as the mid- and long-term goals to be achieved in the areas of immigration and asylum in Turkey by 2012.

Immigration-related harmonization efforts

With respect to the visa and admission legislation, which is very central to the Schengen *acquis*, some attempts were made to reform the current visa regime of the country towards alignment with the *acquis*, and to establish better border management (Apap et al. 2004: 26; Kirişçi 2005b: 350–3). It was within this context that first, as of 1 September 2002, Turkey introduced visa requirements for six Gulf countries (Bahrain, Qatar, Kuwait, Oman, Saudi Arabia and United Arab Emirates) whose citizens are subject to visa requirements in the EU. As a second step, 13 countries (Indonesia, Republic of South Africa, Kenya, Bahamas, Maldives, Barbados, Seychelles, Jamaica, Belize, Fiji, Mauritius, Grenada and Saint Lucia) have been listed for visa requirements, and these came into force between May and July of 2003. Turkey continued its alignment with the EU negative visa list and introduced a visa requirement for citizens of Azerbaijan in November 2003. As a part of this harmonization, it seems that Turkey will have to make similar arrangements for the application of visa requirements to the nationals of Iran, Bosnia-Herzegovina, Kyrgyzstan, Macedonia, Morocco and Tunisia.

It seems clear that in the last four years the idea of European integration has already made a significant impact on Turkey's policies and practices. Accordingly, Turkey has demonstrated strong political will to tackle asylum, irregular migration and human trafficking and smuggling, as well as their labour consequences. There were four legislative developments that constituted direct steps towards harmonization with international standards, and particularly with the EU legislation and implementations (İçduygu 2004: 93–4).

The first development was to fulfil the provisions of the UN Conventions against Transnational Organized Crime and its additional protocols. A draft law on additional articles to the Penal Code and amendments to the Law on Combating Benefits-Oriented Criminal Organizations was prepared by the Ministry of Justice and adopted by the parliament on 3 August 2002. Through this legal arrangement, Law No. 4771 added articles 201/a and 201/b to the Turkish Penal Code to follow article 201.[19] These changes conform to the Palermo Protocol against Trafficking in Persons, which introduces a definition of trafficking in human beings into the Turkish legal system and criminalizes the act of trafficking as such. The law prescribes severe penalties for traffickers: five to ten years' imprisonment. A further provision was adopted by the parliament on the same day to criminalize migrant smuggling, conforming to the Palermo Protocol against Migrant Smuggling. These two separate but related crimes have now been fully addressed by the Penal Code.

The second important legislative decision was related to the UN Convention against Transnational Organized Crime and its two additional protocols including 'The Protocol to Prevent, Suppress and Punish Trafficking, Especially Women and Children' and 'The Protocol against the Smuggling of Migrants by Land, Sea, and Air'. Turkey was among the initial signatories. This Convention and its additional protocols were approved by the Turkish parliament on 31 January 2003 and put into force on 4 February 2003. Again this new legal arrangement was a significant step in developing tools to combat trafficking, smuggling and irregular migration.

The approval of the draft Law on Work Permits for Foreigners (Law No. 4817, dated 27 February 2003) was the third remarkable change in legislation pertaining to irregular migration and its labour outcomes. Although the law was published in the *Official Gazette* on 6 March 2003, it became effective six months after its publication (on 6 September 2003). The Turkish parliament enacted the law in order to concentrate the administration of permits in one authority, thus enabling foreigners to work in Turkey more easily. The law aims to ensure that the work permit process in Turkey meets international standards, in particular those of the EU. One important aspect of this law is to prevent the illegal employment of foreigners by issuing fines. In addition, it allows foreign workers to practise all professions.

According to the previous legal arrangement, foreigners were not able to engage in domestic work. This resulted in the exploitation of thousands of Moldovan women working in the domestic sector in Turkey.

The new Law on Work Permits for Foreigners and its accompanying regulations[20] (the Regulation for the Application of the Law on Work Permits for Foreigners, No. 25214 and dated 29 August 2003, and the Regulation for the Employment of Foreign Nationals in Direct Foreign Investments, No. 25214 and dated 29 August 2003) are the instruments which regulate the employment of foreign nationals in Turkey. The procedure for acquiring a work permit has been simplified: work permits are given by a central authority, the Ministry of Labour and Social Security (art. 3), and are linked to residence permits, which are administered by the Ministry of the Interior (arts 5 and 12).

Regulations for foreigners working without work permits are an important aspect of the new Law on Work Permits for Foreigners. It is required that 'independently working foreigners are obliged to inform the Ministry of the situation within at most fifteen days, from the date they have started working and from the end of the work' (art. 18a), and that 'employers that employ foreigners are obliged to inform the Ministry within at most fifteen days from the end of the said date and from the date when the service contract was terminated for any reason, in the case that the foreign employee does not start working within thirty days from the date when the work permit was given' (art. 18b). The law includes penalties for foreigners who work without permits. For instance, an 'independently working foreigner and the employer employing foreigners, who do not fulfil their obligation of notification according to Article 18 within due time, are fined with an administrative penalty of two hundred and fifty million liras, for each foreigner' (art. 21). In addition to this, 'the foreigner that works independently without a work permit is fined with an administrative penalty of five hundred million liras' and 'an administrative penalty of two billion five hundred million liras is administered to the employer or employer representative that employs a foreigner who does not have a work permit' (art. 21). It is also required that an 'administrative penalty of one billion liras (be) administered to the foreigner who works independently without having a work permit given in accordance with this Law' (art. 21).

Finally, an amendment to article 5 of the Citizenship Law (Law No. 403, dated 11 February 1964) which was made on 4 June 2003, had implications for fighting irregular migration and protecting immigrants' rights. Previously, foreigners (women) could acquire Turkish citizenship immediately by marrying a Turkish national. Under new legislation adopted by the Turkish parliament, foreigners who are married to Turkish citizens will be able to become citizens of the Turkish Republic three years after their marriage. Citizenship is conditional on the continuity of the marriage over three years. Previously, under Turkish law, it was much harder for male foreigners to obtain Turkish citizenship through marriage. This has now been standardized. In addition, under the new law, children of mixed parents (one Turkish, one foreigner) are granted Turkish citizenship. The new legislation 'foreseeing that married couples from different nationalities must live together for three years after their wedding to obtain Turkish citizenship' was enacted to discourage arranged marriages. Under the previous legislation, many irregular women migrants obtained their residence and work permits via arranged marriages.

As a basic tool of 'migration management' in the EU context, readmission agreements are on Turkey's immigration- and asylum-related agenda (Apap et al. 2004: 22; Tokuzlu 2005: 342). Negotiations on the conclusion of a Community readmission agreement between the EU and Turkey started in 2003 but have not yet been finalized. Not surprisingly, in the context of readmission agreements European asylum policy has been criticized for tending to shift the responsibility elsewhere for those persons in need of international protection. Therefore, from Turkey's point of view it is important to ensure that this agreement contains a mechanism for sharing of responsibilities and providing adequate safeguards for persons who are in need of international protection. Meanwhile Turkey also follows a policy of concluding readmission agreements with source countries and then with transit countries and countries of destination: it has already concluded readmission agreements with Greece, Syria, Kyrgyzstan and Romania, and negotiations are ongoing with the Russian Federation, Uzbekistan, Belarus, Hungary, Macedonia, Ukraine, Lebanon, Egypt, Libya and Iran. Readmission agreements were proposed for Pakistan, Bangladesh, India, the People's Republic of China, Tunisia, Mongolia, Israel, Georgia, Ethiopia, Sudan, Algeria, Morocco, Nigeria and Kazakhstan.

Asylum-related harmonization efforts

While the debate on the lifting of the geographical limitation to the 1951 Geneva Convention is still going on with no sign of any change for the near future, there have been remarkable indications of transformation in the asylum system in Turkey (Kirişçi 2005a: 350; Tokuzlu 2005: 340). For instance, one of the major concerns arising from the implementation of the 1994 Asylum Regulation was the time limit for filing an application for refugee status, currently ten days. This requirement is apparently being reconsidered by officials[21] as it often receives harsh criticism from the international community in general and the EU in particular. Another example of the positive steps taken in the area of asylum is the declaration made in the 2005 Action Plan for Asylum and Migration which targets the incorporation of some procedures from the EU asylum laws such as 'subsidiary protection', 'tolerated aliens' and 'residence permits based on humanitarian grounds' into the Turkish asylum system. Furthermore, as again the Action Plan indicates, the implementation of the principle of non-refoulement becomes an issue of concern in the asylum procedure in the country: in fact, according to the constitutional provision that ensures 'all actions and measures taken by the administration can be appealed before justice', all aliens in Turkey may appeal to administrative justice against a deportation; but in order to have a proper implementation of the principle of non-refoulement, the issue must be treated with the same level of sensitivity in the framework of the 1951 Convention, the European Convention on Human Rights and other relevant international standards through national laws in Turkey, particularly in the two new draft laws on asylum and foreigners.

Concluding remarks

Today not only Turkey, but also its European counterparts, face many challenges in relation to the 'management and control of migration' flows involving Turkey. The EU, in particular, is greatly concerned over irregular migration and asylum flows through Turkey, as these have very direct consequences for the whole of Europe. Given the country's candidature for accession to the EU, Turkey has been forced to be proactive in bringing its legislation into harmony with the *acquis communautaire*. Such efforts are being undertaken in the field of migration in general, and with respect to irregular migration and asylum-related issues in particular. It is expected that the country's migration policies and practices will be brought into line with the standards and norms set by the EU. In fact, Turkey has recently taken several steps to ensure convergence with those standards by changing, or planning to change, its relevant policies and practices, thereby consolidating its status as a long-standing accession candidate to the EU. It should be noted that the legal arrangements made in the period of 2002–5, consisting of the introduction of new legislation and practices in the areas of immigration and asylum, signify a significant step in Turkey's commitment to EU membership. It appears that Europeanization of immigration and asylum policies and practices in Turkey is simply a part of the EU-ization process. Consequently, it also appears that the 'material incentives of conditionality'[22] play a crucial role in this process, as the EU authorities repeatedly push various requirements in the area of immigration and asylum issues into the membership process for Turkey.

In determining the degree of the Europeanization, or EU-ization, of immigration and asylum policies and practices in Turkey, we can apply Radaelli's categorization (Radaelli, 2003: 35–8, see also Ette and Faist in this volume) to the Turkish case – and the most obvious conclusion is that no real transformation has yet taken place to indicate a paradigmatic change in the areas of immigration and asylum policies and practices. Apart from the outcome of inertia, suggested by the lack of change observed in the cases of the Law of Settlement and Law of Aliens, the main results of direct or indirect EU directives in domestic implementation are mainly absorption and partly retrenchment. Absorption, which refers to non-fundamental changes but accommodation of new values and practices, has been the major outcome of many aspects of Europeanization of immigration and asylum policies and practices in Turkey. For instance, the implementation of readmission agreements, particularly the one between Greece and Turkey, is often criticized for not achieving full functionality, therefore exemplifying the outcome of absorption. In some areas of this process of change, as in the case of the new Law on Work Permits for Foreigners of 2003, there have been some elements of retrenchment, a form of domestic change that makes the national situation less European. It is reported, for instance, that the relevant offices in the Ministry of Labour, where applications of foreigners for work permits are processed, are not able to inform the applicants about the results of their applications within the time limits stipulated, and in general carry out their tasks in a chaotic administrative structure which poses functional problems.

As discussed throughout this chapter, since 2001 the process of Europeanization, or more specifically EU-ization, has an incredible potential to make the transformation of immigration- and asylum-related policies and practices in Turkey more complex, and multidimensional, the changing nature of which cannot be captured within the limits of conventional understanding of European integration. For this reason, attention should be paid to exploring various ways in which the link between Europeanization and issues of immigration and asylum is constructed both theoretically and practically. In this chapter, an attempt has been made to do so by applying a conceptual framework for analysing relationships between the EU process and the policies and practices of immigration and asylum in Turkey and for understanding how these relationships affect the transformation of these policies and practices in the country. This framework takes the perspective that Europeanization is a political space where diverse national and supranational values and interests interact and negotiate within the dynamics and mechanisms of our globalized world. The key determinants of this process are the factors related to existing as well as developing institutions and processes within the national settings and those institutions and processes embedded in the linkages between national settings and the European core. Indeed, this last point connects our discussion of the Europeanization of immigration and asylum policies and practices to the politics of immigration and asylum. It seems that this political context overwhelmingly colours the climate of the debate in this policy area in Turkey. For instance, those in the EU arguing against Turkish membership often refer, among other things, to the problems of immigration and asylum in Turkey which may run counter to EU norms and experiences; for their part, those in Turkey who are sceptical of EU membership raise the concern that Europeanization in these areas may harm the national homogeneous character of the country.

To conclude, it is possible to make two main observations concerning the impact of the EU process over the transformation of immigration- and asylum-related policies and practices in Turkey. First, the preceding discussion leaves very little room for doubt about the presence of a 'positive' impact on these policies and practices in Turkey. While the strength of this impact is rather moderate, at the same time it is growing, which is probably a reflection of the general opinion that while the EU process is for many quite positive on the whole, at the same time what happens in this context is always something less than expected. From another perspective, the experience of change in the Turkish case is mostly a type of absorption rather than transformation. Second, as far as Turkey's reaction, or resistance, is concerned, the influence of the EU process on immigration- and asylum-related policies and practices seems to vary: for instance, the impact of the EU process on some specific and practical asylum issues was in general stronger than it was on some general and normative immigration concerns. It seems that Turkey's sceptical perspective on the Europeanization of national immigration and asylum policies and practices is strongly linked to the question of burden-sharing versus burden-shifting. Of course, this is again not surprising as the whole Europeanization process often proceeds as a top-down process originating from the core – in this case the EU – which is also often met with the resistance of a bottom-up process coming from a periphery – in this case Turkey. From the Turkish side, indeed, there is a feeling that EU policies and practices for managing migration and the array of related restrictive measures shift the burden of controlling migration to countries on the periphery, like Turkey, with the conclusion of readmission agreements often being cited as a case in point. Likewise, preventing Turkey from turning into a buffer zone between the immigrant-attracting European core and the emigrant-producing peripheral regions has been a similar area of concern for Turkish policy-makers. Therefore, Turkish authorities advocate the need for burden-sharing instead of what is being seen as a case of burden-shifting, especially in relation to a phenomenon such as irregular transit migration or asylum that ultimately targets various European countries. On the other hand, it appears that the EU authorities are urging Turkey to devote more resources and energy to its efforts to manage and control migration and asylum flows across and within its borders. Of course, these demands and considerations are central to EU–Turkish relations and create many areas of concern for both sides, from security and human rights issues to economics and politics. Practically and naturally, however, the likelihood of any progress in this field is strongly linked to the negotiations between the European Commission and the Turkish authorities on burden-sharing.

Notes

1 In a different context, on the issue of Europeanization of civil society Diez et al. (2005) refer to the notion of 'EU-ization' as a dominant form of Europeanization in Turkey's European integration process.

2 For the full text of this draft law (in Turkish) see the following web page: http://www.tbmm.gov.tr/develop/owa/kanun_tasarisi_sd.onerge_bilgileri?k anunlar_sira_no=22917, access date: 7 December 2005.

3 For the full text of this law (in Turkish) see the following web page: http://www.bayindirlik.gov.tr/turkce/kanunlistesi.php, access date: 7 December 2005.

4 For some elaboration, see Kirişçi (1996a, 2000).

5 Since the early 1960s more than 4 million Turkish citizens have migrated to more than 30 countries and about half of them have remained abroad.

Today about 3.5 million Turks have settled abroad, including 2 million in the Federal Republic of Germany. For some details of the current situation of the Turkish emigration, see İçduygu (2005a: 2–5).

6 For some discussion on the occasionally positive discriminatory attitudes towards migrants of Turkish origin, even if they are irregular, see Kaiser (2003).

7 For the details of the visa requirements in Turkey, see the web page of the Turkish Foreign Ministry, www.mfa.gov.tr

8 For further details, see Etçioğlu (2002).

9 See Annex I of the Council Regulation (EC) No 539/2001 of 15 March 2001.

10 In addition, the Law on the Residence and Travel Activities of Foreigners of the same date (Law No. 7564) regulates the conditions for residence and settlement of foreigners.

11 According to article 7 of the law, applications for residence permits by the following persons will be refused without consideration: (a) persons coming to practise a profession prohibited to foreigners; (b) persons not in a position to conform to Turkish law, customs or political conditions, or persons engaging in activities not in conformity with these; (c) persons clearly unable to secure legally the material support necessary for the duration of their desired stay in Turkey; (d) persons who have entered Turkey illegally and (e) persons whose presence in Turkey is disruptive of the general peace and tranquillity.

12 Until 1998, residence permits were issued for a period of at most two years.

13 For a related discussion, see for instance, Kaiser (2003) and Kaiser and İçduygu (2005).

14 Only Turkish citizens may work as state employees in Turkey. Until recently, for the sake of the general welfare, foreigners were banned from certain other professions. These included law, medicine, dentistry, nursing, pharmacy and practising as a notary public. Apart from the professions listed here, some other occupations had been prohibited to foreigners according to the provisions of the Law Regarding Trades and Services Reserved to Turkish Citizens in Turkey, No. 2007 of 11 June 1932. For example, foreigners could not work as itinerant salesmen, musicians, photographers, barbers, typesetters, middlemen, clothing and shoe manufacturers, stockbrokers, sellers of state monopoly products, interpreters and tourist guides, transport workers or construction, iron, and woodworkers. Foreigners were also prohibited from working at water, lighting and heating installations, either temporarily or permanently, and at loading and unloading sites. They could not work as drivers, day labourers, watchmen, janitors, waiters, or household help, as singers or entertainers in bars, nor as veterinarians or pharmacists.

15 For some details, see, for instance, Kirişçi (2002) and İçduygu (2003).

16 For a detailed discussion on the 1994 Regulation on Asylum, see Kirişçi (1996b, 2001); see also BeFrelick (1997).

17 Although Turkey has maintained its basic stance of not recognizing non-Europeans as refugees, the new regulation implied two categories of asylum-seekers to Turkey. The first group are those who come from Europe and can benefit from the protection of the 1951 Convention. The second group are non-European asylum-seekers, who are seeking onward resettlement from

Turkey. Initially, the difficulties in the implementation of this regulation led to some crisis situations between Turkey and the international community. It was often the case that many asylum-seekers had been denied official recognition as asylum-seekers by the authorities, often for having failed to meet arbitrary and restrictive filing requirements unrelated to the merits of their claims. For instance, among other provisions, as the new regulations required non-Europeans to file their asylum claims within five days of entering the country, and, for those arriving with improper documents, to file their claims with the police at the location nearest where they entered the country, for many asylum-seekers it was extremely difficult to meet these requirements, and consequently they could be faced with deportation. While until the late 1990s, the negative consequences of the improper applications of the 1994 Regulation were quite obvious, from 1997 onward the collaborative efforts between the UNHCR Ankara Office, MOI and Ministry of Foreign Affairs made some various improvements in the application of the regulation. These efforts also resulted in some changes: for instance in 1999 the Turkish government increased the five-day time limit of application to ten days.

18 The 1951 Geneva Convention imposes a major obligation on countries that have signed it – that of 'non-refoulement'. Non-refoulement means that no country may deport or expel a person to a country where that person faces persecution, or risk of serious human rights violations.

19 For a detailed elaboration of these new articles, see İçduygu (2003: 77–8).

20 For the full text of this law and related regulations, see MLSS (2003).

21 In a recent study, Tokuzlu (2005: 341) argues:

   Article 4 of the 1994 Asylum Regulation stipulates that individual aliens seeking asylum in Turkey, or requesting residence permits in order to seek asylum in a third country, must apply within ten days of entering the country. The Turkish government had applied this rule strictly and did not accept such applications until 1997 when the Turkish Council of State made a ruling which found the strict interpretation of the provision to be contrary to the Geneva Convention. Since then, the Council of State has settled this contradiction, but this was not reflected in the practice of the Ministry of the Interior until the end of 2004. At this point, the Ministry of the Interior started to receive applications irrespective of whether or not they had been filed within the ten-day period; cases of missing the deadline on the grounds of ill health, accident, or any other reasonable cause or on humanitarian grounds are taken into consideration by the Ministry of the Interior.

22 For a detailed elaboration of the notion of 'material incentives of conditionality' in the context of Turkey's EU integration process, see Kubicek (2005).

References

Apap, J., S. Carrera and K. Kirişçi (2004) 'Turkey in the European Area of Freedom, Security and Justice'. EU–Turkey Working Papers, No. 3. Brussels: Centre for European Policy Studies.

BeFrelick, B. (1997) 'Barriers to Protection: Turkey's Asylum Regulations'. *International Journal of Refugee Law*, Vol. 9: 8–34.

Bulmer, S. and C. Radaelli (2004) 'The Europeanization of National Policy'. *Queens' Papers on Europeanization*, 1/2004.

Diez, T., A. Agnantopoulos and A. Kaliber (2005) 'Turkey, Europeanization, and Civil Society'. *South European Society and Politics*, Vol. 10: 1–15.

Etçioğlu, E. (2002) Seminar on Visa and Readmission Standards for Turkey as a Candidate Country Organized by ICMPD for an EU Odysseus Project. Istanbul: Police Morale and Training Centre, 14–16 January.

Featherstone, K. and C. Radaelli (eds) (2003) *The Politics of Europeanization*. Oxford: Oxford University Press.

İçduygu, A. (2000) 'The Politics of International Migratory Regimes: Transit Migration Flows in Turkey'. *International Social Sciences Journal*, Vol. 165: 357–67.

İçduygu, A. (2003) *Irregular Migration in Turkey*. Geneva: International Organization for Migration.

İçduygu, A. (2004) 'Demographic Mobility over Turkey: Migration Experiences and Government Responses'. *Mediterranean Quarterly*, Vol. 5: 88–99.

İçduygu, A. (2005a) *SOPEMI Report for Turkey*. Istanbul: Koc University.

İçduygu, A. (2005b) 'Turkey: the Demographic and Economic Dimension of Migration'. In P. Fargues (ed.), *Mediterranean Migration 2005 Report*. Florence: CARIM–European University Institute–European Commission, pp. 327–37.

İçduygu, A. and E. F. Keyman (2000) 'Globalization, Security and Migration: the Case of Turkey'. *Global Governance*, Vol. 6: 383–98.

Kaiser, B. (2003) 'Lifeworlds of EU Immigrants in Turkey'. In E. Zeybekoğlu and B. Johansson (eds), *Migration and Labour in Europe. Views from Turkey and Sweden*. Istanbul: MURCIR and NIWL, pp. 269–81.

Kaiser, B. and A. İçduygu (2005) 'Türkiye'deki Avrupa Birliği Yurttaşları' [EU Citizens in Turkey]. In A. Kaya and T. Tarhanli (eds), *Türkiye'de Çoğunluk ve Azınlık Politikaları: AB Sürecinde Yurttaşlık Tartışmaları* [Majority and Minority Policies in Turkey: Citizenship Debates in the EU Process]. Istanbul: Tesev, pp. 171–81.

Kirişçi, K. (1995) 'Refugee Movements and Turkey in the Post Second World War Era'. Research Paper, ISS/POLS 95–01. Istanbul: Bogazici University.

Kirişçi, K. (1996a) 'Refugees of Turkish Origin: "Coerced Immigrants" to Turkey since 1945'. *International Migration*, Vol. 34: 385–412.

Kirişçi, K. (1996b) 'Is Turkey Lifting the "Geographical Limitation"?: the November 1994 Regulation on Asylum in Turkey'. *International Journal of Refugee Law*, Vol. 8: 293–318.

Kirişçi, K. (2000) 'Disaggregating Turkish Citizenship and Immigration Practices'. *Middle Eastern Studies*, Vol. 36: 1–22.

Kirişçi, K. (2001) 'UNHCR and Turkey: Cooperating towards Improved Implementation of the 1951 Convention on the Status of Refugees'. *International Journal of Refugee Law*, Vol. 13: 71–97.

Kirişçi, K. (2002) *Justice and Home Affairs. Issues in Turkish–EU Relations*. Istanbul: Tesev Publications.

Kirişçi, K. (2003) 'Turkey: a Transformation from Emigration to Immigration'. Migration Information Source Paper, Migration Policy Institute.

Kirişçi, K. (2005a) 'Turkey: the Political Dimension of Migration'. In P. Fargues (ed.), *Mediterranean Migration 2005 Report*. Florence: CARIM–European University Institute–European Commission, pp. 349–57.

Kirişçi, K. (2005b) 'A Friendlier Schengen Visa System as a Tool of Soft Power: the Experience of Turkey'. *European Journal of Migration and Law*, Vol. 7: 343–67.

Kubicek, P. (2005) 'The European Union and Grassroots Democratization in Turkey'. *Turkish Studies*, Vol. 1: 361–77.

MLSS (Ministry of Labour and Social Security) (2003) *Yabacıların Çalışma İzinleri Hakkında Kanun ve Yönetmelikler* [Law and Regulations on Work Permits for Foreigners]. Ankara.

Radaelli, C. (2003) 'The Europeanization of Public Policy'. In K. Featherstone and C. Radaelli (eds), *The Politics of Europeanization*. Oxford: Oxford University Press, pp. 27–56.

TMI and UNHCR Ankara (Turkish Ministry of Interior and United Nations High Commissioner for Refugees, Ankara Office) (2005) *Asylum and Migration Legislation*. Ankara: Başkent Matbaası.

Tokuzlu, L. B. (2005) 'Turkey: the Legal Dimension of Migration'. In P. Fargues (ed.), *Mediterranean Migration 2005 Report*. Florence: CARIM–European University Institute–European Commission, pp. 339–47.

11
Driven from the Outside: the EU's Impact on Albanian Immigration and Asylum Policies

Imke Kruse

Introduction

Transnational interdependence has increased since the 1970s, bringing with it new challenges to the problem-solving capacities of nation states. In response to the dilemma of diminished capacity at the national level, some domestic policy fields have been at least partially transferred to supranational responsibility (see, for example, Scharpf 1997; Zürn 2000). One such issue area is migration. During recent years, EU member states have realized that they were no longer able to deal adequately with the phenomenon of international migration on the domestic level and instead needed to combine their efforts regarding immigration and asylum policies on the European level. But in transferring domestic policy fields to the EU, they have simply pushed policy challenges up to the supranational level. Indeed, in the face of the very same problems, the EU itself has only limited capacity to act because it depends on the cooperation of neighbouring countries. This is most obvious in issues related to border control, immigration restrictions and return of illegal migrants. The process of European integration and demarcation of effective borders has thus created a paradox: those countries included in the EU depend on the cooperation of those excluded.

With the most recent enlargement and the upcoming accessions of Bulgaria and Romania, the EU is left surrounded by countries that lack certain prospect of EU membership. Many of these countries are unstable, poor and governed by authoritarian regimes. EU and domestic decision-makers perceive the EU's neighbours as playing a crucial role in security and stability in Europe. In response, the EU seeks to expand its legal boundaries, particularly to non-member countries close to its own terrain. This means that internal policies – especially those like immigration which are of great concern to member states' citizens and their identity – have started to shape the Union's policy towards the outside.

In this chapter, I depart from previous research on EU eastern enlargement in order to bring a better understanding of the EU's external power. On the shoulders of extensive research on Europeanization effects, only recently have a few scholars begun to consider the external dimension of European integration (see, for example, Lavenex and Ucarer 2002). This strand of literature focuses on the interdependence between the EU and non-member countries and brings to the fore the Union's need of cooperation with the outside in order to create an effective common policy. The analysis of the Union's leverage on Albania – a non-candidate country which has only a very long-term EU membership perspective – shows that the process of integration has put the EU in a situation of unavoidable dependence on the cooperation of precisely those countries that are not members of the club. Is the EU able to influence Albanian immigration policies and politics? If so, what is the extent of change caused by the EU? How can we explain the possible Europeanization of Albanian domestic policies and politics? What are the mechanisms of EU influence on non-member countries?

To answer these questions I refer to Europeanization as consisting of

> processes of a) construction, b) diffusion and c) institutionalization of formal and informal rules, procedures, policy paradigms, styles, 'ways of doing things' and shared beliefs and norms which are first defined and consolidated in the EU policy process and then incorporated in the logic of domestic (national and subnational) discourse, political structures and public policies. (Bulmer and Radaelli 2004)

I show that this definition of Europeanization also applies to non-member states that have only a vague or very long-term EU membership perspective. International relations theories offer various mechanisms that seek to account for the ways in which international organizations influence state behaviour. One mechanism that is particularly relevant for the empirical case at hand is conditionality. The notion of conditionality refers to situations in which a state or international organization uses positive incentives to influence a government's behaviour or policies. In the EU's relations with accession countries, non-accession countries with a vague or very long-term membership perspective or countries who wish to acquire at least some prospect of membership, it is membership conditionality that constitutes the Union's negotiation power. The rather basic insight of Europeanization research – namely that significant misfit in policies and politics between an EU member state and the Union results in a high degree of Europeanization of domestic policies and politics – also applies to such non-member countries. In contrast to the EU's influence on its own member states, however, the Europeanization of non-member states functions via the mechanism of conditionality.

The analysis generally corroborates the external incentives model according to which an international organization is unable to influence domestic policies and politics in nation states if strong and credible incentives are absent (see Schimmelfennig and Sedelmeier 2004). Including non-candidate countries in the analysis illustrates that the more unambiguous the membership perspective is, the higher the credibility of the reward and the higher the trust in the EU's commitment. The time frame of membership perspective is less important than the certainty of the reward (for the comparative aspects see Kruse 2005).

This chapter analyses the process of Europeanization of Albanian immigration policies and politics. The main focus is on legislative changes, and the analysis shows that the EU has fundamentally transformed the legal dimension of Albanian policies and politics. The country currently is in a stage of absorbing EU legislation and organizational structure to prepare for EU accession (for the analytic distinction between absorption and transformation, see Radaelli 2003; see also Ette and Faist in this volume). The European Commission cooperates closely with the Albanian administration, assists in drafting laws and provides technical assistance in the context of twinning programmes. In essence, Albania imitates European law and administration (for a similar argument on institutional mimicry see Geddes 2003; Zielonka 2001). However, this chapter also shows that where implementation is concerned Europeanization is rather weak. Although on paper Albanian asylum and immigration law has been widely transformed according to European standards, the practical effects of implementation are lacking. This means that in the Albanian case EU conditionality so far has only affected the legislative dimension but not the implementation dimension.

The chapter starts with an overview of recent developments in EU–Albanian relations. The analysis then examines Albanian efforts in adapting to EU standards regarding irregular migration, trafficking in human beings, border and visa policies, refugee protection and return in more detail.

The institutional framework of EU–Albanian relations

After 44 years under a totalitarian communist regime, in 1991 Albania cut its path to political pluralism and a multi-party system. For decades, the country had been deeply isolated and reclusive, and lacked any economic development and progress. The 1990s witnessed an enormous exodus of Albanians to Italy and Greece, major difficulties in establishing a democratic political system, economic collapse and social unrest and absence of public order. In 1999, a new Constitution came into force in accordance with international democratic standards, but since then local and parliamentary elections in July 2005 have been only partially free. Political life in Albania is of a volatile and confrontational character, and is dominated by deep polarization between the Democratic and the Socialist parties. During the past few years, both intra- and inter-party struggles continuously affected government stability, making political reform difficult if not impossible. The weak political system, together with the government's indifference or even close ties to organized crime, created an ideal environment for organized criminal activity. To add to these difficulties, the role of the parliament is weak, the judiciary is in a poor state, the administration is inefficient and there are hardly any interest groups.

Research on the EU has so far rested on the assumption that the EU has the capacity to transfer its rules only to those non-member countries that have some sort of Western identity or a minimal level of democratic rules (see, for example, Schimmelfennig 2005: 18). As noted, Albania even today still lacks the central features of a liberal Western democracy. Nevertheless, the EU's impact on Albanian policies and politics is very significant. Since 1999, when the EU proposed a Stabilization and Association Process (SAP) for south-eastern Europe, European integration has dominated the political agenda and public discussions in Albania. The European Council (2000) in Feira assured an indisputable long-term membership perspective to all SAP countries. Since then, Albania has benefited from around €238.5 million in CARDS[1] assistance (2000–4). In 2003, €20 million were allocated specifically to actions in the areas of justice and home affairs (JHA). In addition, the CARDS Regional Programme allocated €1 million in 2002 and 2003 each for integrated border management.

Following the SAP, the EU launched negotiations on a Stabilization and Association Agreement (SAA) with Albania in 2003. The European Commission (2001b: 8) had hoped that the opening of such negotiations would be the 'best way of helping to maintain the momentum of recent political and economic reform, and of encouraging Albania to continue its constructive and moderating influence in the region'. The negotiations are still ongoing. A future SAA will affect several migration issues. It requires both the EU and Albania to guarantee non-discrimination in the working environment and in payment and firing of workers who are legally established in their respective territories, and to allow spouses of legally resident workers access to the labour market. Albania is requested to join the ILO Migration for Employment Convention (which took place in March 2005) and the European Convention on the Legal Status of Migrant Workers (which is yet to take place). In addition, the EU is required to apply some of the rules on coordination of social security systems to Albanian nationals legally employed in the EU. Furthermore, Albania will have to cooperate in the fields of asylum, legal and illegal migration, control of external borders, visas and readmission. As a first major step, the Albanian government (2004) adopted a National Strategy on Migration to address EU requirements on the country's way towards accession. A related Action Plan was approved in May 2005 and the Minister of State oversees its implementation.

The EU body that is monitoring Albania's progress in JHA is the Consultative Task Force (CTF). It meets four times a year and provides recommendations to the European Commission and the Albanian government. In 2003, the European Commission (2003: 1) highlighted the importance of more far-reaching reforms in the area of JHA and in particular called for stronger efforts regarding illegal migration, trafficking in human beings, border management and the readmission of third-country nationals. Since then, Albania has repeatedly been criticized for not making substantial progress in reforms (see, for example, Commission of the European Communities 2004: 1). The authors of the Commission's latest Progress Report (Commission of the European Communities 2005: 66) came to the conclusion that, even though notable progress has been made in terms of legislation and the formulation of Action Plans, proper implementation has been hampered by a lack of resources and in some cases of political will.

In June 2003, the Thessaloniki Council of the EU (2003: 11) established the EU–Western Balkans Forum and underlined the European perspective on the western Balkan countries. Within the agenda, the importance of actions against trafficking in human beings with a special focus on victim assistance, training programmes of competent bodies, intelligence and exchange of information, public awareness and strategy development are emphasized. A year later, the Council of the EU (2004) adopted a European Partnership for Albania which, among other things, identifies short- and medium-term priorities in the areas of asylum and migration to be carried out by Albania to make further progress towards membership in the EU. Albania responded with an Action Plan for the Implementation of European Partnership Priorities in September 2004 and provided the Commission with updates on its progress in implementing the Action Plan in December 2004 and March 2005.

Overall, relations between Albania and the EU are indisputably asymmetric in all dimensions. The main rationale for EU engagement in Albania is its interest in stability in the Balkans. To reach this goal, the Union early on held out to all western Balkan countries the prospect of one day joining the club. In the case of Albania, it is a very long-term membership perspective indeed, and the country is far from fulfilling the admission criteria.

Because of Albania's absolute desire to join the EU, the Union has high leverage on Albanian domestic immigration policies. The European Commission cooperates closely with the Albanian administration, assists in drafting laws, provides technical assistance in the context of twinning programmes and monitors implementation of reforms. Therein, the EU plays the game of conditionality: the next steps in integration are made conditional upon certain progress in reform.

Albania's keen interest in joining the EU allows the Union also to wield influence on the country's politics of immigration. In accordance with the great importance placed on close relations to the EU, the Albanian administration established a separate Ministry of European Integration in 2004. The Ministry's main task is to interact with EU institutions and to coordinate negotiations with the Union. Furthermore, European integration dominates the political agenda and public discussions in Albania. According to a 2003 survey, in public administration, in the media and in local NGOs and business groups, support levels for Albania's membership in the EU reach nearly 100 per cent (see, for example, Albanian Institute for International Studies 2003). In general, the EU and Albania's progress in European integration is one of the primary reference points in both Albanian politics and public discourse.

Irregular (transit) migration and trafficking in human beings

Since the transition from communist rule to multi-party democracy in 1991, emigration from Albania has been massive, and the propensity to emigrate higher still (for the data see Papapanagos and Sanfey 2001). According to estimates, 15 per cent of the population, or a total of 500,000–600,000 Albanians, left the country between 1990 and 2000 (see ICMPD 2000: 84). Estimates assume a stock of 400,000 Albanians living illegally in a foreign country and a yearly rate of illegal emigrants of about 20,000–40,000 Albanians (see Gjonca 2002: 34).

The EU is eager for Albania to control its emigration flows, the majority of which are directed towards EU territory. The effectiveness of EU immigration policies is directly related to the effectiveness of Albanian emigration policies and in that sense the EU depends upon Albanian cooperation. Substantial parts of the Albanian National Strategy on Migration concentrate on the management of emigration flows and related legislation: protecting rights of Albanian emigrants abroad, linking Albanian communities abroad, attracting remittances into business investments, establishing a policy for labour migration and facilitating the travel of Albanian citizens with short-term visas (see Albanian government 2004). There are only a very few legal ways to emigrate since Albania signed agreements on labour migration with Germany (1992), Greece (1996) and Italy (1998).[2] The IOM opened a Migrant Assistance Centre in Tirana in 2001 which provides information for potential migrants who wish to emigrate from Albania legally and for those who wish to return and reintegrate into Albanian society. The government adopted a new Law on Emigration in 2003.

Even more important to the EU is Albania's position as a transit country. During the last decade, criminal organizations were engaged in promoting and undertaking illegal migration through Albania. They have strong links with Albanian authorities and with Italian, Greek and Turkish crime rings. According to the Albanian Ministry of Public Order, the main countries of origin for illegal transit migration are Moldova, Lithuania, Iraq, Iran, Turkey, Serbia, Bangladesh, China, Ukraine and Belarus. Illegal migrants reach Albania mainly via land borders, most often via the Albanian–Greek border, but even via borders with Macedonia, Montenegro and Kosovo.

According to estimates, between 150,000 and 250,000 transit migrants followed these routes into Albania between 1993 and 2000, and around 36,000 people transit Albania every year in attempts to migrate to the EU (see Commission of the European Communities 2001a: 10). On the basis of data provided by Albanian and Italian authorities, ICMPD (2000: 88–9) extrapolated that an average of about 16,000 non-Albanians that have crossed Albania are apprehended in Italy on a yearly basis. These apprehended illegal migrants probably represent only about 40 per cent of all illegal migrants coming from Albania, meaning that around 24,000 remain undiscovered and are able to successfully make their way into the EU.

Under EU pressure, the Albanian Council of Ministers adopted in 2003 an Action Plan to Improve the Free Movement of People, which foresees measures to be taken to prevent illegal border crossing and to destroy links between illegal migration and crime. In its November 2003 Brussels JHA ministerial meeting, the EU–Western Balkans Forum also announced the adoption of a programme to combat illegal migration across maritime borders. Illegal migrants who are apprehended by Albanian border guards must usually pay fines of about $50–$100, even though punishment of up to two years' imprisonment would be possible according to law. At present the EU is very much concerned about the general lack of detention facilities, and the result that apprehended people are only rarely kept in detention. The same applies to illegal migrants intercepted at sea and returned to Albania. Even if there were detention facilities in Albania, the government would lack funds to provide apprehended migrants with food and to provide transport of the returnees to their countries of origin. Those apprehended are usually released, which creates great concern on the part of the EU because most of them are likely to try once more to reach EU territory.

Albania is also an important transit and origin country for the business of trafficking in human beings. Official statistics suggest that of the approximately 500,000 Albanians who left the country between 1993 and 2001, about 100,000 were trafficked (Albanian government 2004). In 2000 and 2001, 662 navigational conveyances carrying 18,209 victims of trafficking were intercepted. About 8000 Albanian women were forced into prostitution in several European countries in 2001, and about the same numbers of foreign women – mainly from Russia, Ukraine, Moldova, Romania and Bulgaria – were trafficked through Albania. In addition to these numbers, between 1992 and 2000 an estimated 4000 children were trafficked from Albania to neighbouring countries for exploitation, begging, working in slavery or sexual abuse. Many Albanian girls are caught by the Italian police and immediately repatriated but most of them are trafficked again soon after (Renton 2001: 41–2).

As part of its efforts to adapt to EU standards, Albania has signed the UN Convention against Transnational Organized Crime and its three protocols. Since 2001, trafficking is a criminal offence under Albanian law and the Criminal Code provides that perpetrators will be punished with prison sentences of between 5 and 20 years, and with life imprisonment should they cause the death of a trafficked person. With the help of the EU and several international organizations, the Albanian parliament agreed on a National Strategy to Combat Illegal Trafficking in Human Beings in December 2001 which is coordinated by the Minister of State in cooperation with the Prime Minister (see Council of Ministers of the Republic of Albania 2001). A 'Committee for the fight against trafficking of human beings' reporting directly to the Prime Minister was established, made up of members of the government, directors of state services and specialists from international organizations, particularly the Organization for Security and Cooperation in Europe (OSCE). In addition, a special anti-trafficking police unit was established which successfully carried out some major operations against the trafficking business, especially at the maritime border.

Furthermore, within the framework of the Stability Pact for Southeastern Europe, a Task Force on Trafficking in Human Beings was established in 2000 to develop a regional anti-trafficking strategy addressing a range of tasks such as raising awareness, training and capacity building, law enforcement cooperation, victim protection, return and reintegration, legislative reform and prevention. The task force lobbies for the legalization of the status of trafficked persons, granting them temporary residence, witness protection, the prevention of child trafficking, and combating the root causes of human trafficking and a zero tolerance policy with respect to the demand side.

In view of these activities, the OSCE Anti-trafficking Unit has come to the conclusion that the business of trafficking in human beings through Albania and via the Adriatic/Ionian Sea has been substantially reduced in recent years (see also Commission of the European Communities 2005: 57, 62). Albania has the highest number of arrested traffickers in south-east Europe, although not all are successfully prosecuted. Only recently has the European Commission (2005: 68) called for concrete achievements in the arrest and prosecution of perpetrators. In September 2004, the Albanian government adopted a so-called anti-mafia package consisting of, among other things, a Law on the Protection of Witnesses and Those who Cooperate with the Authorities, which provides a legal definition of trafficking in human beings. Since then, the EU has asked Albania, in vain, to develop operational guidelines on witness protection and to tackle the protection of witnesses in court and remote interviewing. As a first step, six implementing Acts were approved in June and July 2005.

Borders and visas

During the 1990s, Albania had one of the weakest border control systems in Europe. Even though the country is very small – 720 km in land boundaries and 362 km of coastline – it constitutes an important loophole for illegal migrants on their route to Western Europe. For that reason, the EU is very keen that Albania strengthen its border controls in order to reduce flows of illegal migrants heading towards EU territory.

The Albanian border police are basically underpaid, understaffed and unequipped and if violators are caught, the border police lack the financial and infrastructural capacity to detain them because the prison as well as the court systems are still in a very bad state. Nonetheless, the European Commission (2005) recently reported considerable improvement in border control through better management and initial steps in establishing an information and technology infrastructure. Under EU influence, document examination devices are now available at all main border crossings, and mobile surveillance units to control green borders have been introduced. The EU continues to call for a clearer division of responsibilities between border police and customs service for border controls and for further progress in establishing the IT system which provides police and border services with information on stolen passports or visa stickers and which helps register persons transiting the country.

In the context of the SAP, the Albanian government agreed upon a National Strategy on Border Control and its Integrated Management in 2003. The strategy is foreseen to be implemented during 2003–6. With the help of EU twinning programmes, the border police have undergone general restructuring of their legislative framework, composition and organizational structure. During the last few years, Italy has been by far the most important partner in helping the country to control its borders. Both countries signed a border cooperation agreement in 1997, and since then between 100 and 300 officers from the Carabinieri, Guardia di Finanza and Polizia di Stato have been based in Albania. Albanian officers are present on Italian interception vessels and vice versa, and Albanian officers undergo training in Italy. If illegal migrants are intercepted in Albanian or international waters, they are returned to Albania; if in Italian waters, they are passed to

Italy and in most cases returned to Albania afterwards. Only recently has the Albanian–Italian cooperation shifted its focus towards transit migrants rather than illegal Albanian migrants. In contrast, Greece, which is the second most important destination country for Albanian emigrants, does not make comparable efforts to build the Albanian capacity of migration control.

Under the umbrella of the Stability Pact, the EU, NATO and OSCE cooperate in a Consultative Group to develop a common regional approach to border security and management issues in the western Balkans (the so-called 'Ohrid Border Process'). The platform envisages open but controlled and secure borders in the entire region in accordance with European standards and initiatives. This means, on the one hand, facilitation of border crossing for legitimate purposes, especially by the inhabitants of border areas, and on the other hand prevention and prosecution of all illegal cross-border activities.

As far as Albanian visa policy is concerned, the EU has requested Albania in the context of both the SAA and the European Partnership to amend its Law on Foreigners to bring visa legislation closer to EU standards. Respective amendments were put before the Parliamentary Commission of Laws in early 2004 but have not yet been adopted by the parliament. In addition, Albania had to upgrade its travel documents to comply with international standards and recently introduced new ten-year passports containing security features for Albanian citizens. The issuing of travel documents still remains a concern for the EU because most travellers still acquire visas at their port of entry to Albania rather than from Albanian consular offices abroad. In this regard, the European Commission (2005: 64) has also recently called for more progress in computerizing the visa system.

The Albanian government (2003) established a Working Group for the Facilitation of Free Movement of Albanian Citizens in 2002 with the purpose of requesting that EU member states ease or remove the existing visa regime for Albanian citizens. Since then, the government has sought to negotiate and conclude bilateral agreements with different states on visa facilitation or cancellation. In its National Strategy on Migration, however, the government (2004) stated realistically:

> The EU countries remain reluctant to remove Albania from the EU 'black list' … The government will realistically in the short and medium term focus on the facilitation of the visa regime and in a long-term period on the withdrawal of Albania from the 'black list' … The commitment that Albania has shown by concluding the

readmission agreement with the EU and in the combat of irregular migration is a strong argument to ask for visa facilitations in return.

The EU has made it official that liberalization of the visa regime for western Balkan countries will depend upon strengthening the rule of law, combating organized crime, corruption and illegal migration, and strengthening administrative capacities in border control and security of documents.

Refugee protection

Albania signed the Geneva Refugee Convention and its Protocol in 1992. Article 40 of the Constitution establishes the right to asylum, and the principle of non-refoulement is contained in article 39 (3). On paper, the 1998 Law on Asylum meets international standards and regulates both refugee status and temporary protection. In August 2003, a Law on the Integration and Family Reunification of Foreigners granted asylum in Albania was approved. It has been reported by the UNHCR (see Chadbourne 2004: 12), however, that the law has yet to be implemented.

Albania's experience with refugee protection is only recent. During the Kosovo War about 465,000 people came to the country and were granted temporary protection on a humanitarian basis. Most of these refugees returned to their home region afterwards and only a few asked for asylum in Albania. The number of asylum-seekers from other countries is still small – for 2003, the Albanian government talks of some 50 cases. A total of 52 recognized refugees are reported to be residing in Albania so far, which means that the numbers of refugees do not constitute an issue. According to the Directorate for Refugees, which is part of the Ministry of Public Order, Albania is rather a

> place for people coming from the East who want to immigrate to western Europe. So some of them have no interest in staying here and just ask for asylum to so that they may remain here until the opportunity to go to the European Union arises. ... We have many cases of applicants who dropped out of the process mid-stream. They initiated the application, they had the hearing and after that they disappeared. They don't stay here to wait for the decision. (Personal interview, 14 January 2004, Tirana)

Again, this clearly illustrates the EU's dilemma in which the Union depends on the cooperation of non-member governments and is in need of a well-functioning Albanian asylum system to reduce the number of people who continue onward to enter EU member states.

The moment a person arrives at the Albanian border and chooses to apply for asylum, a pre-screening procedure is initiated, which refers foreigners to the responsible authority according to their respective profiles. Asylum-seekers are under the jurisdiction of the Directorate for Refugees and the UNHCR, whereas economic migrants who wish to return to their countries of origin are dealt with by the IOM, while victims of trafficking are handled by the OSCE. Between February 2001 and August 2003, 602 foreigners were pre-screened and referred to the respective authorities (Hoffmann 2003). After the pre-screening, asylum-seekers are transferred to the reception centre in Babrru near Tirana. The EU has asked the Albanian government several times to take on responsibility for the reception centre but to date it awaits official takeover; for the time being the centre is operated by the UNHCR and four Albanian NGOs.

A hearing session is normally held within two weeks by the Directorate for Refugees, after which the directorate has a time period of one month to take a decision. During the procedure, asylum-seekers obtain free legal support from an NGO legal clinic financed by the UNHCR. Asylum-seekers have the right to appeal the decision, within 45 days, to the National Commission for Refugees which is to consist of representatives of the Directorate for Refugees, the Intelligence Service, the Ministry of Foreign Affairs, the Ministry of Public Order, the Ministry of Labour and Social Affairs and the Ministry of Education. After that, asylum-seekers have the right to appeal to the district court in Tirana which is authorized only to decide whether the state decision has been correct in the administrative sense and not in terms of legitimacy of claims.

Albania is often perceived as a safe third country. However, a UNHCR study conducted in 2004 showed unambiguously that it is not (Chadbourne 2004). The UNHCR is concerned about refusal of entry for persons arriving at the borders and complains harshly about non-transparent and insufficient asylum procedures. Time frames are not respected, no regular meetings are scheduled or take place for the determination of refugee status, no provisions have been made for most vulnerable groups and the quality of information on countries of origin is seriously low. Furthermore, an effective appeal opportunity is still unavailable since the National Commission for Refugees has not yet been fully constituted, an internal regulation on the appeal process has not yet been drafted and the information given to the commission for its decision on the appeal is biased, reflecting only the government's position. Reception conditions are inadequate and sustainable local integration of refugees remains unattainable. The EU has repeatedly called upon the Albanian government to bring its asylum procedure in line with international standards – so far without substantial success (see, for example, Commission of the European Communities 2005: 58).

Return

That return is of particular importance to the EU can be seen by the Union's efforts to reach a Community readmission agreement with Albania. In this area, the EU is highly dependent upon the cooperation of non-member countries such as Albania because otherwise its policies on border control, immigration restriction or visa regulations will remain largely ineffective. This also highlights the EU's dilemma and explains why the EU puts particular emphasis on return measures in its relations with Albania.

The Albanian body responsible for return is the Ministry of Public Order. Under its control, the Directorate for Borders and Migration within the General Directorate of Border Police is responsible for the implementation of readmission agreements. A special unit which will deal exclusively with return issues is expected to be created by 2007 (see International Organization for Migration 2004: 62).

More than 300 Albanian nationals voluntarily returned to Albania between 2000 and 2004 through IOM-assisted return programmes. IOM Albania further assists in the voluntary return of illegal migrants apprehended by Albanian authorities on the country's territory, of those who approach the organization in Albania with their wish to return voluntarily, and of rejected asylum-seekers. From these categories, 194 persons were returned voluntarily from Albania between 2001 and 2004.

The National Strategy on Migration foresees information campaigns providing potential voluntary return migrants with information on their status, rights and services offered in Albania upon return. Plans are to distribute this information through diplomatic and consular services as well as emigrant associations and with the help of NGOs and international organizations. Information campaigns will also inform third-country nationals in Albania about voluntary return programmes and possible assistance. The Law on Emigration for Employment Purposes provides for assistance to returnees in case of voluntary return. Unfortunately, the necessary by-laws are still lacking so that this law has not yet been implemented by the Ministry of Labour and Social Affairs.

In comparison, the number of forced returns of Albanian nationals has been much higher in 2003 alone; more than 30,000 individuals were either readmitted from a state's territory or expelled back to Albania at the borders. According to the IOM, the numbers of returns were particularly high in the cases of Italy and Greece where many Albanians live or work illegally and the UK where Albanians were not recognized as refugees. Most Western European countries return Albanian nationals through flights back to Albania; Italy and Greece return them directly over the border or at the ports of Durres and Vlora.

Negotiations on a readmission agreement

In March 2003, the European Commission opened negotiations with Albania on a readmission agreement. After only three rounds of negotiations, the European Commission announced the successful conclusion of negotiations in November 2003. The agreement, which was signed in April 2005, is the first of its kind between the EC and a European non-member country.

Representatives of the Albanian government described their EU counterparts as skilled, expert, and possessing a great deal of negotiation experience. At the same time, they acknowledged their own weaknesses due to a lack of familiarity with issues concerning illegal migration. A representative of the European Commission described the challenge for the Albanian actors as follows:

> It is a new activity for them, all of these articles to create, it is completely new whereas if we look at our own member states they are used to all this. ... The message that the Albanians were always given is, please, don't say yes, yes, yes. Be clear ..., don't think that you have to sign everything. ... It is one of their weak areas, they need to be tougher. (Personal interview, 19 January 2004, Tirana)

The Albanian side saw the readmission agreement not as an especially beneficial tool but rather as an element of the overall integration process with the EU. The reason Albania negotiated the readmission agreement with the EU so quickly was that parallel negotiations of the SAA were going on: the underlying membership perspective put pressure on the country to cooperate.[3]

The only difficult issue during negotiations was the readmission of third-country nationals. The Albanian government had asked for a five-year transitional period before the readmission of third-country nationals was to begin. In the end, both sides agreed upon a two-year transitional period before the EU will begin readmitting third-country nationals to Albania.

The Albanian parliament was not involved in readmission negotiations with the EU. The Parliamentary Commission on European Integration complained about the government's information policy in the context of both the SAA and the readmission negotiations and criticized the European Commission for failing to insist on involving the parliament. According to the Parliamentary Commission, the readmission agreement has not been discussed in parliament even once.[4] Similarly, in 2002 the European Parliament (EP) had expressed its regret at having been neither consulted nor kept informed during readmission negotiations with third countries (European Parliament 2002). A year later, the EP further complained that its opinion had not been taken into proper account, 'either in terms of the provision of information and involvement or in terms of content' (European Parliament 2004: 9). These complaints on the part of both the Albanian and the European parliaments reinforce our understanding of the procedural impact of Europeanization based on what we have already learned about EU member states: namely, that Europeanization strengthens executive authorities and rather discounts or weakens legislative institutions. Readmission policy is an issue for executive institutions and is subject to approval only once it appears as a completed text at the end of negotiations. Both the European and the Albanian parliaments have merely a procedural function, acquiring importance only after the readmission agreement has been signed.

The part of the agreement relating to Albanian nationals enters into force immediately. In contrast, the chapters concerning third-country nationals need ratification by the Albanian parliament. Since the re-admission agreement is understood as an obligation within the context of the SAA and all parties – together with the public – generally support Albania's European integration efforts, the ratification by the parliament is expected to be beyond doubt.

With the signing of the Community readmission agreement, hopes have been raised for deeper integration and visa liberalization for Albania in the future. The problem of readmitting third-country nationals to their country of origin still remains, however. Readmitting third-country nationals to their home countries is a very costly and administratively challenging task. To date Albania has bilateral re-admission agreements in place with Italy (1997), Switzerland (2000), Hungary (2001), Belgium (2001), Bulgaria (2002), Romania (2002), Germany (2002) and Croatia (2003). Only the Albanian–Italian re-admission agreement covers third-country nationals. The UK agreement was signed in October 2003 but has not yet been ratified. Negotiations are ongoing with the Netherlands, Luxembourg, Macedonia, Slovenia, Slovakia and Bosnia-Herzegovina. Albania is also trying to negotiate readmission agreements with Moldova, Ukraine and Turkey but negotiations have not yet begun.[5] The government reports difficulties in launching negotiations on readmission agreements with several countries of origin and some neighbouring countries.

Implementation of the EU–Albanian readmission agreement

The EU–Albanian readmission agreement is the first of its kind signed with a European transit country outside EU borders. Since data about future returnees are scarce and EU member states provide no estimate, the Albanian government faces great difficulties in assessing future numbers of returnees – both its own nationals as well as third-country nationals. This uncertainty leaves the authorities in the dark with regard to necessary personnel and administrative capacities, the desired scope of reintegration programmes, assistance and job training, and the required capacity of detention facilities. In addition, it is difficult to prioritize the countries of origin with which they should initiate negotiations on bilateral readmission agreements since they have little experience and are therefore uncertain about which third-country nationals EU member states are likely to readmit to Albania.

Return of Albanian nationals to Albania by EU member states

The main challenge with respect to return of Albanian nationals is their reintegration into the country. To date no special assistance programmes exist for Albanian nationals upon return – with the exception of vulnerable groups such as victims of trafficking and unaccompanied minors. Article 4 (3) of the Law on Consular Functions foresees financial assistance for Albanian returnees upon approval of the Ministry of Foreign Affairs, and even the National Strategy on Employment and Vocational Training mentions the need to provide opportunities for vocational training to Albanian returnees with economic and/or social problems. However, the law has not yet been applied, and the strategy still awaits its implementation.

Of course, the EU is keenly interested to see Albania implementing the readmission agreement properly. Towards this end, the EU has given money to the IOM to assist the Albanian government in implementing its readmission policy. In the 18-month project, mechanisms to support Albanian returnees figure significantly. These mechanisms are to be made available for both voluntary as well as forced returnees. The Albanian National Employment Service is to participate in developing mechanisms to assist returnees in matching their specific skills with the needs of the labour market in Albania. This project is currently starting to be implemented in employment offices in Durres, Tirana and Elbasan.

Even though international customary law obliges Albania to take back its own nationals, the return of Albanians to their home country creates major difficulties. It is estimated that remittances amount to US$400–600 million annually, and these funds play a major role in the Albanian economy. Many families in Albania depend almost entirely upon money transfers from relatives who work illegally abroad. Their return may very well result in the destruction of their economic basis and aggravation of their already dire circumstances.

Illegal migrants/returnees most often originate from northern or southern rural remote areas, and upon return tend to stay in or around Tirana. As a consequence, their families might leave their villages in the mountains to join their relatives, with the result that the Albanian authorities must deal with internal migration and rapid urbanization. Another important factor in return is re-emigration. At least in the case of forced return, many migrants look for possibilities to go abroad again since they lack any prospects in their home country. In all these dimensions, the return of Albanian nationals carries with it many challenges for the Albanian authorities.

Return of third-country nationals to Albania by EU member states

Albania has almost no experience with returning third-country nationals to their home country or another transit country. According to the Albanian government, up until the end of 2004 there were no recorded cases of return of third-country nationals on the basis of readmission agreements with individual EU member states.[6] Since neither the Albanian government nor the relevant international organizations are in a position to reliably predict the potential numbers of third-country nationals that will be returned to Albania by EU member states, measures providing for the implementation of the readmission of third country-nationals rest upon vague assumptions.

Albanian authorities fear what they call a 'readmission trap' in which Albania is the only south-eastern European country to have signed a readmission agreement with the EU and thus has to readmit many third-country nationals who may have also transited through other countries in the region (see Albanian government 2004: 26). Therefore, it is a high-priority goal to conclude bilateral readmission agreements with neighbouring countries, as well as with other transit states and countries of origin. On several occasions, Albania has asked the EU for its support in convincing neighbouring countries as well as countries of origin to open and carry through on negotiations. The EU-financed IOM project puts an emphasis on improving the knowledge and expertise of Albanian negotiators involved in readmission agreement talks. Both a model readmission agreement and a Readmission Implementation Reference Handbook are to be drafted by summer 2006. The project also envisages additional training for authorities involved in negotiation and implementation of readmission agreements through language training, workshops and study visits to share best practices and experience.

The EU has repeatedly called for the creation of detention facilities for third-country nationals awaiting further removal. The Albanian Ministry of Public Order is in the preparation phase for the creation of a closed reception centre for repatriated third-country nationals. According to the IOM, the decision on where to locate this centre has not yet been taken, and the size of the facility is still under discussion. As of December 2005, five sites had been examined, three were short-listed and one more was also under consideration. According to IOM Albania, a potential location had been decided by the end of December 2005 and a design should be ready by mid-2006. The European Commission has allocated funds for the creation of the centre during 2006 and 2007. A delegation of the Albanian government visited a closed reception facility in the EU in 2004 to obtain information on common standards related to facilities for women or families, medical and social care, and security.

The readmission of third-country nationals to Albania poses a great challenge for the Albanian government. The institutional infrastructure of Albanian authorities is insufficiently developed and the personnel lack any experience in carrying out the various steps of the return procedure. Proper communication between different institutions is not provided for, the technical equipment insufficient and the staff untrained with regard to human rights considerations and respect for migrants and their needs. Here, the EU's pressure has not yet resulted in procedural change. Facilities for adequate lodging and accommodation are non-existent and the return of migrants to their home countries is nearly impossible given the administrative, organizational and financial implications of readmission. Albania therefore runs the risk of being left with substantial numbers of aliens who might pose a social and economic burden for the country and turn it into a country of destination.

Conclusion

With the help of the EU, various international organizations and NGOs, Albania has undergone substantial legislative changes in the area of asylum and migration during the last five years. There now exist National Action Plans as well as legal mechanisms in all relevant fields of migration policy: asylum, child trafficking, trafficking in human beings, witness protection of victims of trafficking, border control, integration of refugees, emigration and immigration. Only an anti-trafficking law remains to be adopted. Europeanization has clearly resulted in changes in the actual policy and in the absorption by the Albanian government of European standards. However, the implementation of legislative instruments is largely insufficient, and the necessary by-laws are still lacking in basically all areas of migration policy.

In the area of illegal (transit) migration, the lack of detention facilities for returnees still causes the EU concern. The deficiencies with regard to trafficking in human beings include lack of qualified police and prosecutors' personnel, lack of shelters for the rehabilitation of victims, and lack of public awareness (see Commission of the European Communities 2004). A better success rate in prosecution of traffickers would be desirable. The efficiency of border control is still unsatisfactory due to low levels of training, limited equipment, poor infrastructure and corruption. In addition, several experts point to the problem of corruption at the border and in the judiciary resulting in wide-ranging levels of punishment (see Commission of the European Communities 2004: 5). In the field of asylum, some institutions are not yet operational and do not meet international standards. Secondary legislation and by-laws have not yet been enacted, and the National Action Plan on Asylum – which was updated by the Directorate for Refugees in February 2005 – has not yet been endorsed by the Council of Ministers. The processing of asylum claims is well below international standards. Because the centralized pre-screening system has yet to be extended to border areas, respect for the principle of non-refoulement cannot be guaranteed.

Thus, Albania's record in establishing proper legislation and institutional structures to deal with migration movements and implementing this legislation is moderate at best. Absorption of legislative standards has not yet been followed by transformation. Nevertheless, legislative developments in the area of asylum and migration and the early steps in their implementation illustrate that the EU successfully used integration conditionality to achieve adaptation to EU standards. In Albania, political and economic life is very much influenced by the EU and its member states, and public discussions are dominated by the desire to join the EU. That gives the EU the status of irreplaceability which helps it to assert its foreign policy goals. For instance, in the case of the re-admission agreement, the incentive of membership was highly credible for the Albanian side because the EU had repeatedly guaranteed a positive membership perspective in several documents and Albania's potential membership is undisputed among EU member states. The conditions for reward are clear and the Albanian government has a catalogue of criteria to process. That means that trust is high on the Albanian side. The fact that Albania is not yet a candidate country and that its membership perspective is very long term has been of little importance because EU accession is the only perspective the country has, and all political parties, economic actors and the society as a whole agree upon the country's main goal: joining the EU one day.

Notes

1 Community Assistance for Reconstruction, Democratization and Stabilization.
2 The agreement with Germany usually foresees up to 1000 Albanian labour migrants per year but it has been suspended for the time being.
3 Personal interviews, 19 September 2003 and 15 October 2003, Brussels.
4 Personal interview, 16 January 2003, Tirana.
5 Information provided by the Albanian Ministry of European Integration in January 2004.
6 Information received by representatives of the Ministry of Public Order and the Ministry of European Integration in personal interviews, November 2004.

References

Albanian government (2003) *Plan of Measures for the Improvement of the Free Movement of Citizens*. Tirana: Working Group for the Facilitation of Free Movement of Albanian Citizens.

Albanian government (2004) *National Strategy on Migration*. Tirana: Albanian government. http://iomtirana.org.al/Arkiva/Final%20eng-version %20%20aproved%20by%20CM-%2019.11.2004.doc (last accessed on 6 June 2006).

Albanian Institute for International Studies (2003) *Albania and European Union: Perceptions and Realities.* Tirana.

Bulmer, S. and C. Radaelli (2004) 'The Europeanization of National Policy?' In *Queen's Papers on Europeanization*, Vol. 1.

Chadbourne, J. (2004) *Meeting the Mark: Asylum in Albania and the Safe Third Country Concept.* Tirana: UNHCR.

Commission of the European Communities (2001a) *European Community CARDS Programme. Albania Country Strategy Paper 2002–2006.* Brussels: European Commission. http://europa.eu.int/comm/external_relations/see/albania /csp/ 02_06_en.pdf (last accessed on 6 June 2006).

Commission of the European Communities (2001b) *Report from the Commission to the Council on the Work of the EU/Albania High Level Steering Group, in Preparation for the Negotiation of a Stabilisation and Association Agreement with Albania.* COM (2001) 300 final. Brussels: European Commission.

Commission of the European Communities (2003) *Albania. Stabilisation and Association Report 2003.* COM (2003) 139 final. Brussels: European Commission. http://europa.eu.int/eurlex/en/com/rpt/2003/com2003_0139en01.pdf (last accessed on 6 June 2006).

Commission of the European Communities (2004) 'Albania: Stabilisation and Association Report 2004'. Commission Staff Working Paper, SEK (2004) 374/2. Brussels: European Commission. http://europa.eu.int/comm/external_rela-tions/see/sap/rep 3/cr_alb.pdf (last accessed on 6 June 2006).

Commission of the European Communities (2005) *Albania 2005 Progress Report.* SEC (2005) 1421. Brussels: European Commission. http://europa.eu.int/comm/enlarge-ment/report_2005/pdf/pa ckage/sec_1421_final_en_progress_report_al.pdf (last accessed on 6 June 2006).

Council of Ministers of the Republic of Albania (2001) *National Strategy to Combat Illegal Trafficking in Human Beings.* Tirana. http://www.osce.org/ attf/pdf/nap_al.pdf (last accessed on 6 June 2006).

Council of the European Union (2000) *Santa Maria Da Feira European Council Presidency Conclusions.* Brussels: European Council. http://ue.eu.int/ueDocs/ cms_Data/docs/pressData/en/ec/00 200-r1.en0.htm (last accessed on 6 June 2006).

Council of the European Union (2003) *Thessaloniki European Council Presidency Conclusions.* Brussels: European Council. http://europa.eu.int/constitution/ futurum/_documents/other/oth200603_en.pdf (last accessed on 6 June 2006).

Council of the European Union (2004) *Council Decisions on the Principles, Priorities and Conditions Contained in the European Partnership with Albania.* 2004/519/EC. Brussels: European Council. http://europa.eu.int/comm/ enlargement/albania/pdf/European_Partnership_Albania_en.pdf (last accessed on 6 June 2006).

European Parliament (2002) *Report on the Proposal for a Council Decision on the Signing of the Agreement between the European Community and the Government of the Special Administrative Region of the People's Republic of China on the Readmission of Persons Residing without Authorisation.* A5-0381/2002. Strasbourg: European Parliament. http://www2.europarl.eu.int/omk/sipade2?PUBREF=//EP//NONSGML+REPORT+A 5-20020381+0+DOC+PDF+V0//EN&L=EN&LEVEL=2&NAV=S& LSTDOC=Y (last accessed on 6 June 2006).

European Parliament (2004) *Report on the Proposal for a Council Decision Concerning the Signing of the Agreement between the European Community and the Macao Special Administrative Region of the People's Republic of China on the*

Readmission of Persons Residing without Authorisation. Final A5-0096/2004. Strasbourg: European Parliament. http://www2.europarl.eu.int/registre/ seance_pleniere/textes_deposes/rapports/2004_P5/0096/P5_A(2004)0096_EN. pdf (last accessed on 6 June 2006).

Geddes, A. (2003) *The Politics of Migration and Immigration in Europe*. London: Sage.

Gjonca, A. (2002) 'Albanische Emigration in den neunziger Jahren – eine neue Ära in der demographischen Entwicklung'. In K. Kaiser, R. Pichler and S. Schwandner-Sievers (eds), *Die weite Welt und das Dorf. Albanische Emigration am Ende des 20. Jahrhunderts*. Vienna: Böhlau, pp. 15–38.

Hoffmann, M. (2003) *Managing the Flows. Albania's Three-Pronged Approach*. Athens: Human Rights Defence Centre (KEPAD).

ICMPD (2000) *How to Halt Illegal Migration to, from and through South East Europe? A Report on the Activities of the Working Group on South East Europe of the Budapest Group, with Proposals on Further Action in the Overall Framework of the Stability Pact Prepared by the Secretariat of the Budapest Group*. Vienna: ICMPD.

International Organization for Migration (2004) *Analysis of Albanian Immigration Legislation and Practice as Compared to EU and International Standards. Gap Analysis on Migration Management in Albania*. Tirana: IOM. http://www.iom.int/en/ PDF_Files/tcm/Albania_GAP.pdf (last accessed on 6 June 2006).

Kruse, I. (2005) 'EU Readmission Policy and Its Implications for Non-Member States'. Dissertation, Otto Suhr Institute for Political Science: Free University Berlin.

Lavenex, S. and E. M. Ucarer (eds) (2002) *Migration and the Externalities of European Integration*. Lanham: Lexington Books.

Papapanagos, H. and P. Sanfey (2001) 'Intention to Emigrate in Transition Countries: the Case of Albania'. *Journal of Population Economics*, Vol. 14: 491–504.

Radaelli, C. (2003) 'The Europeanization of Public Policy'. In K. Featherstone and C. Radaelli (eds), *The Politics of Europeanization*. Oxford: Oxford University Press, pp. 27–56.

Renton, D. (2001) *Child Trafficking in Albania*. New Delhi: Global March Against Child Labour. http://www.globalmarch.org/child-trafficking/virtuallibrary/ child-trafficking-in-albania.pdf (last accessed on 6 June 2006).

Scharpf, F. W. (1997) *Games Real Actors Play: Actor-Centered Institutionalism in Policy Research*. Boulder, Colo.: Westview Press.

Schimmelfennig, F. (2005) 'The International Promotion of Political Norms in Eastern Europe: a Qualitative Comparative Analysis'. Central and Eastern Europe Working Paper No. 61. Cambridge, Mass.: Center for European Studies. http://www.ces.fas.harvard.edu/publications/Schimmelfennig.pdf (last accessed on 6 June 2006).

Schimmelfennig, F. and U. Sedelmeier (2004) 'Governance by Conditionality: EU Rule Transfer to the Candidate Countries of Central and Eastern Enlargement'. *Journal of European Public Policy*, Vol. 11: 661–79.

Zielonka, J. (2001) 'How New Enlarged Borders will Reshape the European Union'. *Journal of Common Market Studies*, Vol. 39: 507–36.

Zürn, M. (2000) 'Multilevel Governance: On the State and Democracy in Europe'. In M. Albert, L. Brock and K. D. Wolf (eds), *Civilizing World Politics: Society and Community beyond the State*. Lanham: Rowman & Littlefield, pp. 149–68.

12

The External Face of Europeanization: Third Countries and International Organizations

Sandra Lavenex

Introduction

'Europeanization' has many faces. As an analytical concept, this term has mainly been applied to study the effects of EU legislation on member states. Yet, it has also been used to describe a variety of processes of social and political change such as the reconfiguration of territorial boundaries in the process of European integration; the strengthening of EU institutions; or, as used in this chapter, as repercussions of the European integration process on the outside world, non-member states and international organizations (Olsen 2002).

The external face of Europeanization is especially salient in the area of international migration and refugee flows which have by definition an external dimension. As this and several other chapters in this volume show, the search for common policies in the EU has triggered the emergence of a dynamic foreign policy agenda which may prove to be more consequential for the governance of migration than protracted harmonization efforts within the EU. This agenda has risen in parallel with the EU's affirmation as an international actor, reflected in the intensification of its cooperation and association relations with third countries and its influence in international organizations and regimes. In many respects, it is an attempt to bind third countries and organizations to EU policy-making in a policy field characterized by complex interdependence and asymmetric relations. In contrast to the candidate countries discussed in the previous chapters, which were the first to experience such 'external governance' (Lavenex 2004; Schimmelfennig and Wagner 2004), the non-member countries have no such carrot of accession inducing their cooperation with the EU. The question that then arises is what mechanisms the EU has at its disposal to promote costly and not always popular policy adaptation in third countries in the absence of membership conditionality.

Opening up the spectrum of Europeanization research to the effects of European policies on non-members, this chapter identifies three mechanisms of external leverage: positive conditionality linked with intergovernmental negotiations; policy transfer through transgovernmental networking; and the mobilization of overarching international organizations such as the International Organization for Migration (IOM) and the UNHCR. With this focus, this chapter departs from the common, narrower use of the concept of Europeanization as an instance of legal transposition of European law at the national level, and understands it in terms of a transformation of the international patterns of governance in the policy field that is induced by EU politics. It concludes with some reflections on the implications of the external face of Europeanization for the wider architecture of global migration governance.

The external dimension in early asylum and immigration policies

The 'external dimension' of EU asylum and immigration policies was officially embraced in 1999 at the Special European Council on Justice and Home Affairs (JHA) in Tampere. In its conclusions the Presidency stated that these concerns should be 'integrated in the definition and implementation of other Union policies and activities', including external relations. Since then, 'partnership with countries of origin' and 'stronger external action' figure prominently in the work plan of the JHA Council. Yet, European cooperation in these matters has always had an external dimension. Already in 1987, the European Parliament (EP) adopted a resolution on the right of asylum which noted the necessity to enhance economic and political cooperation with countries of origin in order to stabilize their economies and to guarantee the protection of human rights (European Parliament 1987: §§ B–E). These ideas were followed further in the Commission's communications of 1991 and 1994, which emphasized the need to fight the root causes of migration through the integration of asylum and immigration policies into all external policies of the Union, including development, trade, human rights, humanitarian assistance and foreign and security policy. Under Maastricht's 'third pillar', however, the Commission and EP lacked formal competence to shape the Council's agenda and these early proposals were not pursued further.

In contrast to a preventive comprehensive approach addressing the factors that cause people to leave their countries of origin, European ministers of immigration have focused on the repression of undesired inflows through externalization (Boswell 2003; van Selm 2002; van der Klaauw 2002). This externalization has also been referred to as 'remote control' (Zolberg 2003) because it shifts the locus of control further afield from the common territory. The earliest instruments were the coordination of visa policies, the introduction of carrier liability and the placing of national liaison officers from the home ministries at airports in countries of origin in order to check that documentation was thoroughly examined. A different unilateral measure with clear external implications was the mobilization of third countries in the control of migration flows to Europe through the adoption of the 'safe third country' rule (Lavenex 1999). Adopted from the early 1990s onward, this rule allows the member states to deny examination of an asylum claim and to send back the applicant to a third country where he or she would have had the possibility to apply for asylum, provided that the state is party to basic international refugee treaties. The next step in the mobilization of third countries into the emerging system of EU-wide cooperation was the conclusion of readmission agreements as agreed in the Declaration of the Edinburgh European Council of 1992.[1] The politics of eastern enlargement provided a framework for binding the newly democratizing countries of Central and Eastern Europe into the EU's emerging system of immigration control. As in other policy fields, the conditionality for membership has proved a powerful instrument of foreign policy and in the promotion of strict immigration control standards beyond the territory of the member states (Byrne et al. 2002; Grabbe 2002; Jileva 2002; Lavenex 1999, 2001; Wallace and Stola 2001). Today, comparable dynamics are also at play with newer and remaining potential candidates for membership, Turkey and the countries of the former Yugoslavia (Kirisci 2002; Kruse and İçduygu in this volume).

Avenues of externalization

Since its official embracement, the evolution of the external dimension has been formidable. A look at the biannual scoreboards on the implementation of the Tampere Programme shows that whereas the internal harmonization agenda remained stable, the external dimension was extended each year to include new measures and countries. This expansion is also visible in the so-called 'multi-presidency programmes' on JHA external relations which the Council has been adopting since 2001.

External migration policies take three main avenues: the first (and not so new) is based on negotiations and consists of the conclusion of readmission agreements. The second could be termed policy transfer and takes the form of the export of EU policies and instruments through transgovernmental networking and support from supranational institutions, including the outsourcing of EU refugee policies through the establishment of so-called Regional Protection Projects. Apart from the use of positive conditionality to trigger cooperation from third countries, these avenues also reflect more socialization-based attempts at policy transfer (on these notions see Kelley 2004 and Schimmelfennig and Sedelmeier 2005). A more recent development, discussed in the next section, which could also be read as an attempt to increase the legitimacy of EU endeavours, is the mobilization of international organizations.

A crucial instrument assuring third countries' participation in fighting undesired irregular immigration is the conclusion of readmission agreements through which they commit themselves to take back their own and third-country nationals returned by the EU. The problem the EU faces with the conclusion of such agreements is that since these 'are solely in the interest of the Community, their successful conclusion depends very much on the "leverage" at the Commission's disposal. In that context it is important to note that, in the field of JHA, there is little that can be offered in return ...' (Commission of the European Communities 2002: 23). Indeed, the difficulties in motivating countries such as Russia, Ukraine or Morocco to sign such agreements show the limits of an unbalanced, EU-centred approach. To respond to this challenge, the Commission has first created a new budget line (B7-667) to support 'Cooperation with third countries in the area of migration'. In 2004, this was replaced by a multiannual financial framework for the years 2004–8 with a total amount of 250 million (the so-called AENEAS Programme). Apart from the general goal to support third countries' efforts to improve the management of migratory flows, the regulation stresses in particular stimulation of third countries' readiness to conclude readmission agreements, and assistance in coping with the consequences of such agreements. Another measure to gain leverage with third countries has been 'increasing complementarity with other Community policies in order to help in achieving the Community's objectives in the field of return and readmission' (Commission of the European Communities 2002: 24). This was achieved essentially by linking association and cooperation agreements with migration control policies as decided in the Conclusions of the Seville European Council of June 2002. Although a Spanish–British initiative to make development aid to third countries conditional on their cooperating on migration control was rejected, the final conclusions did confirm a certain conditionality. First, it was agreed that each future EU association or cooperation agreement should include a clause on 'joint management of migration flows and compulsory readmission in the event of illegal immigration'. The handling of readmission clauses changed when it became obligatory to negotiate a supplementary treaty with the entire Community, not just individual member states. In addition, the EU policy now is that such clauses are mandatory: it will no longer sign any association or cooperation agreement unless the other side agrees to the standard obligations. The Seville Conclusions also decided that inadequate cooperation by a third state could hamper further development of relations with the EU, following a systematic assessment of relations with that country. And, finally, if a non-EU state has demonstrated 'an unjustified lack of cooperation in joint management of migration flows', according to the Council following a unanimous vote, then the Council, after 'full use of existing Community mechanisms', could take 'measures or positions' as part of the EU's foreign policy or other policies, 'while honouring the Union's contractual commitments and not jeopardizing development cooperation objectives' (Council of the EU 2002). Probably realizing the diplomatic contingencies of such negative conditionality, recent readmission negotiations with Albania (see Kruse, this volume), Russia, Ukraine and Morocco have conceded to a long-withheld incentive: linkage with visa facilitation agreements.

A second avenue of external Europeanization occurs less through intergovernmental negotiations than through the networking of civil servants at the transgovernmental level, with the active support of the European Commission. Such networking is promoted in the framework of bilateral Association or Partnership and Cooperation Agreements as concluded with the countries of the European Neighbourhood Policy (ENP),[2] operational cooperation with EU networks of migration or border control officials, and institution-building through expert missions and 'twinnings' between specialized administrations in selected third countries and EU member states, an instrument borrowed from EU enlargement politics (see Commission of the European Communities 2005b). Financial support comes from the EU budget, through the regional TACIS (Eastern Europe) or MEDA (southern Mediterranean) programmes, or thematic budget lines like the AENEAS

Programme. Many of these activities were prepared by Action Plans adopted on illegal immigration, external borders and return policy. A first EU-wide 'Border management control' programme with Morocco, launched already in 2003, includes the execution of joint border patrols and training of officials dealing with migrants. These cooperation measures have become more transversal issues in the ENP and include, apart from operational cooperation at the border, training of officials and support of legal and institutional reforms. Regular biannual meetings in specialized subcommittees composed of EU and third-country officials are to ensure the monitoring of these reforms and, herewith, closer alignment with the EU. The first non-EU candidate country to sign a relevant 'twinning' agreement was Morocco in 2005 with France on the training of the border police. In the long run, the purpose is to lead the EU's neighbours to align legislation with the *acquis* (Commission of the European Communities 2003a: 10). The fact that such cooperation extends to neighbouring countries that, because of their political situation, do not at present qualify for the ENP, shows the importance this posture holds for the EU. Despite the official halt to association relations with Belarus undertaken in 1997, a number of TACIS projects managed by the Commission are in progress that include border infrastructure and management, as well as measures against trafficking in human beings. More recently, it was agreed to conclude with Libya an Action Plan on Illegal Migration covering joint cooperation on search and rescue in the Mediterranean Sea and Saharan desert – despite the fact that Libya, like Belarus, is party neither to the ENP nor to relevant human rights treaties such as the 1951 Geneva Convention (Council of the EU 2005). By embedding these activities within the broader framework of intensified association relations in the ENP, or, in the case of Libya, the prospect of an Association Agreement, the EU makes use of its wider economic and political leverage in promoting external Europeanization.

Whereas readmission agreements and external border cooperation lead to an externalization of the locus of immigration control, the conduct of asylum procedures and the granting of asylum have hitherto remained tied to the territory of the member states. The decision to establish 'Regional Protection Programmes' (RPPs) outside the EU at its external borders (in a first step most likely Ukraine) and in regions of origin (the Great Lake Region) represents a new dimension of externalization, in which not only the control, but the conduct of the public policy itself, in this case the asylum procedure, is being outsourced to a foreign territory. The notion of RPPs contrasts with the older notion of 'safe havens' protected by the international community which were established within regions of conflict and for a limited period of time, as applied, for instance, during the wars in the former Yugoslavia. The idea is now to externalize the formal asylum procedure itself by retaining asylum-seekers in centres closer to their area of origin while their claims are being assessed. From these centres, only recognized refugees are to have access to EU territory and be resettled in a member state, while rejected asylum-seekers are to be returned to their country of origin (Commission of the European Communities 2005a). This recent EU initiative goes back to ideas voiced by member states' governments, first by Austria in 1998, then by UK Prime Minister Blair, backed by Italy and Germany. The international effects of such far-reaching external policies have become immediately salient, as shown in the reaction of the UNHCR, the international organization in charge of safeguarding the international refugee regime. A few days after the British proposal, the UNHCR tabled a 'three-pronged' approach which includes, among other things, stronger protection 'in the region' and, in addition, the idea of closed processing centres, albeit on EU territory. Herewith, the UNHCR agreed to a policy that departs from the fundamental pillar of the post-Second World War refugee regime, that is, the individual commitment and responsibility of liberal democratic countries, under international law, to give access to domestic asylum procedures.

In the next section attention shifts to the international level. The question is how far international organizations themselves become 'EU-ized' and implicated in the external face of Europeanization.

The EU-ization of international organizations

International organizations, in this case the UNHCR and the IOM, play a complex role in the (external) Europeanization of asylum and immigration policies. On the one hand, these organizations follow their own agendas as independent organizations with their own mandates. Theoretically, their work can be a complement to policy harmonization in the EU. Their broader membership, including receiving, transit and sending countries, opens the possibility for a more inclusive agenda than that promoted by EU member states. Yet, overlapping membership can also have the opposite effect of 'EU-izing' overarching international organizations by prompting their alignment with EU policies or turning them into agents in the realization of these policies. This may occur when EU member states, by way of their number and decision-making influence in international organizations, attempt to 'upload' the agenda currently followed in the EU. Apart from international organizations' reliance on the EU member states in terms of constituents and for their ideational support, the latters' financial contributions are a sensitive tool of impact. With the coordination of European policies in the EU, and the crafting of a common approach towards asylum-seekers, refugees and a number of immigration issues, the aggregate weight of European states in these organizations has steadily increased – and today we increasingly witness the effort on the part of the latter to adapt and align their operations to the outlines of emerging European policy.

As their own policy agenda becomes increasingly influenced by the debates in the framework of the EU, we observe two different reactions to Europeanization. The first can be described as an effort to redefine the organizations' own mandates in complement to the EU's activities, that is, getting engaged in those areas in which the EU and its member states put less priority. The other strategy, traditionally more prominent for the IOM, but also increasingly salient in the case of the UNHCR, is more complaisant and consists in the organizations' involvement in the EU's own activities. They thereby become partners and in some cases one could even say subcontractors to the EU and its member states. The mobilization of international organizations has obvious advantages for EU external policies: first, this allows the EU to benefit from the organizations' expertise in terms of established contacts, procedures and knowledge with and about the countries targeted. Second, framing EU requirements in terms of overarching endeavours of international organizations also generates legitimacy, as the latter have the advantage of being regarded as impersonal, value-neutral, not self-interested and hence technocratic actors whose purpose is not the exercise of power but equitable problem-solving. Whether aimed at redressing lacunae left by EU activities (strategy one), or joining the latter (strategy two), both adaptations are deeply reactive in nature, and show the wider ripples of European integration not only on (third) countries but also the structures of international governance.

International organizations as counterweight to EU-ization

At the outset of European intergovernmental cooperation in migration and asylum matters, the role of the international agency responsible for the safeguarding of the international refugee regime, the UNHCR, was very much that of a guardian of the principles, norms and rules agreed in the 1951 Geneva Refugee Convention, its 1967 New York Protocol and the conclusions of the Executive Committee (EXCOM).[3] As Johannes van der Klaauw, former head of the UNHCR Bureau to the European Communities, points out, 'initially, UNHCR adopted a rather reactive stance, commenting on some of the asylum-related resolutions and recommendations adopted in the early 1990s' (2002: 33). In the decade of more or less intergovernmental cooperation which preceded the Treaty of Amsterdam (1999), only loose consultative arrangements existed between successive Presidencies of the Council, preparing the legislative agenda for the next semester, and the UNHCR. Whereas an earlier draft of the Amsterdam Treaty provided for 'close and regular consultations with UNHCR', this reference was later deleted, and in its place Declaration No. 17 was adopted according to which, in asylum matters, the Union is to consult the UNHCR and other concerned international organizations. Since the entry into force of the Treaty, close and regular cooperation has indeed developed between the UNHCR and the Commission in the preparation of Community instruments. The role of the UNHCR has usually been that of redressing the human rights aspects of asylum measures, which were often found wanting in an agenda dominated by the aim to fight the abuse of asylum systems. Whereas the Commission has usually taken the UNHCR's input into consideration in its legislative proposals, that input is later often disregarded in the actual decision-taking process in the Council, which tends to agree on the smallest common denominator (van der Klaauw 2002: 37). This was again confirmed recently with the adoption of the 2005 Asylum Procedures Directive, which the UNHCR soundly condemned for being in breach of fundamental human rights law.

Monitoring the preparations and negotiations on EU asylum legislation has required organizational adaptations. In 1989, a senior liaison post was created in Brussels, and a network of correspondents was set up in UNHCR offices in the member states to follow the Europeanization agenda and to lobby domestic governments on UNHCR recommendations for improvement of draft EC law and policy proposals (van der Klaauw 2002: 46).

Apart from trying to influence the policy-making process within the EU, the second area in which the UNHCR has traditionally provided a counterweight to EU activities is the politics of pre-accession with respect to candidate countries, and, more recently, in other countries tackled by the neighbourhood policies. During the pre-accession process with the countries of Central and Eastern Europe, the UNHCR has played a significant role in supporting the establishment of asylum systems both through legal counselling and institutional or administrative support. It has in particular focused on those elements not covered by EU standards, such as those activities related to the reception of asylum-seekers and integration of recognized refugees (Lavenex 1999). Whereas the EU has usually concentrated on the management of migration flows, 'UNHCR's involvement in non-EU countries ... is much wider in that it aims to ensure the availability of protection and to transform transit countries into countries of destination for refugees' (van der Klaauw 2002: 49). Similar concerns have been voiced regarding EU activities in neighbouring countries as 'its interests seem to be limited to... an effort to reduce secondary movement from these countries to EU member states' and 'attention for asylum matters has had to compete with the EU's priority of combating irregular migration' which has received considerably more attention in political dialogue and operational assistance (UNHCR 2004: 153).

This different emphasis is also visible in the UNHCR's activities in south-eastern and Eastern Europe. In this region, the organization now mainly promotes bilateral, multilateral, NGO and local government support to continue reintegration assistance. This includes issues such as finding alternative solutions for residents in collective centres, or promoting interethnic dialogue between minority refugees, internally displaced persons and returnees with the majority receiving communities. To the east, the UNHCR's main activity has been the CIS Conference Progress which was set up as an inter-agency mechanism between this organization, IOM, the Organization for Security and Cooperation in Europe (OSCE) and the Council of Europe to provide a forum for the countries of the former Commonwealth of Independent States (CIS) to discuss problems of population displacement, review population movements in the region and reach an understanding on persons of concern. Started in 1996, this process has had a considerable impact on problems in the region, such as for example the regularization of the legal status of formerly deported people and, subsequently, the reduction of statelessness as well as the creation of asylum systems (UNGA 2003).

With the linkage of the issue of refugee protection to broader issues of development, democratization/human rights promotion and also conflict resolution/peace-building, the UNHCR's original focus on asylum and refugee protection was widened to the question of migration management in general, where it cooperates also with other UN agencies such as the United Nations Development Programme (UNDP).

This broadened mandate has also brought it closer to the second major international organization in the field, the non-UN agency the IOM.

The predecessor organization to the IOM was set up 1951 with an originally limited mandate inspired by the post-Second World War situation in Europe, covering humanitarian intervention, logistical assistance to migrants and activities such as the provision of language training and cultural orientation for migration. Since 1989, the organization has continuously widened its field of activities, and is now the main agent and promoter of global and regional attempts at migration management. IOM activities nowadays cover, apart from direct assistance to migrants, technical assistance for member states dealing with migration issues, the management of return migration, information campaigns in countries of origin, the fight against irregular migration and migrant trafficking, emergency and post-conflict programmes and the promotion of political dialogue on migration. As of December 2005, the IOM had 116 member states and 22 observers. This is an increase of 11 members over a year earlier, and nearly double the membership in 1998 (67 states). Likewise, IOM's operational budget has seen a steep increase from US$218.7 million in 1998 to more than US$1 billion in 2005 (estimated); field locations increased from 119 in 1998 to more than 280 in 2005; projects increased from 686 in 1998 to more than 1400 in 2005; and operational staff increased from approximately 1100 in 1998 to about 5000 at present.[4]

These numbers reflect a significant rise in the importance of the IOM over the last decade. A particular emphasis of this organization has become the initiation and monitoring of regional intergovernmental consultation processes on migration policy and management. Such processes include the Mediterranean Transit Migration Dialogue, the Manila Process, the South American Migration Dialogue, the Migration Dialogues for Southern and Western Africa and other newly established panels (see Thouez and Channac 2005). In addition, the IOM provides sending and transit countries participating in these dialogues with staff training, expertise and logistical support.

International organizations as agents of EU-ization

With the official embracement of the external dimension of the EU JHA policy, the links between the EU and relevant international organizations have intensified. In the policy areas of asylum and immigration, we observe an increasing convergence in the agendas of relevant organizations with EU activities – and in many cases the international organizations have become crucial partners in the implementation of policies agreed in the EU. On the one hand, the IOM and the UNHCR have increasingly filled the role of subcontractors to the EU in the realization of particular Community programmes. On the other hand, these organizations have come to occupy a crucial role in broader multilateral consultative processes which, following a more participatory approach, are nevertheless instrumental to EU interests in managing migration better.

Already during the EU's eastern enlargement, the UNHCR was involved in the transfer of the asylum *acquis*. It participated in the preparations and implementation of the PHARE 'horizontal' programme in asylum, which was aimed at adapting the legislation and institutions in applicant countries to those of the EU. It also participated in the preparations and implementation of bilateral assistance programmes for each of the ten applicant countries, as well as Turkey. As different scholars and practitioners have noted, although the UNHCR's activities were partly financed by the EU, they were not without tension with those activities carried out by the EU and its member states (Lavenex 1999; van der Klaauw 2002: 39). Later, the UNHCR also became a major player in the European Commission's CARDS programme that underpins the EC's Stabilization and Association Process for the Balkans. With the creation of new financial means to address third countries beyond the circle of aspirants for membership, this kind of project-based cooperation has gained a new dimension. A look at the projects financed under the so-called Budget-line B7-667 created in 2001 to support action in third countries of origin and transit in the area of migration (see above) documents the dominant role of international organizations as beneficiaries. As summarized in Table 12.1, the UNHCR and the IOM together account for more than 50 per cent of all projects funded by this programme. In the

Table 12.1 Number of IOM and UNHCR projects financed under Budget-line B7-667[1]

Year	IOM	UNHCR	Total number of projects
2001	3	3	15
2002	6	2	13
2003	4	6	22

[1]At the time of writing, data on allocation of the successor programme AENEAS were not yet available.
Source: Commission website at http://www.europa.eu.int/comm/justice_home/funding/cooperation/funding_cooperation_en.htm#

successor AENEAS Programme, too, the IOM and the UNHCR took up roughly 40 per cent of the budget in the year 2004 (Commission of the European Communities 2006).

Funding for international organizations linked to EU programmes is of course only a detail when viewed against the overall funding relationship between European countries, the EU and these organizations. Although no detailed information is available on the IOM's funding, the fact that 95 per cent of its total budget is earmarked for specified operations suggests the influence of wealthy Western states, and increasingly also the European Commission (IOM 2005). In the case of the UNHCR, the European Commission itself has become the third largest donor, behind the USA and Japan, in 2004. Yet European sources are clearly in the lead when one adds the contributions from the member states and from private donors from these countries. Again, many of these contributions are earmarked funds, which must be spent as the donor requires (van Selm 2005: 5).[5]

A relatively new form of partnership which has gained prominence with the EU's new Neighbourhood Policy concerns the role of the European Commission and these international organizations in overarching multilateral consultation processes linking EU member states with third countries. Insofar as these activities build on previous consultation networks, the novelty rests in the leading role assumed by the Commission, and herewith a change of emphasis towards West European concerns and interests.

Such a shift is particularly salient in the case of the Söderköping Process which followed up the CIS Conference discussed above.[6] The so-called Söderköping Process was originally initiated in early 2001 by the UNHCR and the Swedish Migration Board as an initiative to promote a dialogue on asylum and irregular migration problems after EU enlargement among the countries situated along Europe's future eastern border. The Söderköping Process began with the participation of five countries – Sweden, Belarus, Lithuania, Poland and Ukraine, and also included the UNHCR and the IOM. They were later joined by Hungary, Slovakia, Moldova and Romania. In order to provide a more solid basis for funding, and to institutionalize the process, the UNHCR submitted a project proposal to the European Commission to fund the establishment of a Secretariat for this purpose. The Secretariat became operational in May 2003 within the premises of the UNHCR office in Kiev. With EU involvement, the process has gained a new emphasis. Originally meant to serve as a forum for dialogue where the participating countries can discuss their concerns in the migration/asylum/border management area and look for solutions in addressing these concerns, the forum became more targeted towards EU policy transfer in 2004. Its main function is described as 'transferring experience of the newly acceded EU member states and the candidate country to the WNIS [Western Newly Independent States] in aligning their migration and asylum related legislation, policies and practices with the EU *acquis* standards and further networking among the participants'. The aim is to 'Strengthen the role of Belarus, Moldova and Ukraine as increasingly important partners of the EU in managing migration and providing protection to asylum-seekers and refugees' (Cross-Border Cooperation/Söderköping Process 2003: 11).

To the south, a similar multilateral project has unfolded under the lead of the IOM – the so-called '5+5 Dialogue' for the western Mediterranean which takes place between Algeria, France, Italy, Libya, Malta, Mauritania, Morocco, Portugal, Spain and Tunisia. Launched in 2001, this dialogue focuses on the fight against irregular migration and trafficking in human beings, but also deals with questions of immigrant integration and co-development. This broader agenda reflects the impact of long-standing relations across the Mediterranean, including migration flows. This situation differs from that in Eastern Europe which, for the period of European unification until 1989, entertained very limited contacts with EU members. Although officially the EU has only observer status at these consultations, session documents repeatedly refer to the need for 'examining the financing possibilities available within the framework of European Union instruments' (5+5 Dialogue 2004). At the end of 2005, the Commission suggested linking the informal dialogue more closely with the overall framework of the Barcelona Process and the work of the relevant subcommittees and promoting cooperation especially in areas such as the fight against illegal migration and trafficking (Commission of the European Communities 2005c).

It seems that with the deepening external dimension, international organizations have become useful vehicles for transporting European concerns and policy solutions via multilateral frameworks to sending and transit countries. Whereas these organizations depend on the EU and its member states for funding and support, the Commission increasingly recognizes their catalytic functions in facilitating dialogue with their member countries which are not party to the Union. This 'deal' is gradually leading to a sort of enhanced partnership between the EU and the international organizations. Whereas earlier attempts by the UNHCR to conclude an 'EU–UNHCR Partnership Framework' had been repeatedly declined (van der Klaauw 2002: 48), consensus was finally reached in 2005, with a focus on activities concerning non-member states. On 15 February of that year, a 'Strategic Partnership Agreement' was signed with the External Relations and European Neighbourhood Policy Commissioner, Benita Ferrero-Waldner. The agreement is intended to consolidate, develop and better structure the existing cooperation between the UNHCR and the European Commission with respect to the protection of, and assistance for, refugees and other people of concern to the UNHCR outside the borders of the EU. A second accord was signed the same day with EC Vice President Franco Frattini, who is Commissioner for Justice, Freedom and Security, to consolidate general consultation on asylum and refugee matters. The words of Judith Kumin, the UNHCR's Representative in Brussels, who was closely involved in negotiating both agreements, on the occasion of their conclusion, are indicative of the Europeanization of international refugee politics, including the UNHCR:

> Cooperation and coordination between the EC and UNHCR can help both parties achieve more effective results. It is symbolic that, on the very day that they were signed, UNHCR and the European Commission are jointly chairing an important session of strategic consultations on Afghanistan, highlighting the scope and will for further collaboration.[7]

Conclusions

Whereas traditionally, studies of European integration and Europeanization have focused on the relationship between member states and European supranational competencies, the transnational nature of asylum and migration flows suggests a widening of the concepts to account for their international effects. This external dimension has become compelling with the dynamic evolution of EU 'foreign' asylum and immigration policies and their repercussions for international governance structures, in relation both to third countries and to international organizations. As I have argued elsewhere, the EU's external agenda has not only traditionally included asylum and immigration policies, it is far more dynamic and possibly also consequential than cumbersome internal harmonization efforts (Lavenex 2006). Highlighting the continuity between contemporary developments and the early instruments adopted under intergovernmental cooperation and the politics of EU enlargement, this chapter scrutinized the mechanisms through which the EU seeks to involve third parties in its 'management' of the migration issue. It was shown that in the absence of membership conditionality, which, as different chapters in this volume indicate, may exert an influence even when the prospect of accession is distant and uncertain, new instruments of external leverage have taken shape. These are the use of positive incentives in intergovernmental negotiations such as the linkage of financial aid and visa facilitation to the conclusion of readmission agreements; the embedding of JHA cooperation in the broader framework of cooperation and association relations, including the promotion of transgovernmental networks; and, finally, the mobilization of international organizations active in the field, such as the IOM and the UNHCR. Gradually, these organizations have shifted from being a complement or counterweight to activities of the EU member states to a role as partners and subcontractors in the EU's widening external migration cooperation. This shift reflects the member states' and, increasingly, the European Commission's pivotal roles as major donors to these organizations, thereby gaining a disproportionate influence on their agendas. At the same time, these organizations' wider membership, their expertise acquired over time, and their technocratic image as neutral functional agencies are important resources contributing not only to the efficiency but also the potential legitimacy of the EU's extraterritorial endeavours.

In sum, whereas the 'Europeanization' of a genuinely transnational phenomenon such as migration necessarily has an external face, an active foreign policy agenda is crafting a distinctive profile. The repercussions of European policy-making are thus felt not only at the level of states and their respective legislation, but also at the level of the structures of international governance. The effects on international organizations and third countries highlighted in this chapter shed a new light on the notion of the EU being a 'normative power' (Manners 2002), and suggest new avenues for Europeanization research.

Notes

1 These recommended that member states 'work for bilateral or multilateral agreements with countries of origin or transit to ensure that illegal immigrants can be returned to their home countries' (European Council 1992: 23).
2 The European Neighbourhood Policy which was implemented in 2004 with five East European countries (Armenia, Azerbaijan, Georgia, Moldova and Ukraine) and the countries of the Euro-Mediterranean Partnership (Algeria,

The Europeanization of National Policies and Politics of Immigration

Morocco, Tunisia, Libya, Egypt, Israel, the Palestinian Authority, Lebanon, Syria and Jordan).

3 The EXCOM meets annually to review and approve the UNHCR's programmes and budget, advise on international protection, and adopt conclusions on international protection which contain specific norms and rules on detailed aspects of refugee protection. It currently counts 68 member states.

4 Data on www.iom.int, 10.2.2006.

5 See also UNHCR's financial information at http://www.unhcr.ch/cgi-bin/texis/vtx/partners?id=3b963b874, 10.2.2006.

6 This initiative was named the 'Söderköping Process' after the town of Söderköping in Sweden where the first meeting was held.

7 See UNHCR News at http://www.unhcr.ch/cgi-bin/texis/vtx/news/opendoc.htm?tbl=NEWS&page=home&id=4212384f4, 10.2.2006.

References

Boswell, C. (2003) 'The "External Dimension" of EU Immigration and Asylum Policy'. *International Affairs*, Vol. 79, No. 3: 619–38.

Budapest Group (2004) Minutes of the first meeting of the project 'Re-direction of the Budapest Process towards the CIS Region', St Petersburg, 11–12 October.

Byrne, R., G. G. Noll and J. Vedsted-Hansen (2002) *New Asylum Countries? Migration Control and Refugee Protection in an Enlarged European Union*. The Hague: Kluwer Law International.

Commission of the European Communities (2002) *Green Paper on a Community Return Policy on Illegal Residents*. 10.4.2002, COM (2002) 175 final, Brussels.

Commission of the European Communities (2003a) *Communication on Wider Europe – Neighbourhood: a New Framework for Relations with our Eastern and Southern Neighbours*. 11.3.2003, COM (2003) 104 final, Brussels.

Commission of the European Communities (2003b) *Report on the Implementation of the Council Conclusions on Intensified Co-operation on the Management of Migration Flows with Third Countries of 18 November 2002*. 9.7.2003, SEC(2003) 815, Brussels.

Commission of the European Communities (2005a) *Communication on Regional Protection Programmes*. 1.9.2005, COM (2005) 388 final, Brussels.

Commission of the European Communities (2005b) *Communication on the External Dimension of the Area of Freedom, Security and Justice*. 12.10.2005, COM (2005) 491, Brussels.

Commission of the European Communities (2005c) *Communication on Priority Actions for Responding to the Challenges of Migration: First Follow-up to Hampton Court*. 30.211.2005, COM (2005) 621 final, Brussels.

Commission of the European Communities (2006) *Communication on the Thematic Programme for the Cooperation with Third Countries in the Areas of Migration and Asylum*. 25.1.2006, COM (2006) 26 final, Brussels.

Council of the European Union (1992) *Presidency Conclusions from the Edinburgh European Council*. 11–12.12.1992.

Council of the European Union (2002) *Presidency Conclusions from the Seville European Council*. Brussels, 24.10.2002, Doc. 13463/02 POLGEN.

Council of the European Union (2005) *Draft Council Conclusions on Initiating Dialogue and Cooperation with Libya on Migration Issues*. Doc No. 9413/1/05 REV 1 of 27 May 2005.

Cross-Border Cooperation/Söderköping Process (2003) 'Migration and Asylum Management Challenges for Countries Along the Enlarged European Union Border', Kiev, 7–8 July, conference materials. http://soderkoping.org.ua/site/page108.html (last accessed 10 February 2006).

European Parliament (1987) *Report on the Right of Asylum*. Rapporteur: H. O. Vetter, Doc. A2-227/86/A and B of 23.2.1987.

5+5 Dialogue (2004) Third Ministerial Conference on Migration in the Western Mediterranean, Algiers, 15–16 September, Summary of Conclusions by the Presidency. http://www.iom.int/en/PDF_Files/5+5/en/summary_of %20 conclusions_by %20the_presidency_en.pdf (last accessed on 13 August 2005).

Grabbe, H. (2002) 'Stabilizing the East while Keeping out the Easterners: Internal and External Security Logics in Conflict'. In S. Lavenex and E. M. Uçarer (eds), *Migration and the Externalities of European Integration*. Lanham, Md: Lexington Books, pp. 91–104.

International Organization for Migration (IOM) (2005) 'Facts and Figures', March, online at http://www.iom.int/en/pdf %5Ffiles/who/iom %5Ffacts %5Fand %5Ffigures %5Fmar05.pdf (last accessed on 13 August 2005).

Jileva, E. (2002) 'Larger than the European Union: the Emerging EU Migration Regime and Enlargement'. In S. Lavenex and E. M. Uçarer (eds), *Migration and the Externalities of European Integration*. Lanham, Md: Lexington Books, pp. 75–89.

Kelley, J. (2004) *Ethnic Politics in Europe: the Power of Norms and Incentives*. Princeton, NJ: Princeton University Press.

Kirisci, K. (2002) 'Immigration and Asylum Issues in EU–Turkish Relations: Assessing EU's Impact on Turkish Policy and Practice'. In S. Lavenex and E. M. Uçarer (eds), *Migration and the Externalities of European Integration*. Lanham, Md: Lexington Books, pp. 125–42.

Klaauw, J. van der (2002) 'European Asylum Policy and the Global Protection Regime: Challenges for UNHCR'. In S. Lavenex and E. M. Uçarer (eds), *Migration and the Externalities of European Integration*. Lanham, Md: Lexington Books, pp. 33–53.

Lavenex, S. (1999) *Safe Third Countries. Extending EU Asylum and Immigration Policies to Central and Eastern Europe*. Budapest and New York: Central European University Press.

Lavenex, S. (2001) 'The Europeanisation of Refugee Policies: Normative Challenges and Institutional Legacies'. *Journal of Common Market Studies*, Vol. 39, No. 5: 851–74.

Lavenex, S. (2004) 'EU External Governance in Wider Europe'. *Journal of European Public Policy*, Vol. 11, No. 4: 680–700.

Lavenex, S. (2006) 'Asylum Policy'. In Paolo Graziano and Maarten Vink (eds), *Europeanisation: New Research Agendas*. London: Palgrave Macmillan (forthcoming).

Lavenex, S. and E. M. Uçarer (eds) (2002) *Migration and the Externalities of European Integration*. Lanham, Md: Lexington Books.

Lavenex, S. and E. M. Uçarer (2004) 'The External Dimension of Europeanisation'. *Cooperation & Conflict*, Vol. 39, No. 4: 417–43.

Manners, I. (2002) 'Normative Power Europe: a Contradiction in Terms?' *Journal of Common Market Studies*, Vol. 40, No. 2: 235–58.

Olsen, J. P. (2002) 'The Many Faces of Europeanisation'. *Journal of Common Market Studies*, Vol. 40, No. 5: 921–52.

Schimmelfennig, F. and U. Sedelmeier (2005) *The Europeanisation of Central and Eastern Europe*. Ithaca, NY: Cornell University Press.

Schimmelfennig, F. and W. Wagner (2004) 'Preface: External Governance in the European Union'. *Journal of European Public Policy*, Vol. 11, No. 4: 665–8.

Selm, J. van (2002) 'Immigration and Asylum or Foreign Policy: the EU's Approach to Migrants and Their Countries of Origin'. In Sandra Lavenex and Emek M. Uçarer (eds), *Migration and the Externalities of European Integration*. Lanham, Md: Lexington Books, pp. 143–60.

Selm, J. van (2005) 'European Refugee Policy: Is there such a thing?' New Issues in Refugee Research Working Paper No. 115, UNHCR.

Thouez, C. and F. Channac (2005) *Convergence and Divergence in Migration Policy: the Role of Regional Consultative Processes*. Geneva: Global Commission on International Migration (GCIM) Global Migration Perspectives Paper Series. http://www.gcim.org/ir_gmp.htm (last accessed on 10 February 2006).

United Nations General Assembly (UNGA) (2003) *Follow-up to the Regional Conference to Address the Problems of Refugees, Displaced Persons, Other Forms of Involuntary Displacement and Returnees in the Countries of the Commonwealth of Independent States and Relevant Neighbouring States*. Report of the Secretary General, Doc. A/58/281 of 14.8.2003.

UNHCR (2004) *UNHCR Toolbox. The EU Enlargement Process and the External Dimension of the EU JHA Policy*. Geneva: UNHCR.

Wallace, C. and D. Stola (2001) *Patterns of Migration in Central Europe*. London: Macmillan.

Zolberg, A. (2003) 'The Archeology of "Remote Control"'. In A. Fahrmeir, O. Faron and P. Weil (eds), *Migration Control in the North Atlantic World*. New York: Berghahn Books, pp. 195–222.

Index